PISTACHIOS
HAZELNUTS

hamlyn

CONTENTS

SERVES 6
PREPARATION TIME: 1 HOUR
COOKING TIME: 10 MINUTES
CHILLING TIME: MINIMUM 4 HOURS

PISTACHIO **BLANCMANGE**

250 ml (8 fl oz) milk
250 g (8 oz) unsalted pistachios
10 leaves gelatine (20 g/¾ oz)
120 g (4 oz) caster sugar
Almond essence (optional)
250 ml (8 fl oz) double cream, chilled
Flavourless oil (such as groundnut)

To serve: white peaches or strawberries

1 Heat 250 ml (8 fl oz) of water with the milk in a pan to just below boiling point.

2 Process the pistachios in a food processor, gradually adding the hot milk and water. Leave to cool. Line a sieve with two layers of muslin, place it over a pan and strain the pistachio mixture through it, then gather up the residue in the muslin and squeeze thoroughly to extract as much of the liquid as possible. Measure 450 ml (¾ pint) of this pistachio milk, adding water if necessary to make up the quantity.

3 Soften the gelatine in a little cold water, squeezing out when ready to use. Heat the pistachio milk with the sugar and a few drops of almond essence, if using, stirring well to dissolve the sugar. When the mixture has almost come to the boil, add the gelatine and stir until fully dissolved. Leave to cool.

4 Lightly oil 6 ramekins or attractive glasses.

5 Whip the cream and fold into the cold mixture, then pour into the ramekins and leave to set for at least 4 hours in the refrigerator. To serve, dip the ramekins briefly in hot water and turn out the blancmanges (or serve in the glasses, if using). Accompany the blancmange with slices of ripe white peaches or little cultivated 'wild' strawberries.

SERVES 6
PREPARATION TIME: 10 MINUTES + SETTING TIME
COOKING TIME: 10 MINUTES

PISTACHIO **NOUGATINE**

150 g (5 oz) caster sugar
150 g (5 oz) pistachios
   (salted it you like a touch of salt flavour in sweets)

To serve: vanilla ice cream or raspberry sorbet

1 Line a baking sheet with nonstick baking paper.

2 Put the sugar into a pan with 100 ml (3½ fl oz) of water. Bring to the boil and cook until it turns a light golden colour.

3 Remove from the heat and add the pistachios, stir in well, then pour the mixture onto the prepared baking sheet. Leave to harden, then chop fairly small and serve sprinkled on ice cream or sorbet. It is also delicious on a plain cheesecake.

SERVES 4
PREPARATION TIME: 10 MINUTES
COOKING TIME: 20 MINUTES
FREEZING TIME: MINIMUM 7 HOURS

KULFI

3 tablespoons unsalted pistachios
4 tablespoons caster sugar
1.5 litres (2½ pints) milk
Seeds from 4 cardamom pods
2 tablespoons ground almonds

1 Grind the pistachios in a food processor with 1 tablespoon of sugar, or chop them as finely as possible.

2 Pour the milk and the cardamom seeds into a pan, bring to the boil, then lower the heat and let it simmer gently, stirring occasionally, until it has reduced by around one third. Add the rest of the sugar and stir until dissolved.

3 Filter the milk and discard the seeds before adding the pistachios and the almonds. Leave to cool.

4 When cold, pour the mixture into a freezerproof container and put in the freezer. Leave for 1 hour then take out and beat briskly. Freeze for a further hour and beat again. Repeat the operation a third time then return to the freezer for several more hours or overnight. Remove from the freezer for about 15–20 minutes before serving.

Cook's tip Kulfi is Indian ice cream.

12

PREPARATION TIME: 20 MINUTES
COOKING TIME: 35 MINUTES

PISTACHIO NUT **CAKE**

Butter, for greasing
100 g (3½ oz) unsalted pistachios
150 g (5 oz) caster sugar
1 teaspoon fennel seeds,
    or 2 tablespoons orange flower water
2 eggs
150 g (5 oz) plain yogurt
4 tablespoons olive oil
180 g (6 oz) plain flour
2 teaspoons baking powder

1 Preheat the oven to 180°C (350°F) Gas Mark 4. Grease a cake tin 20 cm (8 inches) in diameter.

2 Finely grind half of the pistachios with 1 tablespoon of sugar in a blender or food processor; chop the remainder roughly with a knife. Process the fennel seeds separately, if using.

3 Whisk the eggs with half the remaining sugar until pale and frothy. Add the yogurt, olive oil and half the fennel seeds, or half the orange flower water.

4 Sift the flour with the baking powder and fold into the egg mixture without over-mixing.

5 Reserve a little of the chopped pistachios and add the rest to the mixture, together with the ground nuts. Pour into the cake tin and sprinkle with the remaining pistachios. Put in the oven and bake for 35 minutes or until a metal skewer inserted in the centre emerges quite clean. Leave to cool for 5 minutes before turning out onto a wire rack to cool.

6 Dissolve the rest of the sugar in a scant ½ cup of simmering water, add the remaining fennel or orange flower water and boil to make a syrup. Filter to remove the seeds and use to glaze the cake.

MAKES 24 'CIGARS'
PREPARATION TIME: 1 HOUR + SETTING TIME
COOKING TIME: 15 MINUTES

PISTACHIO NUT **'CIGARS'**

FOR THE FILLING
50 g (2 oz) unsalted butter
250 g (8 oz) unsalted shelled pistachios
250 g (8 oz) ground almonds
175 g (6 oz) icing sugar
3 tablespoons orange flower water
Finely grated peel of ½ orange
½ teaspoon ground cinnamon

FOR THE 'CIGARS'
3 sheets filo pastry
150 g (5 oz) unsalted butter + extra for greasing, all melted
2 tablespoons orange flower water (optional)
4 tablespoons icing sugar (optional)

1 To make the filling: melt the butter. Briefly process the pistachios with 1 tablespoon of sugar in a food processor. Add all the other ingredients and process them again, briefly.

2 Preheat the oven to 190°C (375°F) Gas Mark 5. Brush a baking sheet(s) with melted butter or line with nonstick baking paper.

3 Brush a sheet of filo pastry with melted butter and cut in half to make two long rectangles. Cut each of these into 4 smaller rectangles and place a little of the filling on each. Fold in the longer sides and roll into a cigar shape. Place these on the baking sheet and brush over with more butter. Continue the process with the remaining sheets.

4 Put in the oven and bake for 12–15 minutes or until nicely browned. Remove from the oven and, when cold, serve as they are or roll them first in the orange flower water and then in the icing sugar. Repeat this process several times, then leave the coating to harden.

SERVES 4
PREPARATION TIME: 5 MINUTES
COOKING TIME: 30 MINUTES

RICE WITH
PISTACHIO NUT MILK

4 tablespoons plain shelled pistachios
4–5 tablespoons caster sugar
1 litre (1¾ pint) milk
1 cinnamon stick
1 vanilla pod
150 g (5 oz) short-grain rice
1 tablespoon orange flower water or rosewater
Little dried roses for decoration
    (from Middle Eastern delicatessens)

1 Grind the pistachios with a little sugar in a food processor and set aside a little for decoration.

2 Put the milk into a pan with the cinnamon stick and the vanilla pod, split and the seeds scraped into the milk. Bring to the boil, sprinkle in the rice, then lower the heat and leave to simmer, stirring frequently. The rice should cook in about 25 minutes; however, it should remain 'al dente' (slightly firm).

3 Add the orange flower water or rosewater, the rest of the sugar and the ground pistachios and stir carefully. Add a little more milk if the consistency seems too dry and cook a little more.

4 Discard the stick and vanilla pod and serve warm or cold, decorated with the remaining ground pistachios and the petals from the dried roses.

SERVES 6
PREPARATION TIME: 45 MINUTES + RESTING TIME
COOKING TIME: 35 MINUTES

APRICOT & PISTACHIO **TART**

FOR THE PASTRY
200 g (7 oz) plain flour
1 teaspoon salt
1 tablespoon caster sugar
Vanilla essence
100 g (3½ oz) butter, cut into small pieces
50 g (2 oz) amaretti or boudoir biscuits

FOR THE PISTACHIO NUT CREAM
30 g (1 oz) softened butter
30 g (1 oz) crème fraîche
3 tablespoons caster sugar
60 g (2½ oz) ground unsalted shelled pistachios
1 egg
Ripe apricots or a tin of apricots in syrup

1 To make the pastry: sift together the flour, salt and sugar in a bowl. Add a few drops of vanilla essence and the butter and rub into the flour until the mixture resembles breadcrumbs. Add 3–4 tablespoons of very cold water to bind and mix together with a knife. Form into a rough ball without kneading, put into a polythene bag, and refrigerate for at least 1 hour.

2 Preheat the oven to 180°C (350°F) Gas Mark 4.

3 Roll out the pastry and line a tart tin 23 cm (9 inches) in diameter.

4 Crumble the biscuits and spread them over the bottom of the tart to absorb the juice from the fruit and prevent it soaking into the pastry.

5 To make the pistachio nut cream: beat the butter in a bowl with a spatula to give it a creamy consistency. Mix in the crème fraîche, sugar, ground pistachios and the egg and pour into the pastry case. Cut the apricots into quarters and arrange them on the cream.

6 Put in the oven and bake for about 35 minutes.

SERVES 6
PREPARATION TIME: 45 MINUTES
COOKING TIME: 30 MINUTES

PISTACHIO NUT **PARIS-BREST**

125 g (4 oz) superfine sugar
75 g (3 oz) coarsely ground pistachios
2 tablespoons whole unsalted pistachios, chopped

FOR THE CONFECTIONER'S CUSTARD
500 ml (17 fl oz) milk
5 egg yolks
100 g (3½ oz) caster sugar
2 tablespoons plain flour
2 tablespoons cornflour
100 g (3½ oz) very soft butter + plus extra for greasing

FOR THE CHOUX PASTRY
125 ml (4 fl oz) milk
125 ml (4 fl oz) water
1 teaspoon salt
1 tablespoon caster sugar
100 g (3½ oz) butter, cut into small pieces
150 g (5 oz) plain flour
4 eggs, beaten

1 Put the 125 g (4 oz) of sugar into a pan with 3 tablespoons of water and cook to a golden caramel. Add the ground pistachios and quickly stir in to coat them with the caramel. Pour onto a sheet of nonstick baking paper and leave to harden. Pound in a mortar or grind in a food processor to form a praline with the consistency of fine sand.

2 To make the confectioner's custard: heat the milk. Whisk the egg yolks with the sugar, then add the flour and cornflour and continue to whisk. Pour on a little of the just-boiling milk, whisking constantly, then gradually add the rest of the milk, still whisking. Pour the mixture back into the pan and cook over medium heat, stirring constantly and scraping the base of the pan. When bubbles start to rise to the surface, cook gently for a further 2–3 minutes, then pour into a bowl, cover closely with clingfilm and leave to cool. When quite cold, add the pistachio praline and the very soft butter.

3 Preheat the oven to 200°C (400°F) Gas Mark 6. Grease a baking sheet or line with nonstick baking paper.

4 To make the choux pastry: put the milk in a pan with the water, salt, sugar and butter. Remove from the heat just before it boils, add the flour all at once and stir vigorously with a spatula. When all the flour has been absorbed, return to the heat and cook, stirring constantly, until it comes away from the sides of the pan. Transfer to a large bowl and gradually beat in the eggs with the spatula. It should be such a consistency that a line drawn in it with a finger closes again very slowly.

5 With a piping bag fitted with a nozzle, pipe a disc of dough on a baking sheet (or 6 small circles). Build up several layers of dough to make a thick disc.

6 Sprinkle the chopped nuts over the dough, lower the oven temperature to 180°C (350°F) Gas Mark 4 and bake for 20 minutes, until the pastry is risen and nicely browned. Cool on a wire rack. Slice the disc through the centre, spread the bottom half with cream and top with the other half.

SERVES 4
PREPARATION TIME: 30 MINUTES
COOKING TIME: 20 MINUTES
FREEZING TIME: MINIMUM 4 HOURS

MACAROONS
WITH PISTACHIO ICE CREAM

FOR THE ICE CREAM
300 ml (½ pint) double cream
120 g (4 oz) unsalted shelled pistachios
60 g (2½ oz) caster sugar
300 ml (½ pint) milk
4 egg yolks
1 tablespoon cornflour

FOR THE MACAROONS
300 g (10 oz) icing sugar
80 g (3 oz) ground almonds
100 g (3½ oz) unsalted pistachios, finely ground
    with a little icing sugar to stop them turning to a paste
5 egg whites
30 g (1 oz) caster sugar

To serve: tinned Morello cherries

1 To make the ice cream: whip the cream to firm peaks and put in the refrigerator. Grind half the pistachios to a fine powder with the sugar and chop the rest. Heat the milk with the ground pistachios. In a bowl, whisk the egg yolks with the cornflour. Pour the almost boiling milk onto the egg mixture, stirring constantly. Return to the pan and cook gently, stirring constantly, until it thickens. Transfer to a bowl and leave to get cold, then fold in the whipped cream. Freeze in an ice-cream maker.

2 To prepare the macaroons: sift together the icing sugar, ground almonds and ground pistachios; repeat the process twice. Whisk the egg whites until stiff, then gently fold in the almond-sugar-pistachio mixture, which will make the egg whites collapse slightly.

3 Preheat the oven to 180°C (350°F) Gas Mark 4, using the fan option if available. Line a baking sheet with nonstick baking paper.

4 With a piping bag or a spoon, form little discs about 6 cm/2½ inches in diameter on the baking sheet. Place a second baking sheet under the first one, so that the bases do not cook too quickly, and put in the oven, lowering the temperature immediately to 140°C (275°F) Gas Mark 1. Bake for about 10 minutes: they should form a crust on the outside but the centres should still be a little soft. Cool on a wire rack.

5 Decorate each macaroon with Morello cherries and serve with a scoop of the ice cream, which should be removed from the freezer and kept in the refrigerator for 20–30 minutes before serving, to soften it a little.

SERVES 6
PREPARATION TIME: 35 MINUTES + RESTING TIME
COOKING TIME: 45 MINUTES

PISTACHIO NUT **STOLLEN**

50 g (2 oz) unsalted pistachios
40 g (1½ oz) candied orange or citron peel
2 tablespoons rum
75 g (3 oz) raisins
Vanilla essence
200 ml (7 fl oz) milk
50 g (2 oz) butter + extra for greasing
2 tablespoons caster sugar
380 g (12 oz) plain flour + extra for dusting
½ teaspoon salt
25 g (1 oz) fresh yeast or a sachet of dried yeast
1 egg
Finely grated rind of 2 limes
75 g (3 oz) pistachio nut paste
75 g (3 oz) almond paste

FOR THE GLAZE
75 g (3 oz) unsalted butter, melted
5 tablespoons icing sugar

1 Chop half of the pistachios. Chop the candied peel and put to macerate in the rum with the raisins and a few drops of vanilla essence. Grind the rest of the pistachios in a food processor (lightly by pulsing and/or with a little icing sugar to prevent the nuts going oily).

2 Warm the milk. Melt the butter gently with the sugar. Sift the flour into a bowl with the salt and add the ground pistachios. Make a well in the centre and pour in the melted butter.

3 Dissolve the yeast in the warm milk (follow the maker's instructions if using dried yeast) and pour that into the well also. Add the egg and the grated lime rind. Mix gradually into a dough with a wooden spoon or by hand. The dough should be soft enough to be kneaded by hand or in a food processor for 5 minutes. Incorporate the macerated fruit with any unabsorbed rum and the chopped pistachios. Cover the bowl with clingfilm and leave to rest for 3 hours, away from draughts: the dough should double in volume.

4 Put the dough on a floured work surface and roll it out into a 25-cm (10-inch) square, or into two smaller squares. Form 2 sausages with the almond and pistachio paste, a little shorter than the square. Lay them in the centre of the square and roll the dough around them, sealing the edges well. Slide the stollen onto a buttered baking sheet, keeping the join underneath. Cover with clingfilm and leave to rest for a further hour.

5 Preheat the oven to 200°C (400°F) Gas Mark 6 and bake the stollen for about 40 minutes: the top should be browned and should sound hollow when tapped. Leave to cool on a wire rack. When it is quite cold, brush it over generously with melted butter and dredge with icing sugar.

Cook's Tip Stollen is a sweet German Christmas bread.

MAKES 12
PREPARATION TIME: 25 MINUTES
COOKING TIME: 20 MINUTES

FLAPJACKS

125 g (4 oz) butter + extra for greasing
60 g (2½ oz) brown sugar
1 tablespoon runny honey
3 tablespoons plain flour
250 g (8 oz) oat flakes or a mixture of 5 different cereals
50 g (2 oz) chopped hazelnuts
50 g (2 oz) raisins or other dried fruit

1 Preheat the oven to 180°C (350°F) Gas Mark 4. Grease a shallow square baking tin.

2 Melt the butter slowly in a small pan with the sugar and honey. Mix with a fork and take off the heat.

3 Add the flour, oat flakes, hazelnuts and raisins.

4 Pour into the tin, put in the oven and bake for 20 minutes. Cut into squares and leave to get quite cold, then store in an airtight tin.

SERVES 6
PREPARATION TIME: 30 MINUTES
COOKING TIME: 35 MINUTES
CHILLING TIME: 1 HOUR

PLUM & HAZELNUT **TART**

FOR THE PASTRY
200 g (7 oz) plain flour
1 teaspoon salt
1 tablespoon caster sugar
100 g (3½ oz) unsalted butter, cut into small pieces
1 vanilla pod

FOR THE HAZELNUT CREAM
30 g (1 oz) softened butter
30 g (1 oz) crème fraîche
3 tablespoons caster sugar
100 g (3½ oz) ground hazelnuts
1 egg
10 ripe red plums or greengages or small yellow plums

1 To make the pastry: mix the flour, salt and sugar in a bowl. Add the butter and the seeds scraped from the vanilla pod. Rub in with the fingertips until the mixture resembles breadcrumbs. Add 3 tablespoons of cold water and mix together with a knife. Finish forming the pastry into a rough ball, without kneading, then put into a polythene bag and refrigerate for at least 1 hour.

2 Preheat the oven to 180°C (350°F) Gas Mark 4.

3 Roll out the pastry and use it to line a tart tin about 23 cm (9 inches) in diameter.

4 For the hazelnut cream: mix the butter with the crème fraîche, the sugar, the ground hazelnuts and the egg. Spread this in the pastry case. Wash, pit and cut the fruit in half and arrange it on the cream. Put in the oven and bake for about 35 minutes, until the pastry and the cream are both lightly browned.

PREPARATION TIME: 20 MINUTES
COOKING TIME: 35 MINUTES

HAZELNUT & ARGAN **CAKE**

Butter, for greasing
100 g (3½ oz) hazelnuts
75 g (3 oz) caster sugar
2 eggs
150 g (5 oz) plain yogurt
4 tablespoons argan oil (available from supermarkets)
180 g (6 oz) plain flour
2 teaspoons baking powder
Ground cinnamon

1 Preheat the oven to 180°C (350°F) Gas Mark 4. Grease a cake tin 20 cm (8 inches) in diameter.

2 Pulse the hazelnuts in a food processor or chop them roughly.

3 Whisk the sugar and eggs until the mixture is very pale. Add the yogurt and the argan oil. Sift the flour with the baking powder and a pinch of ground cinnamon and fold in carefully. Finish with the hazelnuts, keeping a few back to sprinkle over the cake.

4 Pour the mixture into the tin, sprinkle the remaining hazelnuts on the top, put in the oven and bake for 35 minutes. The cake should be browned and a metal skewer inserted in the centre should emerge quite clean. Leave to cool for 5 minutes before turning out onto a wire rack to cool.

Cook's Tip Argan oil comes from the nuts of the Moroccan argan tree. Its flavour is similar to walnut oil, but milder.

SERVES 6
PREPARATION TIME: 25 MINUTES
COOKING TIME: 1 HOUR
RESTING TIME: SEVERAL HOURS OR OVERNIGHT IF POSSIBLE

RICH HAZELNUT **SQUARES**

125 g (4 oz) medium semolina
125 g (4 oz) butter + extra for greasing
175 g (6 oz) hazelnuts
150 g (5 oz) caster sugar
6 egg yolks
Nutmeg
Seeds scraped from 1 vanilla pod
Finely grated rind of 1 orange
2 egg whites

1 Heat up a dry frying pan and pour in the semolina. Stir it for a few seconds while it colours slightly, then transfer to a bowl and leave to cool for 5 minutes before adding the butter.

2 Coarsely grind the hazelnuts without reducing them to a powder.

3 Preheat the oven to 140°C (275°F) Gas Mark 1. Grease a shallow 20-cm (8-inch) square baking tin.

4 Whisk together the sugar and egg yolks until light and fluffy, then add a pinch of freshly grated nutmeg and the vanilla seeds, grated orange rind, the semolina and the hazelnuts.

5 Whisk the egg whites until stiff and gently fold into the mixture.

6 Pour the mixture into the baking tin, put in the oven and bake for about 1 hour. The cake should remain sticky in the centre. Leave to cool in the tin. For best results, leave overnight before cutting into squares.

SERVES 6
PREPARATION TIME: 20 MINUTES + RESTING TIME
COOKING TIME: 25 MINUTES
CHILLING TIME: 20 MINUTES

HONEY & HAZELNUT
CRISP BISCUITS

200 g (7 oz) whole hazelnuts
   or 150 g (5 oz) hazelnuts + 50 g (2 oz) pine nuts
2 eggs + 1 yolk
150 g (5 oz) caster sugar
3 tablespoons honey
Finely grated rind of 1 orange
200 g (7 oz) plain flour
1 teaspoon baking powder
A little butter to grease the baking sheet

1 Preheat the oven to 190°C (375°F) Gas Mark 5. Spread the nuts on a baking sheet and put them on a high shelf of the oven for 5 minutes, then take them out. Put them in a tea towel and rub off as much of the skins as possible.

2 Whisk 1 egg with the egg yolk, sugar and honey. Add the grated orange peel. Sift the flour with the baking powder and stir into the mixture. Finally add the nuts. Refrigerate the pastry for about 20 minutes to let it settle and become firm.

3 Grease a baking sheet. Form 2 long 'sausages' 4–5 cm (1½–2 inches) in diameter and lay them on the baking sheet, spaced well apart to leave room for expansion during baking. Beat the remaining egg and brush over the 'sausages'. Put in the oven and bake for about 15 minutes. The pastry should be set but not too brown.

4 Remove from the oven, leaving the oven on, and slide onto a cutting board. Cut diagonally into slices about 1.5 cm (¾ inch) thick. Lay the biscuits flat on the baking sheet, return to the oven, and bake for a further 10 minutes or so. Leave to cool on a wire rack: they will become very hard, like Italian biscotti. Delicious with coffee or hot chocolate.

SERVES 4
PREPARATION TIME: 20 MINUTES
COOKING TIME: 10 MINUTES

HAZELNUT **WAFFLES**

100 g (3½ oz) hazelnuts
350 g (10 oz) plain flour, either all white
  or half white and half wholemeal
40 g (1½ oz) butter
1½ teaspoons baking powder
1 tablespoon caster sugar
150 ml (¼ pint) milk
150 g (5 oz) yogurt mixed with 2 tablespoons milk
2 eggs
Salt

To serve: brown sugar, whipped cream and/or mascarpone

1 Preheat the oven to 190°C (375°F) Gas Mark 5.

2 Spread the hazelnuts on a baking sheet and put them on a high shelf of the oven for 5 minutes, then take them out. Put them in a tea towel and rub off as much of the skins as possible. Chop them finely without reducing them to a powder and mix with 1 tablespoon of flour.

3 Melt the butter. Sift the rest of the flour with the baking powder, sugar and a pinch of salt. Mix together the melted butter, the milk, the diluted yogurt and the egg yolks in a large bowl and mix in the dry ingredients with a whisk.

4 Whisk the egg whites until stiff and gently fold them into the mixture. Finally add the hazelnuts.

5 Cook on a preheated waffle iron for 3–4 minutes. Serve with sugar, whipped cream and mascarpone.

SERVES 4
PREPARATION TIME: 35 MINUTES
COOKING TIME: 10 MINUTES
RESTING TIME: OVERNIGHT

PRALINE **CHARLOTTE**

6 leaves gelatine (12 g/½ oz)
4 egg yolks
2 teaspoons cornflour
400 ml (14 fl oz) milk
4 tablespoons caster sugar
80 g (3 oz) praline (ground caramel-coated nuts,
  see recipe page 20)
300 ml (½ pint) double cream, chilled
30 boudoir biscuits
150 ml (¼ pint) orange juice
1 handful hazelnuts

1 Put the gelatine to soften in a little cold water. Squeeze out when ready to use.

2 Whisk the egg yolks with the cornflour and sugar. Heat the milk to almost boiling point. Whisking constantly, add the milk to the egg mixture, then return the mixture to the pan and cook over gentle heat, stirring constantly until it thickens. Add the drained gelatine and stir until completely dissolved. Add the praline and leave to get cold.

3 Whip the cream and fold into the praline cream.

4 Dip the boudoir biscuits into the orange juice and use to line a charlotte mould. Pour in half the cream then add a layer of biscuits. Finish with the remainder of the cream and a final layer of biscuits. Leave overnight to set, if possible. Turn out of the mould and decorate with chopped hazelnuts.

SERVES 4
PREPARATION TIME: 30 MINUTES + 1 HOUR STRAINING
COOKING TIME: 10 MINUTES
CHILLING TIME: MINIMUM 4 HOURS

HAZELNUT MILK **ICE CREAM**

150 g (5 oz) hazelnuts
500 ml (17 fl oz) milk
3 tablespoons caster sugar
4 egg yolks
200 g (7 oz) mascarpone

1 Preheat the oven to 190°C (375°F) Gas Mark 5. Spread the hazelnuts on a baking sheet and put them on a high shelf of the oven for 5 minutes, then take them out. Put them in a tea towel and rub off as much of the skins as possible.

2 Heat the milk in a pan. Grind the hazelnuts in a food processor, adding the hot milk a little at a time through the feeder tube, then leave to cool.

3 Line a sieve with two layers of muslin and place over a pan. Pour the hazelnut and milk mixture into it and leave to drain for 1 hour, then gather up the muslin around the residue and squeeze out as much liquid as possible. Measure 450 ml (¾ pint) of the hazelnut milk, adding a little water to make up the quantity if necessary.

4 Whisk the sugar and egg yolks together, pour on the hazelnut milk and stir well, then pour the mixture into a clean pan and heat gently, stirring constantly, until it thickens. Leave to cool.

5 Beat the mascarpone to make it smooth and add to the hazelnut cream. Freeze in an ice-cream maker.

SERVES 6
PREPARATION TIME: 10 MINUTES
COOKING TIME: 35 MINUTES
SETTING TIME: 2 HOURS

HAZELNUT &
BROWN SUGAR FUDGE

100 g (3½ oz) hazelnuts
60 g (2½ oz) butter + extra for greasing
300 ml (½ pint) milk
500 g (1 lb) brown sugar or soft brown sugar
Seeds scraped from 1 vanilla pod

1 Preheat the oven to 190°C (375°F) Gas Mark 5. Spread the hazelnuts on a baking sheet and put them on a high shelf of the oven for 5 minutes, then take them out. Put them in a tea towel and rub off as much of the skins as possible.

2 Butter a shallow 15-cm (6-inch) square cake tin. Gently heat the milk, sugar and butter in a pan. Bring to the boil, stirring constantly, and leave to simmer gently for about 30 minutes.

3 Drop a tiny quantity of this mixture in a bowl of cold water; if it forms a soft ball it is ready, if not cook a little more and test again.

4 Take the pan off the heat and add the vanilla seeds and the hazelnuts. Beat the mixture until it forms a thick cream, then pour into the tin and leave to set at room temperature. Cut into squares.

SERVES 6
PREPARATION TIME: 25 MINUTES
COOKING TIME: 10 MINUTES

HAZELNUT **ROULADE**

30 g (1 oz) butter + extra for greasing
4 eggs, separated
120 g (4 oz) caster sugar
120 g (4 oz) plain flour
250 g (8 oz) mascarpone
100 g (3½ oz) powdered praline
   (ground caramel-coated nuts, see recipe page 20)
Hazelnut syrup

1 Preheat the oven to 200°C (400°F) Gas Mark 6. Grease a Swiss roll tin or a baking sheet lined with nonstick baking paper.

2 Melt the butter.

3 Whisk the egg yolks with the sugar until light and frothy. Sift the flour and add to the mixture. Whisk the egg whites until stiff, gently fold in and finally stir in the melted butter.

4 Pour into the greased Swiss roll tin or onto the lined baking sheet. Put in the oven and bake for 10 minutes, when the cake should be just lightly browned. Turn out onto a damp tea towel, peel off the paper and leave to cool.

5 Beat the mascarpone until smooth and add the praline, keeping a little to sprinkle on top of the cake. Dilute the hazelnut syrup with a little water and sprinkle over the cake, then spread the mascarpone on it and roll, using the tea towel to make sure it rolls tightly and evenly. Trim the ends and place on a dish. Sprinkle with the remaining praline.

English translation and adaptation: JMS Books LLP
Layout: cbdesign

First published in France in 2007 under the title
La Boîte à gâteau, by Hachette Livre (Marabout)
Copyright © 2007 Hachette Livre (Marabout)
Editorial: Catherine Berranger and Charlotte Müller-Buch

An Hachette Livre UK Company
www.hachettelivre.co.uk

First published in Great Britain in 2008 by
Hamlyn, a division of Octopus Publishing Group Ltd
2–4 Heron Quays, London E14 4JP
www.octopusbooks.co.uk

Copyright © English edition
Octopus Publishing Group Ltd 2008

Original French edition copyright
© HACHETTE LIVRE (Marabout) 2007

ISBN 978 0 600 61876 8

A CIP catalogue record for this book is available from
the British Library

Printed and bound in China

1 3 5 7 9 10 8 6 4 2

This book contains dishes that are made with raw or lightly cooked eggs.
These should be avoided by vulnerable people such as pregnant and
nursing mothers, invalids, the elderly, babies and young children.

APPLES & PEARS
CINNAMON

hamlyn

CONTENTS

SERVES 4
PREPARATION TIME: 25 MINUTES
COOKING TIME: 1 HOUR

EASY PEASY **PEAR CAKE**

5 ripe pears
125 g (4 oz) butter + extra for greasing
3 eggs
75 g (3 oz) caster sugar
Vanilla essence
125 g (4 oz) plain flour
Salt

1 Preheat the oven to 180°C (350°F) Gas Mark 4.

2 Grease a tart tin. Gently melt the butter in a pan. In a bowl, whisk the eggs with the sugar and a few drops of vanilla essence, to taste. Add the melted butter, then sift in the flour with a pinch of salt and mix well.

3 Peel the pears, cut in quarters and remove the core. Pour a little of the mixture into the tart tin and arrange the pear quarters on it, then cover with the rest of the mixture. Bake for 45–60 minutes until the top is golden brown.

SERVES 4
PREPARATION TIME: 20 MINUTES + RESTING TIME
COOKING TIME: 40 MINUTES

PEAR & CHOCOLATE
CRISP TART

FOR THE SHORTCRUST PASTRY
200 g (7 oz) plain flour
100 g (3½ oz) butter, cut into small pieces,
   + extra for greasing
1 teaspoon salt

FOR THE FILLING
4 tablespoons sugar
100 g (3½ oz) dark chocolate
4 pears
1 egg
125 ml (4 fl oz) single cream

1 To make the shortcrust pastry: sift the flour into a large bowl with the salt and the butter. Rub the butter into the flour with the fingertips until the mixture resembles breadcrumbs. Add 100 ml (3½ fl oz) of cold water and mix to a soft dough with a round-bladed knife, adding more water if necessary. Form it into a ball by hand without kneading it, put it in a polythene bag and leave to rest in the refrigerator for at least 1 hour.

2 Preheat the oven to 190°C (375°F) Gas Mark 5. Grease a tart tin and sprinkle it with 2 tablespoons of the sugar, then line it with the pastry. Chop the chocolate and scatter it over the pastry. Peel the pears, cut in quarters, remove the core and thinly slice before arranging them on top of the chocolate. Lightly beat the egg with the cream and 1 tablespoon of the sugar. Spread this mixture over the pears and chocolate, place the tart in the oven and bake for 30–35 minutes.

3 Sprinkle over the remaining sugar and caramelize the top under a very hot grill.

SERVES 4
PREPARATION TIME: 20 MINUTES
COOKING TIME: 1¼ HOURS

APPLE & PEAR **CHARLOTTE**

2 oranges
1 lemon
4 tablespoons sugar
2 apples
2 pears
12 slices rustic-style bread with crusts removed
100 g (3½ oz) butter + extra for greasing

To serve: custard

1 Preheat the oven to 190°C (375°F) Gas Mark 5. Peel the oranges and the lemon with a sharp knife, removing all the white pith. Cut up the flesh over a plate to save the juice, removing any pips, and put in a pan together with the juice and the sugar. Bring to the boil, stirring to dissolve the sugar, then lower the heat and leave to reduce to a syrup.

2 Peel, core and slice the apples and pears and gently stew them in the syrup for about 10 minutes to soften.

3 Grease a charlotte mould. Butter the bread slices and line the bottom and sides of the mould with them. Fill with the fruit mixture and enclose with more bread slices. Put in the oven and bake for 50 minutes, by which time the bread will be nicely browned. Turn the charlotte out of the mould and serve with custard.

SERVES 4
PREPARATION TIME: 20 MINUTES
COOKING TIME: 15 MINUTES

DELICATE **PEAR TARTS**

1 sheet pre-rolled butter puff pastry
4 firm pears
1½ tablespoons butter, for greasing
2 tablespoons sugar
Finely ground seeds from 4 cardamom pods

To serve: 4 scoops of fromage frais ice cream
   (see recipe page 44)

1 Preheat the oven to 220°C (425°F) Gas Mark 7. Cut out 4 circles of pastry (using a saucer) and draw a circle 5 mm (¼ inch) from the edge of each with the point of a knife, without cutting through the pastry.

2 Generously butter a baking sheet and sprinkle with 1 tablespoon of the sugar, then lay the pastry circles on it.

3 Peel, core and finely slice the pears and arrange them on the pastry circles. Mix the remaining sugar with the ground cardamom and sprinkle over the tarts.

4 Place in the oven and bake for 12–15 minutes. Serve with ice cream.

SERVES 4
PREPARATION TIME: 10 MINUTES
COOKING TIME: 50 MINUTES

CLAFOUTIS WITH
CARAMELIZED APPLES

4–5 apples
30 g (1 oz) unsalted butter
5 tablespoons sugar
80 g (3 oz) plain flour
200 ml (7 fl oz) milk
200 ml (7 fl oz) crème fraîche
4 eggs
1½ tablespoons butter, for greasing

1 Preheat the oven to 200°C (400°F) Gas Mark 6.

2 Peel the apples and cut them into quarters. Melt the unsalted butter in a frying pan and spoon off any scum that rises to the surface. Add the apple quarters and brown on one side then turn them over, sprinkle with 1 tablespoon of the sugar and fry on the other side until lightly caramelized.

3 Make a batter with the flour, milk, crème fraîche, eggs and the remaining 4 tablespoons of sugar.

4 Grease a medium-size ovenproof dish with the butter. Arrange the apples in the dish and pour over the batter.

5 Put in the oven and bake for 40 minutes until the clafoutis is set and the top golden brown and domed.

Cook's Tip A traditional clafoutis is made with black cherries that come from the Limousin region in France. There are many variations using other fruits.

SERVES 6
PREPARATION TIME: 20 MINUTES
COOKING TIME: 1¼ HOURS

DUTCH APPLE **SQUARES**

400 g (14 oz) unsalted butter + extra for greasing
500 g (1 lb) plain flour
2 teaspoons baking powder
250 g (8 oz) oat flakes
200 g (7 oz) soft brown sugar
1 teaspoon cinnamon
Pinch of ground nutmeg
7 russet apples
1 lemon, cut in half
100 g (3½ oz) raisins
100 g (3½ oz) dried cranberries
75 g (3 oz) Brazil nuts, walnuts or almonds, chopped
  (or a mixture)
150 g (5 oz) apricot jam
Salt

1 Preheat the oven to 180°C (350°F) Gas Mark 4. Grease a fairly shallow square or rectangular cake tin.

2 Melt the rest of the butter and leave it to cool a little, then add the flour, mixed with the baking powder and a pinch of salt, the oat flakes, sugar and spices. Put three-quarters of this mixture into the tin and tap to level it.

3 Peel the apples, rub with lemon juice, and grate coarsely. Spread the grated apples, raisins and cranberries over the mixture in the tin, cover with the remaining mixture and scatter over the nuts. Put in the oven and bake for 1–1¼ hours.

4 Melt the jam in a pan over low heat, stir in the remaining lemon juice and spread it over the cake once it has cooled. Cut into squares.

SERVES 6
PREPARATION TIME: 30 MINUTES
COOKING TIME: 1 HOUR

MERINGUE-TOPPED
APPLE CAKES

175 g (6 oz) softened butter + extra for greasing
250 g (8 oz) caster sugar
4 eggs, separated
100 g (3½ oz) ground almonds
300 g (10 oz) plain flour
7 cooking apples

1 Preheat the oven to 190°C (375°F) Gas Mark 5. Grease 6 tartlet tins (or 1 large tart tin about 23 cm/9 inches in diameter).

2 In a large bowl, beat 150 g (5 oz) of the butter with 100 g (3½ oz) of the sugar. Beat in the egg yolks, add the ground almonds and finally sift in the flour and mix well. Divide this mixture between the tartlet tins. Put in the oven and bake for about 30 minutes.

3 Peel, quarter and core the apples. Melt the remaining butter in a frying pan and spoon off any scum that rises to the surface. Add the apple quarters and brown on one side, then turn them over, sprinkle on 4 tablespoons of the sugar and fry on the other side until the sugar is lightly caramelized.

4 Whisk the egg whites until firm, then add the remaining sugar and whisk again.

5 Increase the temperature of the oven to 220°C (425°F) Gas Mark 7. Lay the apples in the baked tartlet cases, leaving a small border, then spread the meringue mixture over the top and onto the border, forming it into whorls with the spoon. Return to the oven for 15–20 minutes to brown the meringue peaks.

SERVES 4
PREPARATION TIME: 15 MINUTES
COOKING TIME: 10 MINUTES

PEAR GRATIN
WITH ASTI SPUMANTI

6 ripe pears (or pears poached in syrup)
1 lemon, cut in half
4 very thin slices of brioche or panettone
4 egg yolks
50 g (2 oz) caster sugar
150 ml (¼ pint) sparkling white wine
   (Asti or Clairette from the town of Die)
1 tablespoon Poire Williams (pear liqueur), optional

1 Peel, core and thinly slice the pears. Rub with lemon to prevent them discolouring.

2 Put the slices of brioche onto small heatproof plates or in shallow heatproof ramekins. Arrange the pear slices on the brioche.

3 Whisk the egg yolks with the sugar in a heatproof bowl, place over a pan of simmering water and continue to whisk until the mixture begins to turn to foam, then add the sparkling wine and continue to whisk until it forms quite a firm cream. Add the pear liqueur, if using.

4 Preheat the grill. Spread the cream over the pears and quickly flash-grill them. Serve immediately.

SERVES 4
PREPARATION TIME: 25 MINUTES
COOKING TIME: 40 MINUTES

APPLE & PEAR PIE

3 apples
2 pears
40 g (2 oz) apricot jam
Calvados (optional)
2 sheets pre-rolled butter puff pastry
1 egg, beaten
1 tablespoon caster sugar

To serve: 4 tablespoons crème fraîche

1 Preheat the oven to 200°C (400°F) Gas Mark 6.

2 Peel and core the apples and the pears; cut into very thin slices and mix with the jam and a dash of Calvados, if using.

3 Lay one sheet of pastry on a baking sheet lined with nonstick baking paper and spread the fruit mixture over it, leaving a small border. Moisten this border with water, cover with the second sheet of pastry and press down firmly by thumb or the tines of a fork to seal it. Cut a small opening in the centre of the pastry to allow the air to escape.

4 With a pointed knife, draw curls or a rosette on the surface, but not right through the pastry, then brush with beaten egg and sprinkle with the sugar. Put in the oven and bake for 40 minutes. Serve warm or cold with the crème fraîche.

SERVES 6
PREPARATION TIME: 40 MINUTES + RESTING TIME
COOKING TIME: 1 HOUR

BISTRO-STYLE
APPLE TART

FOR THE PASTRY
150 g (5 oz) plain flour
1 teaspoon baking powder
1 tablespoon caster sugar
1 egg
75 g (3 oz) unsalted butter, cut into small pieces
Salt

FOR THE APPLE FILLING
6–8 apples
1½ tablespoons butter
50 g (2 oz) caster sugar
½ teaspoon cinnamon
1 lemon
4 tablespoons apricot jam
Shop-bought glaze

1 Sift the flour with a pinch of salt and baking powder into a bowl. Add the butter and rub this into the flour with the fingertips. Make a well in the centre and mix in the sugar and the egg. Form into a ball with a round-bladed knife, knead briefly, then wrap in clingfilm and refrigerate for 1 hour.

2 Preheat the oven to 180°C (350°F) Gas Mark 4. Roll out the pastry and line a tart tin 23 cm (9 inches) in diameter. Cover the pastry with a circle of nonstick baking paper, weight down with dried beans or pie weights and bake for 10 minutes, then remove the beans and paper and return to the oven for a further 5 minutes.

3 Peel and core 2–3 apples and cut in fairly thick slices. Put in a pan with the butter, half the sugar and the cinnamon. Cook over moderate heat, stirring frequently, for 10–15 minutes to reduce the apples to a compote. Spread this compote in the cooled pastry case.

4 Prepare the remaining apples and slice very finely. Arrange the slices, slightly overlapping, on top of the compote in a rosette design. Squeeze half the lemon and sprinkle the juice over the apples to prevent them discolouring.

5 Put the jam into a small pan with the rest of the sugar, a little lemon juice and 2 tablespoons of water. Heat sufficiently to dissolve the sugar, then pass the jam through a sieve and return to the pan. Boil until it thickens slightly, then brush over the apples. Return the tart to the oven and bake for 35 minutes.

6 Make up the shop-bought glaze according to the instructions on the packet and pour over the cooked tart.

SERVES 6
PREPARATION TIME: 30 MINUTES
COOKING TIME: 1 HOUR

GRANDMA'S CAKE

225 g (8 oz) plain flour
2 teaspoons baking powder
1 teaspoon ground cinnamon
1 teaspoon ground ginger
120 g (4 oz) butter + extra for greasing
120 g (4 oz) soft light brown sugar
175 g (6 oz) honey
2 teaspoons orange marmalade
2 eggs, beaten
125 ml (4 fl oz) milk

FOR THE CREAM
60 g (2½ oz) softened unsalted butter
120 g (4 oz) icing sugar
½ egg yolk
½ teaspoon ground cinnamon
Ground nutmeg
Ground cloves

1 Preheat the oven to 180°C (350°F) Gas Mark 4. Grease and line a round or rectangular cake tin.

2 Sift the flour with the baking powder and spices. Heat the butter, the sugar, honey and marmalade in a small pan until completely melted. Add the flour and the beaten eggs to the mixture, then finally add the milk and stir well. Pour the mixture into the prepared cake tin, put in the oven, and bake for 1 hour. Leave the cake in the tin to cool down, then turn out onto a wire rack to cool completely.

3 To make the cream: beat the butter with the sugar and the half yolk. Add a good pinch of each of the spices.

4 Slice the cake in half horizontally, spread the cream over one half and place the second half on top.

SERVES 4
PREPARATION TIME: 15 MINUTES
COOKING TIME: 50 MINUTES

PLUM & CINNAMON
CRUMBLE

500 g (1 lb) plums
2 teaspoons ground cinnamon
4 tablespoons soft light brown sugar
150 g (5 oz) plain flour
100 g (3½ oz) butter, cut into small pieces
1 egg yolk
3 tablespoons flaked almonds

To serve: crème fraîche

1 Preheat the oven to 180°C (350°F) Gas Mark 4.

2 Wash and stone the plums and put in a small ovenproof dish with 1 teaspoon of cinnamon and 2 tablespoons of the sugar. Bake in the oven for 25 minutes.

3 Put the flour, remaining cinnamon, and the butter into a bowl. Rub the butter into the flour with the fingertips until the mixture resembles fine breadcrumbs. Add the remaining sugar and the egg yolk and mix with a fork.

4 Spread the crumble mixture over the plums, sprinkle with the almonds, put in the oven and bake for about 25 minutes or until the top is brown.

5 Serve either warm or very cold, with the crème fraîche.

MAKES A TART 16–18 CM (6–7 INCHES) IN DIAMETER
PREPARATION TIME: 25 MINUTES
COOKING TIME: 1¾ HOURS

CINNAMON **TART**

1 sheet pre-rolled puff pastry
Butter for greasing
1 egg white

FOR THE CINNAMON CREAM
800 ml (1¼ pints) milk
1 cinnamon stick
3 eggs + 3 yolks
100 g (3½ oz) soft light brown sugar
2 teaspoons ground cinnamon

1 Preheat the oven to 200°C (400°F) Gas Mark 6.

2 Butter a fairly deep cake tin 16–18 cm (6–7 inches) in diameter, or a classic tart tin of a larger diameter.

3 Line the tin with the pastry, cover with a circle of nonstick baking paper, weight with some dried beans or pie weights and bake for 25 minutes. Remove the paper and the beans and return to the oven for a further 5 minutes. Remove from the oven and lower the temperature to 150°C (300°F) Gas Mark 2. Lightly beat the egg white and brush it over the base of the pastry case.

4 Meanwhile prepare the cream: put the milk and the cinnamon stick into a pan and bring gently to a simmer, then remove from the heat. Cover and leave to infuse for 10–20 minutes, then discard the cinnamon stick. In a heatproof bowl whisk the eggs and the yolks with all but 2 tablespoons of the sugar, then slowly add the milk, whisking constantly. Pour this cream through a sieve into the pre-cooked pastry base and bake for 1¼ hours – the flan should be set but still slightly quivery in the centre.

5 Mix the rest of the sugar with the ground cinnamon and sprinkle over the tart. Serve warm or cold.

SERVES 4
PREPARATION TIME: 10 MINUTES
COOKING TIME: 1 HOUR

FIG & CINNAMON **CLAFOUTIS**

8 ripe figs
Butter for greasing
100 g (3½ oz) soft light brown sugar
3 teaspoons ground cinnamon
75 g (3 oz) plain flour
200 (7 fl oz) milk
200 ml (7 fl oz) crème fraîche
4 eggs
Salt

1 Preheat the oven to 200°C (400°F) Gas Mark 6.

2 Wash the figs and cut a cross in the pointed ends. Cut a little from the bases to level them, then sit them in a well-greased, ovenproof dish. Sprinkle over 1 tablespoon of the sugar and 1 teaspoon of the ground cinnamon and put in the oven for 20 minutes.

3 Make a batter with the flour, milk, crème fraîche, eggs, a pinch of salt and all but 2 tablespoons of the remaining sugar.

4 Pour this batter over the figs and return them to the oven for 40 minutes. The cream should be set and the top should be browned and domed. Mix the rest of the sugar and cinnamon together and sprinkle over the clafoutis.

SERVES 6
PREPARATION TIME: 30 MINUTES
COOKING TIME: 1–1¼ HOURS

CHOCOLATE CINNAMON
GATEAU

100 g (3½ oz) good quality milk chocolate
50 g (2 oz) plain flour
½ teaspoon baking powder
2 tablespoons cocoa powder
1 heaped teaspoon ground cinnamon
4 eggs, separated
100 g (3½ oz) caster sugar
2 tablespoons milk
50 g (2 oz) ground almonds or hazelnuts
75 g (3 oz) raisins macerated in 2 tablespoons rum

To serve: ice cream

1 Preheat the oven to 160°C (325°F) Gas Mark 3. Line a cake tin 20 cm (8 inches) in diameter with a circle of nonstick baking paper.

2 Melt half the chocolate in a heatproof bowl set over a pan of barely simmering water, or in the microwave. Chop the rest of the chocolate.

3 Sift the flour with the baking powder, cocoa and cinnamon into a bowl.

4 In another bowl, whisk the egg yolks with the sugar until they are pale and frothy. Mix in the melted chocolate, milk and the ground nuts. Whisk the egg whites until stiff, carefully fold into the mixture, then very delicately fold in the sifted dry ingredients. Lastly, add the chopped chocolate and raisins.

5 Transfer to the cake tin, put in the oven and bake until a metal skewer inserted in the centre comes out quite clean (about 1¼ hours). Leave the cake in the tin for a few minutes before turning out onto a wire rack to cool. Delicious with chocolate or cinnamon ice cream.

SERVES 4
PREPARATION TIME: 10 MINUTES
COOKING TIME: 20 MINUTES
CHILLING TIME: IF REQUIRED, ABOUT 2 HOURS

RISOGALO

4 teaspoons cornflour
500 ml (17 fl oz) whole milk
1 cinnamon stick
100 g (3½ oz) short-grain rice
75 g (3 oz) caster sugar
2 teaspoons ground cinnamon

1 Mix the cornflour into about 200 ml (7 fl oz) of the milk and heat slowly until the mixture thickens.
2 In a separate pan, very slowly bring the remaining milk to the boil together with the cinnamon stick.
3 Sprinkle in the rice and leave to simmer gently for 15 minutes, stirring frequently. Add all but 1 tablespoon of the sugar, and the cornflour and milk mixture. Leave to simmer for a further 5 minutes, check that the grains are soft, then remove from the heat and discard the cinnamon stick.
4 Divide between 4 bowls, dust with ground cinnamon and the remaining sugar and leave to get thoroughly cold before serving.

Cook's Tip Risogalo is a Greek rice pudding, often served as a breakfast dish.

SERVES 4–6
PREPARATION TIME: 20 MINUTES
COOKING TIME: 6 MINUTES

WELSH CAKES

300 g (10 oz) plain flour
1 teaspoon ground cinnamon
1½ teaspoons baking powder
50 g (2 oz) caster sugar
160 g (5½ oz) butter, cut into small pieces,
   + extra for greasing
100 g (3½ oz) raisins
1 egg
Milk

1 Sift the flour with the cinnamon and the baking powder into a large bowl. Add the sugar and the butter and rub into the flour with the fingertips until the mixture resembles fine breadcrumbs.

2 Add the raisins and the egg and mix to a dough, using a round-bladed knife. Add a little milk if the dough seems too dry.

3 Roll out on a floured work surface to a depth of 5 mm (¼ inch). Cut out circles with a 5-cm (2-inch) pastry cutter.

4 Heat up a very heavy-based frying pan (a pancake pan is ideal). When it is very hot, grease it with a buttered sheet of kitchen paper and reduce the heat a little. Cook the Welsh cakes for about 3 minutes on each side. The pan should not be too hot, or the heat too fierce, otherwise the cakes will burn on the outside before the centres are cooked. However, they should become quite brown – even almost blackened in parts. Serve immediately with butter and a cup of tea.

SERVES 4
PREPARATION TIME: 15 MINUTES
COOKING TIME: 30 MINUTES

MELT-IN-THE-MOUTH
SHORTBREAD BISCUITS
WITH CINNAMON & OLIVE OIL

250 g (8 oz) plain flour
125 g (4 oz) caster sugar
Finely grated rind of half a lemon
125 ml (4 fl oz) olive oil
1 teaspoon ground cinnamon
Butter for greasing

1 Preheat the oven to 180°C (350°F) Gas Mark 4. Grease a baking sheet or line it with nonstick baking paper.

2 Sift the flour and sugar into a bowl. Add the grated lemon rind, make a well in the centre and pour in the oil. Form into a ball of dough with the minimum of handling.

3 Roll small quantities (about walnut-size) between the palms to form balls of equal size. Make a little indentation in each to flatten slightly, then place them on the baking sheet, spaced well apart. Dust with cinnamon, put in the oven and bake for 25–30 minutes.

SERVES 2
PREPARATION TIME: 10 MINUTES
COOKING TIME: 6 MINUTES

FRENCH CINNAMON TOAST

2 eggs
400 ml (14 fl oz) milk
2 tablespoons brown sugar
4 slices of day-old brioche with raisins
3 tablespoons butter
1 teaspoon ground cinnamon

To serve: Yogurt ice cream and plums

1 Beat the eggs in a bowl. In another bowl mix the milk and half the sugar. Dip the slices of brioche first into the milk then into the beaten egg.

2 Melt the butter in a frying pan over moderate heat and fry the slices of brioche for 3 minutes on each side. Sprinkle with sugar and cinnamon and serve immediately.

Cook's Tip This makes a very good breakfast but it can be served in rather more elegant form as a dessert with the addition of yogurt ice cream and pitted ripe plums, either raw or stewed.

SERVES 4
PREPARATION TIME: 30 MINUTES
COOKING TIME: 25 MINUTES
CHILLING AND FREEZING TIME: ABOUT 8 HOURS

CINNAMON ICE CREAM
ON A CRISPY FILO BASE

FOR THE CINNAMON AND VANILLA ICE CREAM
300 ml (½ pint) milk
1 vanilla pod
1 cinnamon stick
4 egg yolks
60 g (2½ oz) caster sugar
1 tablespoon cornflour
400 g (14 oz) good fromage frais, well drained

FOR THE CRISP BASE
4 sheets filo pastry
50 g (2 oz) butter (or 3 tablespoons olive oil)
   + a little extra for greasing
2 tablespoons sugar
½ teaspoon ground cinnamon

1 First make the ice cream: pour the milk into a pan, split the vanilla pod in half, scrape the seeds into the milk, then add the pod and the cinnamon stick and bring to the boil. Remove from the heat, cover and leave to infuse for 15 minutes.

2 Beat the egg yolks, sugar and cornflour together in a heatproof bowl. Remove the vanilla pod and cinnamon stick from the milk and return it almost to boiling point. Stirring constantly, pour the hot milk onto the egg yolk mixture, return it to the pan and cook gently, stirring all the time, until the custard thickens.

3 Set aside to cool, then chill in the refrigerator. When the custard is quite cold, mix in the fromage frais. Put in an ice-cream maker to churn, and then freeze.

4 For the crispy bases, preheat the oven to 190°C (375°F) Gas Mark 5. Grease or oil a baking sheet.

5 Melt the butter. Cut the sheets of filo pastry into 6–7-cm (2½–3-inch) squares, brush with melted butter or olive oil and stack in 4 piles. Sprinkle with sugar and cinnamon and arrange on the baking sheet. Bake for about 10 minutes, just long enough to brown the pastry. Serve each person with a little filo pastry base, still hot, topped with a scoop of cinnamon ice cream.

English translation and adaptation: JMS Books LLP
Layout: cbdesign

First published in France in 2007 under the title
La Boîte à gâteau, by Hachette Livre (Marabout)
Copyright © 2007 Hachette Livre (Marabout)
Editorial: Catherine Berranger and Charlotte Müller-Buch

An Hachette Livre UK Company
www.hachettelivre.co.uk

First published in Great Britain in 2008 by
Hamlyn, a division of Octopus Publishing Group Ltd
2–4 Heron Quays, London E14 4JP
www.octopusbooks.co.uk

Copyright © English edition
Octopus Publishing Group Ltd 2008

Original French edition copyright
© HACHETTE LIVRE (Marabout) 2007

ISBN 978 0 600 61876 8

A CIP catalogue record for this book is available from
the British Library

Printed and bound in China

1 3 5 7 9 10 8 6 4 2

This book contains dishes that are made with raw or lightly cooked eggs.
These should be avoided by vulnerable people such as pregnant and
nursing mothers, invalids, the elderly, babies and young children.

MANGO
COCONUT

hamlyn

CONTENTS

SERVES 4
PREPARATION TIME: 25 MINUTES
COOKING TIME: 10 MINUTES
CHILLING TIME: MINIMUM 4 HOURS

MANGO **BAVAROIS**

Oil or butter for greasing
1 sponge base
2–3 ripe mangoes (or a bag of frozen mango quarters)
5 leaves gelatine (10 g)
250 ml (8 fl oz) milk
4 egg yolks
4 tablespoons caster sugar
250 ml (8 fl oz) double or whipping cream
1 small glass orange or passion fruit juice,
   with a little rum if desired
Mint leaves

1 Grease or oil 4 small glasses, moulds or bowls. Cut circles of sponge the size of the serving dishes and set aside.

2 Peel, pit and purée the mangoes, reserving 4 quarters for serving. Soak the gelatine in a bowl of cold water; squeeze out when ready to use.

3 Heat the milk to almost boiling point. Beat the egg yolks and sugar in a heatproof mixing bowl, then pour in the hot (not boiling) milk, stirring constantly. Pour the mixture back into the pan and cook over low heat, stirring constantly, until the custard thickens and coats the back of the spoon. Drain the gelatine and completely dissolve in the hot custard. Allow to cool a little.

4 Add the mango purée. Whip the chilled cream and fold into the mixture. Pour into the serving dishes. Cover with a round of sponge lightly soaked in fruit juice (and alcohol, if using). Put in the refrigerator for at least 4 hours, long enough to set.

5 To turn out: dip the dishes briefly in a bowl of hot water and loosen the edges with a thin knife. Serve with the remaining mangoes cut in strips and decorated with torn-up mint leaves.

Cook's tip Bavarois (Bavarian cream) is a delicate egg custard aerated with whipped cream and set with gelatine.

SERVES 4
PREPARATION TIME: 15 MINUTES + DRAINING TIME
CHILLING TIME: SEVERAL HOURS

SHRIKHAND

12 small plain yogurts
2 very ripe mangoes
4 tablespoons caster sugar
Finely ground seeds of 4 cardamom pods
Pomegranate seeds for decoration (optional)

1 Put the yogurts in two layers of muslin, tie a knot and hang from a wooden spoon placed across a large bowl. Leave the yogurt to drain in a cool place for 5 hours.

2 Peel, pit and purée the mangoes.

3 Mix the drained yogurt with the sugar and ground cardamom seeds.

4 Fold in the mango purée, but leave decorative streaks, no need to mix in thoroughly.

5 Serve chilled, decorated with pomegranate seeds, if using.

Cook's tip Shrikhand is an Indian dessert made of strained yogurt with dried or fresh fruit.

SERVES 4
PREPARATION TIME: 35 MINUTES
CHILLING TIME: SEVERAL HOURS

TIRAMISU WITH MANGO

1 sponge base
Orange juice (and a little rum, if desired)
3 ripe mangoes
250 g (8 oz) mascarpone
2 eggs, separated
4 tablespoons caster sugar
Flaked almonds, lightly toasted

1 Cut the sponge in pieces and place in a fairly shallow dish (glass if possible). Drizzle with the orange juice (and rum, if using).

2 Peel, pit and purée half the mango flesh and cut the remainder in strips.

3 Spread the purée over the soaked sponge and arrange the strips on top.

4 Beat the mascarpone with the egg yolks and sugar. Whisk the egg whites until stiff and gently fold into the mixture. Spread over the mangoes.

5 Place in the refrigerator for several hours if possible. Decorate with the almonds before serving.

SERVES 4
PREPARATION TIME: 40 MINUTES + RESTING TIME
COOKING TIME: 35 MINUTES

MANGO & PEANUT **TART**

FOR THE PASTRY
200 g (7 oz) plain flour
100 g (3½ oz) butter, cut in pieces + extra for greasing
1 tablespoon caster sugar
Salt

FOR THE FILLING
3 tablespoons ground almonds
3 tablespoons peanut butter
2 tablespoons crème fraîche
2 tablespoons caster sugar
1 egg
Rum
3 ripe mangoes

1 To make the dough: sift together the flour and a pinch of salt into a large bowl, add the butter and rub into the flour with your fingertips to the consistency of coarse breadcrumbs. Stir in the sugar, add 100 ml (3½ fl oz) of cold water and mix in with a palette knife. The dough will come together. Finish by hand (adding a little water if necessary), and form into a rough ball but do not work the dough too much. Put in a polythene bag in the refrigerator for at least 1 hour.

2 Preheat the oven to 190°C (375°F) Gas Mark 5.

3 In a bowl, mix the ground almonds, peanut butter, crème fraîche, sugar, egg and rum.

4 Peel and pit the mangoes and cut into strips.

5 Roll out the dough and line a greased tart tin 20–23 cm (8–9 inches) in diameter. Spread the almond and peanut butter cream over the pastry base. Arrange the mango strips on top of the cream.

6 Put into the oven and bake for 35 minutes, long enough for the pastry and cream to turn slightly golden.

SERVES 4
PREPARATION TIME: 20 MINUTES
COOKING TIME: 35 MINUTES
RESTING TIME: PREFERABLY OVERNIGHT

MANGO CAKE

Butter for greasing
120 g (4 oz) flour + extra for dusting
4 eggs, separated
120 g (4 oz) caster sugar for the cake + 3–4 tablespoons
   for the whipped cream
120 ml (4 fl oz) double or whipping cream
120 g (4 oz) mascarpone
2 ripe mangoes
1 glass muscat or orange rum
125 g (4 oz) white almond paste
Icing sugar for dusting

1 Preheat the oven to 180°C (350°F) Gas Mark 4. Grease and flour a baking tray (20 x 30 cm/8 x 12 inches, but no bigger). Instead you could use a rectangular cake tin. The cake will be a bit thicker, but it's nice that way too.

2 In a bowl (over a pan of simmering water, it will be quicker), beat together the egg yolks and the 120 g (4 oz) of sugar. The mixture should become very light and frothy. Sift the flour and fold in with a large spoon. Whisk the egg whites and fold in carefully. Pour onto the baking sheet or into the cake tin, put into the oven and bake for about 20 minutes, reducing the temperature to 160°C (325°F) Gas Mark 3 after 15 minutes. Turn out and leave to cool on a wire rack.

3 Whip the chilled cream with the remaining sugar. Beat the mascarpone to make it smooth, then mix with the whipped cream.

4 Peel and pit the mangoes. Purée the flesh of one and fold the purée into the cream. Cut the second mango in strips.

5 Cut the cake in two. Spread three-quarters of the cream over one half. Cover with the strips of mango and top with the remaining cream. Cover with the other half of the cake. Roll out the almond paste (on a work surface dusted with icing sugar). Cover the cake with the almond paste and refrigerate for several hours, or overnight. Trim the ends of the cake with a sharp knife to neaten them. This cake is best eaten the next day.

SERVES 6–8
PREPARATION TIME: 30 MINUTES
COOKING TIME: 1¼ HOURS

PUFF PASTRY TART
WITH MANGO CREAM

1 sheet pure butter puff pastry
5 fresh mangoes or frozen mango quarters
  (you need about 1 kg /2 lb flesh)
2 eggs
300 ml (½ pint) single cream
125 g (4 oz) caster sugar

1 Preheat the oven to 190°C (375°F) Gas Mark 5. Line a tart tin 25 cm (10 inches) in diameter with the pastry. Cover with nonstick baking paper and dried beans and bake for 15 minutes, then remove the beans and paper and bake for a further 5 minutes. Set aside to cool.

2 Reduce the oven temperature to 160°C (325°F) Gas Mark 3.

3 Peel, pit and purée the mango flesh. Beat this purée together with the eggs, cream and sugar. Pour over the tart base, put in the oven and bake for about 1 hour. The mixture should still be quivery when it comes out of the oven. Allow to cool and set before serving.

SERVES 6
PREPARATION TIME: 30 MINUTES
COOKING TIME: 30 MINUTES

CHOUX WITH MANGOES

150 ml (¼ pint) milk
150 ml (¼ pint) water
1 tablespoon caster sugar
100 g (3½ oz) butter, cut in pieces
150 g (5 oz) plain flour
3 eggs, beaten
3 tablespoons almonds, quite finely chopped
300 ml (½ pint) double cream
4½ tablespoons icing sugar + extra for decoration
2 ripe mangoes
Salt

1 Preheat the oven to 200°C (400°F) Gas Mark 6.

2 To make the choux pastry: in a pan, heat the milk, water, sugar, butter and a pinch of salt. Remove from the heat just before it boils. Add all the flour at once and mix vigorously with a spatula. As soon as the flour has been thoroughly mixed in, put the pan back on the heat to dry out the mixture. Stir until the dough comes away from the sides of the pan. Transfer to a large bowl and gradually add the beaten eggs, 'cutting' the dough with a spatula. It should not be too soft. If the dough looks right (it will gently close up if you run your finger through it), do not add all the egg.

3 Using a piping bag (medium nozzle), pipe a circle of choux pastry 23 cm (9 inches) in diameter on a baking sheet lined with nonstick baking paper (you can draw a circle on the paper with a plate or put a mould on the baking sheet as a guide). Pipe several layers on top of one another to make it thick enough. If you don't have a piping bag, put spoonfuls of pastry in a circle, one on top of the other.

4 Sprinkle with the chopped almonds. Put in the oven, bake for 10 minutes, then increase the oven temperature to 220°C (425°F) Gas Mark 7 and cook for a further 15–20 minutes until the pastry is golden brown. Leave to cool on a wire rack.

5 Whip the chilled cream and add half the icing sugar.

6 Peel and pit the mangoes. Purée one and mix with half the whipped cream. Cut the second mango in small pieces.

7 Cut the pastry circle in 6 and cut each segment in half horizontally. Spread the bottom halves with mango cream, cover with mango pieces and a layer of whipped cream and put the tops back on. Put the 6 segments together on a serving plate to re-form the gateau. Dust with icing sugar and serve quite quickly.

SERVES 4
PREPARATION TIME: 25 MINUTES
COOKING TIME: 1 HOUR

EASY **MANGO CAKE**

125 g (4 oz) butter + extra for greasing
3 eggs
85 g (3½ oz) caster sugar
Vanilla extract
125 g (4 oz) plain flour
3 mangoes
4 tablespoons grated coconut
Salt

1 Preheat the oven to 180°C (350°F) Gas Mark 4. Grease a tart tin.

2 Melt the butter gently in a pan. Beat together the eggs, sugar, a few drops of vanilla extract, to taste, and a pinch of salt. Add the melted butter, then the flour.

3 Peel and pit the mangoes and cut each half in three.

4 Spoon sufficient dough into the tart tin to cover, arrange the pieces of mango on top and cover with the remaining dough, pressing firmly round the edge to seal.

5 Sprinkle with grated coconut. Put into the oven and bake for between 45 minutes and 1 hour. The top should be golden brown.

SERVES 4
PREPARATION TIME: 20 MINUTES

MANGO SPLIT

2 ripe mangoes
150 ml (¼ pint) double or whipping cream
Vanilla extract
4 small bananas
Juice of 1 lime
4 scoops vanilla ice cream
4 scoops mango ice cream
Decorations of your choice: grated chocolate, mini-parasols
   sparklers, etc.

1 Peel and pit the mangoes. Purée the flesh of one and cut the other in pieces.

2 Whip the chilled cream with a few drops of vanilla extract to taste.

3 Cut the bananas in half lengthways and arrange on small plates. Drizzle with lime juice. Put the mango pieces in the middle with one scoop of each flavour of ice cream, then drizzle with mango purée. Top with whipped cream, decorate as desired and serve immediately.

SERVES 6
PREPARATION TIME: 35 MINUTES
COOKING TIME: 2–3 HOURS

MANGO & PASSION FRUIT
PAVLOVAS

5 egg whites
350 g (11½ oz) caster sugar
Vanilla extract
150 ml (¼ pint) double or whipping cream
250 g (8 oz) fromage frais
3 mangoes
3 passion fruit

1 Preheat the oven to 120°C (250°F) Gas Mark ½.

2 Make 1 large meringue or 6 small ones. Whisk the egg whites until stiff, gradually adding 300 g (10 oz) of sugar, then a few drops of vanilla extract, to taste.

3 On a baking sheet lined with nonstick baking paper, form 1 large disc or 6 small ones. You can draw round a plate or a saucer to guide you. Put into the oven and bake for 2–3 hours. The meringues should dry out; the cooking time will depend on their size.

4 Whip the chilled cream with the remaining sugar. Stir the fromage frais and fold into the cream. At the last moment, cover the meringue(s) with cream.

5 Peel, pit and cut the mangoes in strips and arrange on top of the cream.

6 Squeeze the juice and seeds of the passion fruit directly onto the pavlova and serve immediately.

SERVES 4
PREPARATION TIME: 40 MINUTES + OVERNIGHT
RISING TIME: 2 HOURS
COOKING TIME: 45 MINUTES

COCONUT **KUGELHOPF**

FOR THE FIRST DAY'S DOUGH
50 ml (2 fl oz) milk
75 ml (3 fl oz) coconut milk
15 g (½ oz) fresh baker's yeast
120 g (4 oz) plain flour

FOR THE SECOND DAY'S DOUGH
100 g (3½ oz) dried papaya and pineapple chunks
50 g (2 oz) dried coconut chunks
   (or slices, if you can't get chunks)
2 tablespoons rum
1 vanilla pod
50 g (2 oz) Brazil nuts
100 g (3½ oz) soft butter + 40 g (1½ oz) for greasing
3½ tablespoons caster sugar
2 eggs + 2 egg yolks
Finely grated rind of 1 lemon
225 g (7½ oz) plain flour
Salt
Icing sugar

1 Day one: Warm the milk and coconut milk together. In a large bowl, stir the yeast into the warm milk. Mix in the flour to give a fairly soft dough. Cover and leave to rest overnight at room temperature.

2 Day two: Soak the papaya, pineapple and coconut chunks in the rum. Split the vanilla pod lengthways and scrape the seeds into the fruits. Chop the nuts (reserving three whole ones).

3 Put a kugelhopf mould in the refrigerator. Melt the 40 g (1½ oz) of butter, then allow to cool but not set. Brush the mould with a pastry brush, put back in the refrigerator for the butter to set, then brush with a second layer.

4 In a large bowl, beat together the soft butter and sugar with a spatula. Add the whole eggs and the yolks, grated lemon rind and a pinch of salt, while continuing to beat. Finally mix in the flour and the previous day's dough. Beat vigorously by hand, lifting the dough to stretch it as much as possible. If necessary, add a tiny bit more flour to stop it sticking to the sides of the bowl and make it easier to work. Knead for 3–4 minutes (you can use a food processor instead). Lastly, mix in the papaya, pineapple, coconut and chopped nuts. Cover the bowl with greased clingfilm and leave the dough to rise for 1½ hours or longer in a draught-free place. It should double in volume.

5 Put the dough on a lightly floured work surface and press it with the palm of your hand. Cut the remaining Brazil nuts in half lengthways and place them in the grooves at the bottom of the mould. Fill halfway up with dough. Cover with the greased clingfilm and set aside to rise for a further 30 minutes. It should rise to the top of the mould.

6 Preheat the oven to 200°C (400°F) Gas Mark 6. Put the kugelhopf into the oven and bake for about 30 minutes. Test by inserting a metal skewer (it should come out clean). Bake for a further 10 minutes if necessary. Turn out and leave to cool on a wire rack. Dust with icing sugar to serve.

SERVES 6
PREPARATION TIME: 20 MINUTES + SOAKING TIME
COOKING TIME: 25 MINUTES + 10 MINUTES RESTING TIME

GLUTINOUS **RICE**

400 g (13 oz) glutinous rice
400 ml (14 fl oz) coconut milk
100 g (3½ oz) caster sugar
Salt
4 tablespoons grated coconut

1 Rinse the rice in clean water and drain. Put to soak in a pan with at least 500 ml (17 fl oz) of cold water for 1 hour (or overnight).

2 Bring the pan of rice to the boil. Stir once, boil for 5 minutes, then reduce the heat to the minimum, cover tightly and cook for 20 minutes. Remove from the heat and set aside to rest for 10 minutes, keeping the lid on.

3 Mix the coconut milk, sugar and a pinch of salt in another pan. Bring to the boil and simmer, stirring almost continuously, until the liquid has reduced by about one-third. Pour into a large bowl (reserving a little for finishing) and add the rice. Mix in carefully.

4 Heat a frying pan without fat or oil. As soon as it is hot enough, toast the coconut in it for a few seconds. Serve spoonfuls of rice in small bowls with the reserved coconut milk and the toasted coconut.

MAKES 12
PREPARATION TIME: 15 MINUTES
COOKING TIME: 30 MINUTES

MIDDLE EASTERN
CAKES

150 g (5 oz) grated coconut
150 g (5 oz) fine semolina
2 teaspoons baking powder
3 small plain yogurts
1 vanilla pod or bitter almond extract
2 tablespoons flaked or crushed almonds
150 g (5 oz) caster sugar
1 tablespoon butter + extra for greasing
Juice from 1 lemon
300 ml (10 fl oz) water

1 Preheat the oven to 170°C (340°F) Gas Mark 3–4.

2 Mix together the coconut, semolina and baking powder. Add the yogurts and the seeds scraped from the vanilla pod or a few drops of bitter almond extract.

3 Grease a shallow square cake tin (as used for brownies) or muffins cups and pour in the mixture. Fill no more than three-quarters full because it swells during cooking. Smooth the surface. Sprinkle with almonds and bake for 30 minutes.

4 In a small pan, heat the sugar, butter, lemon juice and water. Stir to dissolve the sugar.

5 Turn out the cake and prick with a metal skewer. Pour over the hot syrup. To serve, cut in squares, if you made it in one large tin.

SERVES 6
PREPARATION TIME: 25 MINUTES
COOKING TIME: 1 HOUR
CHILLING TIME: OVERNIGHT

MINI COCONUT
CHEESECAKES

150 g (5 oz) shortbread biscuits
50 g (2 oz) butter
40 g (1½ oz) grated coconut
300 g (10 oz) fromage frais
300 g (10 oz) cream cheese
  (such as Saint-Moret or Philadelphia)
150 g (5 oz) caster sugar
4 eggs
Finely grated rind and juice of 1 lime or lemon
200 ml (7 fl oz) coconut milk

1 Preheat the oven to 180°C (350°F) Gas Mark 4.

2 Put the biscuits in a polythene bag and crush with a rolling pin. Melt the butter and mix with the biscuit crumbs and coconut. Spoon this mixture into deep individual moulds (disposable foil moulds are very suitable). Put into the oven and bake for 10 minutes. Remove from the oven and reduce the temperature to 140°C (275°F) Gas Mark 1.

3 In a food processor or with an electric beater, stir the cheeses (no more than 30 seconds), add the sugar, then the eggs one at a time, and then the grated peel and lemon or lime juice. Lastly add the coconut milk.

4 Pour into the moulds. Place the moulds on a baking sheet, put in the oven and bake for 45 minutes, then turn off the oven, leaving the cheesecakes in it with the door ajar to cool. Remove from the oven, allow to get cold, and store in the refrigerator until the next day.

SERVES 6
PREPARATION TIME: 25 MINUTES
COOKING TIME: 1¾ HOURS

COCONUT **FLAN**

FOR THE PASTRY
240 g (8 oz) plain flour
2 tablespoons caster sugar
1 teaspoon salt
120 g (4 oz) butter, cut into pieces,
   + a little for greasing
1 vanilla pod
1 egg white

FOR THE FILLING
400 ml (14 fl oz) milk
400 ml (14 fl oz) coconut milk
1 vanilla pod
2 whole eggs + 2 yolks
2 tablespoons cornflour, Maizena if possible
100 g (3½ oz) caster sugar + a little for decoration

1 Preheat the oven to 190°C (375°F) Gas Mark 5.

2 To make the pastry: sift the flour and salt together into a bowl, add the butter and rub in with your fingertips to the consistency of coarse breadcrumbs. Stir in the sugar and the seeds scraped from the vanilla pod. Moisten with 3–4 tablespoons of very cold water and mix together with a knife. Finish bringing the dough together by hand, without working it too much. Form into a rough ball, wrap in clingfilm and set aside to rest in a cool place for at least 1 hour. You can also make the pastry in a food processor.

3 Grease a flan tin, roll out the pastry and line the tin. Cover the pastry base with a sheet of nonstick baking paper, fill with dried beans, put into the oven and bake for 25 minutes. Remove the beans and paper and bake for a further 10 minutes, Brush the base with lightly beaten egg white. Turn the oven down to 150°C (300°F) Gas Mark 2.

4 To make the filling: gently simmer the milk and coconut milk with the split vanilla pod. Beat the eggs and egg yolks with the sugar and cornflour, then beat in the hot milk. Scrape the vanilla seeds into the mixture before pouring it through a sieve into the cooked flan case. Put into the oven and bake for about 1 hour 15 minutes. The filling should have set but still be a little quivery in the middle. Sprinkle with a little sugar. Serve warm or cold.

SERVES 4
PREPARATION TIME: 25 MINUTES
COOKING TIME: 50 MINUTES

QUEEN OF PUDDINGS
WITH COCONUT

150 g (5 oz) stale white bread or brioche
Vanilla extract
1 tablespoon caster sugar
Finely grated rind of ½ lemon
200 ml (7 fl oz) milk
50 g (2 oz) butter + extra for greasing
300 ml (½ pint) coconut milk
4 eggs, separated
2 tablespoons bramble jelly
100 g (3½ oz) caster sugar
Salt

1 Preheat the oven to 180°C (350°F) Gas Mark 4. Grease an ovenproof dish that it not too deep or wide.

2 Process the bread into coarse breadcrumbs and tip into a mixing bowl. Add a few drops of vanilla extract with the tablespoon of sugar and the grated lemon rind.

3 In a small pan, heat the milk with the butter. Just before it boils, pour the hot milk over the breadcrumbs, then add the coconut milk. Lastly beat in the egg yolks

4 Pour the mixture into the greased baking dish, put into the oven and bake for about 30 minutes. The cream should be just starting to firm.

5 Warm the jelly gently and spread it over the cream, when it has cooled a little. Whisk the egg whites until stiff with a pinch of salt, add the sugar (reserving 2 teaspoons) and whisk again. Spread the meringue over the cream, sprinkle with the remaining sugar and put in the oven for about 15 minutes, just long enough for the meringue to brown in places. Serve hot.

SERVES 6
PREPARATION TIME: 20 MINUTES
COOKING TIME: 15 MINUTES

CONGOLAIS

Butter for greasing
3 egg whites
150 g (5 oz) caster sugar
Vanilla extract
200 g (7 oz) grated coconut

1 Preheat the oven to 200°C (400°F) Gas Mark 6. Grease several baking sheets or cover with nonstick baking paper.
2 Beat together the egg whites, sugar and a few drops of vanilla extract in a large pan over low heat, until the mixture is frothy. Remove from the heat and continue beating until it is almost cold.
3 Add the coconut and mix with a spatula. Place small spoonfuls of dough on the baking sheets. Put into the oven and bake for 15 minutes.

Cook's tip Congolais are small biscuits made with meringue and grated coconut.

SERVES 4
PREPARATION TIME: 1 HOUR
COOKING TIME: 15 MINUTES
FREEZING TIME: 4 HOURS (DEPENDING ON THE ICE-CREAM MAKER)

COCONUT ICE CREAM
WITH FRESH COCONUT

3 coconuts
Peel of 1 lime
1 cinnamon stick
500 ml (17 fl oz) milk
4 egg yolks
75 g (3 oz) caster sugar

1 Break open the coconuts, scoop out the flesh, remove the brown skin and grate the flesh.

2 Bring 1 litre (1¾ pints) water to the boil with the lime peel and cinnamon stick. Remove from the heat and add the grated coconut. Set aside to cool.

3 Put a small quantity of pulp in a double layer of muslin and squeeze to extract the coconut milk. Do the same with the remaining pulp, a little at a time.

4 To make an egg custard: first heat the milk. Mix together the egg yolks and sugar in a heatproof bowl then pour over the milk, stirring constantly. Pour back into the pan over low heat, stirring constantly until the custard coats the back of the spoon. Leave to cool.

5 Mix the cooled egg custard with the coconut milk. Freeze in an ice-cream maker.

MAKES 12
PREPARATION TIME: 30 MINUTES
COOKING TIME: 35 MINUTES

COCONUT &
PASSION FRUIT CAKES

FOR THE CAKES
180 g (6 oz) soft butter + extra for greasing
100 g (3½ oz) caster sugar
Vanilla extract
3 eggs
225 g (7½ oz) plain flour
2 teaspoons baking powder
150 g (5 oz) grated coconut

FOR THE ICING
100 g (3½ oz) soft butter
300 g (10 oz) icing sugar
1 teaspoon vanilla extract
Milk
Salt
3 passion fruit
100 g (3½ oz) sliced coconut

1 Preheat the oven to 160°C (325°F) Gas Mark 3. Grease a 12-cup muffin tin very thoroughly or line with paper cases.

2 Beat together the butter, sugar and a few drops of vanilla extract until the mixture becomes very fluffy. Add the eggs one at a time, then sift in the flour and baking powder together.

3 Fold in the coconut, mixing carefully. Fill the muffin cups or paper cases three-quarters full with the mixture and bake for 35 minutes (If you insert a metal skewer, it should come out clean). Turn out and leave to cool on a wire rack.

4 To make the icing: mix together all the ingredients (except the coconut slices) with a little milk and a pinch of salt, finishing with the passion fruit flesh. Ice the cakes and decorate with coconut slices.

SERVES 6
PREPARATION TIME: 35 MINUTES
COOKING TIME: 1 HOUR 20 MINUTES

COCONUT & CHOCOLATE
POUND CAKE

250 g (8 oz) soft butter + extra for greasing
250 g (8 oz) brown sugar
4 eggs
1 glass orange juice (preferably freshly squeezed)
250 g (8 oz) plain flour + extra for dusting
2 teaspoons baking powder
200 g (7 oz) dark or white chocolate
   (or a mixture of both), chopped
150 g (5 oz) grated coconut (or half grated and half in chunks)

1 Preheat the oven to 180°C (350°F) Gas Mark 4. Grease and flour a 1-kg (2-lb) capacity loaf tin or line it with nonstick baking paper.

2 Beat together the butter and sugar until the mixture becomes very fluffy (it's easier with an electric whisk). Beat in the eggs one at a time. Mix in the orange juice. Sift the flour and baking powder together into a bowl. Using a large spoon, blend the flour into the butter-sugar-egg mixture, working carefully and 'cutting' the dough.

3 Add the chocolate (reserving a little for the top of the cake) and the coconut. Do not overmix.

4 Tip the dough into the loaf tin and put the remaining chocolate on top. Put into the oven and bake for about 1¼ hours. Test by inserting a metal skewer into the cake. It should come out clean. Leave to rest for 15 minutes before turning out. Eat warm or cold.

Cook's tip A pound cake is traditionally made with equal quantities of butter, sugar, eggs and flour.

English translation and adaptation: JMS Books LLP
Layout: cbdesign

First published in France in 2007 under the title
La Boîte à gâteau, by Hachette Livre (Marabout)
Copyright © 2007 Hachette Livre (Marabout)
Editorial: Catherine Berranger and Charlotte Müller-Buch

An Hachette Livre UK Company
www.hachettelivre.co.uk

First published in Great Britain in 2008 by
Hamlyn, a division of Octopus Publishing Group Ltd
2–4 Heron Quays, London E14 4JP
www.octopusbooks.co.uk

Copyright © English edition
Octopus Publishing Group Ltd 2008

Original French edition copyright
© HACHETTE LIVRE (Marabout) 2007

ISBN 978 0 600 61876 8

A CIP catalogue record for this book is available from
the British Library

Printed and bound in China

1 3 5 7 9 10 8 6 4 2

This book contains dishes that are made with raw or lightly cooked eggs.
These should be avoided by vulnerable people such as pregnant and
nursing mothers, invalids, the elderly, babies and young children.

ALMOND
NOUGAT

hamlyn

CONTENTS

SERVES 6
PREPARATION TIME: 1 HOUR
COOKING TIME: 10 MINUTES
CHILLING: MINIMUM OF 4 HOURS, PREFERABLY OVERNIGHT

PANNA COTTA
WITH ALMOND MILK

250 ml (8 fl oz) water
250 ml (8 fl oz) milk
250 g (8 oz) whole almonds
10 leaves gelatine (20 g)
120 g (4 oz) caster sugar
Bitter almond extract (optional)
250 ml (8 fl oz) double cream
Flavourless oil (such as groundnut) for greasing
Poached apricots for serving

1 Heat the water and milk in a pan. Remove from the heat just before it boils. Grind the almonds in a food processor, gradually adding the hot water and milk. Allow to cool. Line a sieve with two layers of muslin and place it over a pan. Pour the almond, milk and water mixture into the sieve and leave to drain. Then wrap it in the muslin and twist very tightly to squeeze out as much liquid as possible. Measure 450 ml (¾ pint) of the almond milk, adding a little water if necessary.

2 Soak the gelatine in a little cold water; squeeze out when ready to use. Heat the almond milk with the sugar and a few drops of almond extract, if using, stirring to dissolve the sugar. Add the squeezed-out gelatine and dissolve it completely in the mixture just before it boils. Set aside to cool.

3 Whip the chilled cream and fold it into the cooled mixture. Pour into 6 small ramekins or 6 glasses (brushed with oil if you want to turn out the panna cottas), or into a nice big mould with a capacity of 1 litre (1¾ pints) (also lightly oiled). Refrigerate for at least 4 hours, or overnight.

4 Dip the moulds quickly in hot water to turn out, or leave in the ramekins or glasses if they look attractive. Serve with poached apricots.

SERVES 6
PREPARATION TIME: 1 HOUR
COOKING TIME: 20 MINUTES
REFRIGERATION TIME: MINIMUM 5 HOURS
RESTING TIME: MINIMUM 5 HOURS

ALMOND MILK
ICE CREAM

4 egg yolks
4 tablespoons caster sugar
150 ml (¼ pint) double cream

FOR THE ALMOND MILK
250 ml (8 fl oz) water
250 ml (8 fl oz) milk
250 g (8 oz) whole almonds
(Instead you could use 450 ml/¾ pint ready-made
   almond milk from a specialist or health food store)

1 Lightly toast the whole almonds for 3–4 minutes in an oven preheated to 190°C (375°F) Gas Mark 5.

2 Heat the water and milk in a pan. Remove from the heat just before it boils. Grind the almonds in a food processor, gradually adding the hot water and milk. Allow to cool.

3 Line a sieve with two layers of muslin and place it over a pan. Pour the almond, milk and water mixture into the sieve and leave to drain. Then wrap it in the muslin and twist very tightly to squeeze out as much liquid as possible. Measure 450 ml (¾ pint) of the almond milk, adding a little water if necessary.

4 Make an egg custard with the almond milk. Beat the egg yolks with the sugar. Heat the almond milk before pouring it over the egg mixture, stirring constantly. Cook over low heat, stirring, until it thickens and coats the back of the spoon. Allow to cool.

5 Whip the chilled cream and mix with the custard. Freeze in an ice-cream maker.

SERVES 6
PREPARATION TIME: 30 MINUTES
COOKING TIME: 35 MINUTES

ALMOND & APRICOT
MOELLEUX

250 g (8 oz) soft butter + extra for greasing
150 g (5 oz) caster sugar + 2 tablespoons for decoration
4 eggs
Finely grated rind and juice of 1 lemon
100 g (3½ oz) plain flour
75 g (3 oz) ground almonds
100 g (3½ oz) soft dried apricots, very finely chopped
3 tablespoons flaked almonds

To serve: almond milk ice cream (see page 8)

1 Preheat the oven to 180°C (350°F) Gas Mark 4. Grease a cake tin 20–23 cm (8–9 inches) in diameter and line with a sheet of nonstick baking paper.

2 Beat together the butter and sugar (preferably with an electric beater) until the mixture turns pale and fluffy.

3 Beat the eggs one at a time into the butter and sugar mixture. Add the grated lemon rind.

4 Sift the flour and ground almonds together and stir carefully into the previous mixture in two or three lots, using a large spoon or a whisk, without working the dough too much. Lastly add the lemon juice and apricots. Mix just enough to blend them in.

5 Pour into the cake tin, put into the oven and bake for 30–35 minutes. (Test the cake by inserting a metal skewer. If it comes out clean, the cake is ready). Turn out onto a wire rack to cool. Sprinkle with sugar and flaked almonds. Serve with almond milk ice cream.

Cook's tip Moelluex is a very moist cake with a soft 'sunken' centre.

SERVES 6
PREPARATION TIME: 20 MINUTES
COOKING TIME: 35 MINUTES

'BROKEN BISCUITS'
WITH ALMONDS & CHOCOLATE

75 g (3 oz) whole almonds
125 g (4 oz) butter, cut in pieces + extra for greasing
300 g (10 oz) plain flour
½ teaspoon baking powder
2 egg yolks
75 g (3 oz) caster sugar
75 g (3 oz) dark or milk chocolate, roughly chopped
Cocoa for dusting

1 Preheat the oven to 180°C (350°F) Gas Mark 4. Spread out the almonds on a baking sheet and toast for 6 minutes, but watch carefully as they can brown very quickly. Grease a tart tin 20–23 cm (8–9 inches) in diameter, if possible with a loose base.

2 Sift together the flour and baking powder. Rub the butter into the flour with your fingertips to the consistency of coarse breadcrumbs. Mix in the egg yolks.

3 Lastly add the sugar, chocolate, and toasted almonds.

4 Spoon the mixture into the tart tin, level off the surface, put into the oven and bake for 30 minutes.

5 Turn out onto a wire rack to cool. Break in pieces and dust lightly with cocoa. Serve with coffee.

MAKES ABOUT 20
PREPARATION TIME: 2 MINUTES
COOKING TIME: 15 MINUTES

AMARETTI

150 g (5 oz) ground almonds
200 g (7 oz) icing sugar
Bitter almond extract
2 egg whites
3 tablespoons caster sugar
A little butter for greasing

1 Preheat the oven to 220°C (425°F) Gas Mark 7. Grease a baking sheet or cover with a sheet of nonstick baking paper.

2 Mix the ground almonds with the icing sugar, a few drops of almond extract and the egg whites (DO NOT whisk!). Form this mixture into a 'sausage' 3 cm (1¼ inches) in diameter.

3 Cut in slices 1 cm (½ inch) thick and arrange, spaced well apart, on the baking sheet (bake several batches if the sheet is too small). Sprinkle with caster sugar, put into the oven and bake for 15 minutes. The amaretti should be slightly golden. Leave to cool on a wire rack.

Cook's tip Amaretti are Italian macaroons. You can eat them on their own, use in desserts (trifles, verrines) or crumble over ice cream or fromage frais.

MAKES 6 CASSATAS
PREPARATION TIME: 25 MINUTES
CHILLING TIME: 4 HOURS

MINI ALMOND PASTE
& RASPBERRY CASSATAS

Icing sugar for dusting
250 g (8 oz) almond paste (see page 18)
1 round sponge base
2 tablespoons Muscat or Grand Marnier
300 g (10 oz) fromage frais or cream cheese
100 g (3½ oz) mascarpone
Finely grated rind of ½ lemon
1 vanilla pod
3 tablespoons caster sugar
1 punnet raspberries

1 Roll out the almond paste on a work surface dusted with icing sugar. Dust 6 small moulds or ramekins with icing sugar.

2 Cut rounds of paste to fit the base of the moulds and strips the height of the moulds, and line the bases and sides of the moulds. Cut rounds for the lids and set aside.

3 Cut rounds of sponge the size of the moulds and place on top of the almond paste bases. Drizzle the sponge with the alcohol.

4 Beat together the fromage frais and mascarpone. Add the grated lemon rind, the seeds from the vanilla pod, scraped out with the point of a knife, and the caster sugar. Fold in the raspberries (reserving a few for decoration) and fill the moulds with this mixture. Cover the moulds with the almond paste lids.

5 Set aside in a cool place for 1 hour, then turn out onto a large serving dish or small dessert plates. Put in the refrigerator for 2 or 3 hours. Dust with icing sugar before serving.

MAKES ABOUT 625 g (1¼ LB) ALMOND PASTE
PREPARATION TIME: 20 MINUTES
COOKING TIME: 3 MINUTES

ALMOND **PASTE**

500 g (1 lb) whole almonds, skinned
1 tablespoons caster sugar
150 g (5 oz) icing sugar + a few
   spoonfuls for dusting the worktop
Bitter almond extract (optional)
Vanilla essence
Food colourings (optional)

1 To skin the almonds: plunge twice in boiling water. After that, the skin should come away easily when you pinch between your fingers.

2 Preheat the oven to 190°C (375°F) Gas Mark 5.

3 Spread the almonds on a baking sheet to dry thoroughly and toast lightly in the oven for 3–4 minutes (you need not do this if you want to make a classic almond paste – without the slightly toasted flavour.) Grind the almonds with the caster sugar, adding it a little at a time. Take care: it is best to pulse the almonds as you want to achieve a fine powder, absolutely not an oily paste. (In fact you could use ground almonds but you run the risk of their not being so fresh.)

4 Add the icing sugar and a few drops of the extracts (and colourings, if desired). Knead the paste until smooth, dusting with icing sugar so you can work it, roll it out and shape it. Use for all kinds of pastries. You can colour the paste to make decorations (flowers, fruits…).

MAKES ABOUT 20
PREPARATION TIME: 25 MINUTES
RESTING TIME: 1 HOUR
COOKING TIME: 4 X 17 MINUTES

TUILES AUX AMANDES

1 whole egg + 2 egg whites
125 g (4 oz) caster sugar
40 g (1½ oz) plain flour
1 vanilla pod
Finely grated rind of ½ orange or 1 lemon or lime
150 g (5 oz) flaked almonds
Butter for greasing

1 Mix together the egg and the sugar, then the egg whites. Add the sifted flour, seeds scraped from the vanilla pod and the finely grated peel. Mix in the almonds with a spatula, taking care not to break them. Set the mixture aside to rest for 1 hour in a cool place.

2 Preheat the oven to 150°C (300°F) Gas Mark 2. Grease several baking sheets.

3 Put little blobs of dough spaced well apart on the baking sheets and flatten into discs with a fork dipped in water. Put into the oven and bake for 15–17 minutes. You will have to bake several batches.

4 Have small tumblers ready for use by the oven. When the tuiles start to turn golden, remove from the oven immediately. Lay them on the sides of the tumblers to give the tuile its traditional curve. When the tuiles have hardened, put them to cool on a wire rack.

Cook's tip Tuiles are crisp, thin biscuits, so named because they look like tiny roof tiles. Tuile is the French word for tile.

SERVES 4
PREPARATION TIME: 20 MINUTES
COOKING TIME: 15 MINUTES

CROISSANTS BOURDALOUE

60 g (2¼ oz) soft butter
50 g (2 oz) caster sugar
1 egg
60 g (2¼ oz) ground almonds
1 tablespoon rum
1 vanilla pod
4 stale butter croissants
2 home-poached pears

1 Preheat the oven to 180°C (350°F) Gas Mark 4. Line a baking sheet with nonstick baking paper.

2 Beat together the butter and sugar. Mix in the egg, ground almonds, rum and seeds scraped from the vanilla pod with the point of a knife.

3 Cut the croissants in half horizontally. Spread with two thirds of the almond cream.

4 Drain the pears, core and cut in slices and lay them on the croissants. Put the tops on and spread the remaining cream over the croissants.

5 Put into the oven and bake for 10–15 minutes. The cream on top should be golden.

SERVES 6
PREPARATION TIME: 20 MINUTES
COOKING TIME: 1 HOUR

ALMONDY
TARTE ANGLAISE

150 g (5 oz) butter
1 roll (sheet) pure butter puff pastry
2 tablespoons raspberry or blackcurrant jam (not jelly)
1 egg white + 4 egg yolks
120 g (4 oz) caster sugar
50 g (2 oz) ground almonds

1 Preheat the oven to 200°C (400°F) Gas Mark 6.

2 Melt the butter then allow to cool. Roll the pastry out a little thinner and use it to line a baking tin 20–23 cm (8–9 inches) in diameter. Spread the jam over the pastry.

3 Beat together the egg white and sugar until the mixture is very white and frothy. Add the egg yolks and mix well. Add the cooled butter and the ground almonds. Mix and pour over the tart base.

4 Put in the oven and bake for 1 hour, but watch carefully: the filling should have set, but if the top browns too quickly, cover with kitchen foil during cooking.

5 Leave to rest for 15 minutes. Serve warm or cold.

6 You can also make individual tartlets.

SERVES 4
PREPARATION TIME: 15 MINUTES
COOKING TIME: 15 MINUTES
FREEZING TIME: 6 HOURS

SEMIFREDDO
WITH NOUGAT

150 g hard nougat (Spanish turrón duro or Italian torrone)
2 eggs, separated
2 tablespoons caster sugar
150 ml (¼ pint) milk
1 vanilla pod
100 ml (3½ oz) double or whipping cream

1 Chop or crush the nougat as fine as possible, almost to a powder (you can do this in a food processor).

2 Beat the egg yolks together with the sugar. Heat the milk with the seeds scraped from the vanilla pod. As soon as the milk boils, pour it over the egg mixture, stirring constantly. Pour the mixture back into the pan and thicken over low heat, stirring constantly until the cream coats the back of the spoon.

3 Pour into a clean bowl, add the powdered nougat, mix well and leave to cool.

4 Whisk the egg whites until stiff and fold very carefully into the mixture. Whip the chilled cream and fold this in also. Pour into a mould or a lined rectangular freezerbox and put in the freezer for at least 6 hours.

5 Take out of the freezer 15–20 minutes before serving. Serve in slices (perhaps with a fruit coulis).

Cook's tip Semifreddo is a soft iced dessert with a texture halfway between mousse and ice cream.

SERVES 6
PREPARATION TIME: 25 MINUTES
COOKING TIME: 10 MINUTES
RESTING TIME: 30 MINUTES

HOME-MADE NOUGAT
WITH BRAZIL NUTS

200 g (7 oz) Brazil nuts
200 g (7 oz) orange flower honey (optional)
800 g (1¾ lb) caster sugar + 1 tablespoon for the egg whites
1 tablespoon orange flower water
2 teaspoons cream of tartar
3 egg whites
Rice paper (or nonstick baking paper)

1 Chop the nuts.

2 Put the honey, sugar, orange flower water and 100 ml (3½ fl oz) of water in a large pan. Bring to the boil, stirring to dissolve the sugar. Add the cream of tartar and continue cooking this syrup until it reaches the 'balling' stage: if you plunge a teaspoonful of mixture into a bowl of cold water, it should form a malleable, not too sticky ball. Remove from the heat and leave to cool for 3–4 minutes.

3 Whisk the egg whites until stiff, then add the 1 tablespoon of sugar and continue whisking until they are firm and shiny. Pour the sugar syrup over the egg whites in a thin stream, whisking constantly. Continue beating until the mixture cools.

4 Mix in the nuts.

5 Pour into a rectangular mould lined with rice paper. Smooth the surface with a spatula dipped in hot water and cover with a sheet of rice paper. Leave to set for 30 minutes before cutting in rectangles or squares. This nougat can also be made with almonds, pistachios, etc.

SERVES 4
PREPARATION TIME: 30 MINUTES
REFRIGERATION TIME: MINIMUM 4 HOURS

NOUGAT-STYLE
FROMAGE FRAIS

100 g (3½ oz) mixed dried fruit and nuts
   (raisins, almonds, hazelnuts, etc.)
100 ml (3½ fl oz) orange juice or a mixture of rum and orange
100 ml (3½ fl oz) double or whipping cream
3 leaves gelatine (approx. 6 g)
100 g (3½ oz) fromage frais
2 tablespoons caster sugar
2 teaspoons orange flower water
3 egg whites

1 Chop the dried fruit and nuts, cover with orange juice and leave to soak.

2 Whip the chilled cream. Soak the gelatine in cold water; squeeze out when ready to use.

3 Mix the fromage frais with the well-drained fruit and nuts and the sugar.

4 Heat the orange flower water and the orange juice in which the fruits were soaked. Dissolve the gelatine in it before mixing it all with the fromage frais. Whisk the egg whites and add to the mixture, along with the whipped cream.

5 Leave to set in the refrigerator for at least 4 hours or freeze for 4 hours. Take it out 15 minutes before serving if you chose the freezer option. Very good with a mango coulis.

SERVES 4
PREPARATION TIME: 15 MINUTES
COOKING TIME: 5 MINUTES

STRAWBERRIES
WITH HALVA

750 g (1½ lb) strawberries
3 tablespoons caster sugar
1 lemon
150 g (5 oz) good quality halva (available in delicatessens, health
   food stores and some supermarkets)

1 Wash and hull the strawberries.

2 In a small pan, heat the sugar and lemon juice (plus a little peel, if desired) with 100 ml (3½ fl oz) water. Stir to dissolve the sugar and simmer for a few minutes, long enough to give you a fairly runny syrup. Set aside to cool.

3 Cut the strawberries in pieces. Cut the halva in slightly smaller pieces. Fill small glasses with a few strawberries, pieces of halva, then a few more strawberries. Drizzle with the cold syrup and serve.

Cook's tip The acidity of the strawberries goes well with the very sugary, melting taste of the halva.

SERVES 4
PREPARATION TIME: 40 MINUTES
COOKING TIME: 15 MINUTES
CHILLING TIME : MINIMUM 4 HOURS

JIJONA TURRÓN **CHARLOTTE**

5 leaves gelatine (10 g)
500 ml (17 fl oz) milk
1 vanilla pod
4 tablespoons caster sugar
4 egg yolks
200 ml (7 fl oz) double cream
50 g (2 oz) Jijona turrón (soft Spanish nougat, available in
   delicatessens and some supermarkets), crumbled
About 30 boudoir biscuits or sponge fingers
Apple juice

1   Soak the gelatine in cold water; squeeze out when ready to use.

2   Heat the milk with the seeds scraped from the vanilla pod. Beat together sugar and egg yolks, pour over the nearly boiling milk, stirring constantly, pour back into the pan and cook over low heat, stirring constantly until it thickens and coats the back of the spoon.

3   Dissolve the softened gelatine completely in the hot custard, then leave to cool.

4   Whip the chilled cream. Mix together the custard, whipped cream and crumbled nougat.

5   Line a charlotte mould with the boudoir biscuits soaked briefly in apple juice. Pour in half the cream, add a layer of soaked biscuits and finish with the remaining cream. Cover and place in the refrigerator to set. Turn out and serve.

SERVES 4
PREPARATION TIME: 25 MINUTES
COOKING TIME: 15 MINUTES
FREEZING TIME: 4 HOURS

TWO NOUGAT **ICE CREAM**

50 g (2 oz) Jijona turrón (soft Spanish nougat)
50 g (2 oz) turrón de Alicante (variety of hard Spanish nougat)
500 ml (17 fl oz) milk
4 egg yolks
2 tablespoons caster sugar
300–400 g (10–13 oz) Greek yogurt
Salt

1 Crumble the soft nougat by crushing with a fork. Chop the hard nougat, but not too finely.

2 Heat the milk. Beat together the egg yolks, sugar and a pinch of salt. Pour the hot milk over this mixture, stirring constantly, then pour back into the pan, and cook over low heat, stirring constantly, until the custard coats the back of the spoon.

3 Stir the soft nougat into the hot custard. Allow to cool before adding the yogurt. Freeze in an ice-cream maker. While the ice cream is still soft, add the chopped, hard nougat.

SERVES 4
PREPARATION TIME: 35 MINUTES
CHILLING TIME: SEVERAL HOURS

TIRAMISU WITH NOUGAT

1 sponge base
Strawberry or raspberry syrup
500 g (1 lb) raspberries
100 g (3½ oz) Jijona turrón (soft Spanish nougat)
250 g (8 oz) mascarpone
2 eggs, separated
2 tablespoons caster sugar
Flaked almonds, lightly toasted

1 Break the sponge base in pieces, put them in the bottom of a fairly shallow dish and drizzle with well-diluted syrup so that it is not too sweet.

2 Crush the raspberries with a fork, crumble the nougat and spread both over the sponge.

3 Beat together the mascarpone, egg yolks and sugar. Whisk the egg whites and fold into the mixture. Spread over the nougat and raspberries.

4 Place in the refrigerator for several hours if possible. Decorate with the almonds before serving.

SERVES 4
PREPARATION TIME: 15 MINUTES
RESTING TIME: 5 HOURS

ORIENTAL YOGURT

10 small natural yogurts
1 tablespoon tahini (sesame paste)
Honey
60 g (2¼ oz) soft or hard nougat (your choice)

1 Wrap the decanted yogurts in two layers of muslin, tie a knot and hang on a wooden spoon laid across a large bowl. Leave to drain for 5 hours.

2 Beat the yogurt, then mix with the tahini. Sweeten, to taste, with a little honey.

3 Crumble the nougat and gently fold into the yogurt, reserving a little for decoration.

4 Serve in small glasses.

SERVES 4
PREPARATION TIME: 30 MINUTES

GRAPE & NOUGAT
TARTLETS

75 g (3 oz) nougat
250 g (8 oz) mascarpone
12 ready-made mini shortcrust tartlets
1 bunch grapes, deseeded and halved
12 small mint leaves

1 Crumble the nougat.
2 Stir the mascarpone with a spatula until smooth and spoon into the tartlets.
3 Add a few grapes to each, sprinkle with the crumbled nougat and decorate each one with a mint leaf before serving.

SERVES 4–6
PREPARATION TIME: 20 MINUTES
COOKING TIME: 3 MINUTES
CHILLING TIME: MINIMUM 4 HOURS

NEW YEAR'S DAY **JELLY**

6 leaves gelatine (12 g)
450 ml (¾ pint) sparkling wine (such as Cava or Asti)
1 lemon
2 tablespoons caster sugar
125 g (4 oz) Jijona turrón (soft Spanish nougat)
250 g (8 oz) raspberries (optional)

1 Soak the gelatine in a little cold water; squeeze out when ready to use.

2 Heat 200 ml (7 fl oz) of the wine with 1 tablespoon (or to taste) of lemon juice and the sugar.

3 Dissolve the gelatine completely in the hot wine, away from the heat, then pour in the remaining wine.

4 Cut the nougat in pieces the size of the raspberries. Fill 4 or 6 glasses with nougat and raspberries. Pour over the jelly and put in the refrigerator for at least 4 hours to set.

English translation and adaptation: JMS Books LLP
Layout: cbdesign

First published in France in 2007 under the title
La Boîte à gâteau, by Hachette Livre (Marabout)
Copyright © 2007 Hachette Livre (Marabout)
Editorial: Catherine Berranger and Charlotte Müller-Buch

An Hachette Livre UK Company
www.hachettelivre.co.uk

First published in Great Britain in 2008 by
Hamlyn, a division of Octopus Publishing Group Ltd
2–4 Heron Quays, London E14 4JP
www.octopusbooks.co.uk

Copyright © English edition
Octopus Publishing Group Ltd 2008

Original French edition copyright
© HACHETTE LIVRE (Marabout) 2007

ISBN 978 0 600 61876 8

A CIP catalogue record for this book is available from
the British Library

Printed and bound in China

1 3 5 7 9 10 8 6 4 2

This book contains dishes that are made with raw or lightly cooked eggs.
These should be avoided by vulnerable people such as pregnant and
nursing mothers, invalids, the elderly, babies and young children.

RASPBERRIES
SUMMER BERRIES

hamlyn

CONTENTS

SERVES 4
PREPARATION TIME: 20 MINUTES
COOKING TIME: 35 MINUTES
CHILLING TIME: OVERNIGHT IF POSSIBLE

RASPBERRY **GATEAU**

Butter, for greasing
120 g (4 oz) plain flour + extra for dusting
4 eggs, separated
120 g (4 oz) caster sugar + 3–4 tablespoons extra for the
   whipped cream
120 ml (4 fl oz) double cream, chilled
120 g (4 oz) mascarpone
250 g (8 oz) fresh raspberries
4 tablespoons Muscat, Grand Marnier or raspberry syrup
125 g (4 oz) white or pink almond paste/marzipan
Icing sugar, for dusting

1 Preheat the oven to 180°C (350°F) Gas Mark 4. Grease and flour a cake tin no larger than 30 x 20 cm (12 x 8 inches) or a round cake tin (the gateau will be a little thicker but just as good).

2 Whisk the yolks with the caster sugar in a bowl placed over a pan of simmering water, to speed the process, until the mixture becomes very light and frothy. Sift the flour into a bowl then fold into the egg and sugar mixture with a metal spoon. Whisk the egg whites until stiff and fold into the mixture very carefully. Pour the mixture into the prepared tin and bake for about 35 minutes, reducing the temperature to 160°C (325°F) Gas Mark 3 after the first 15 minutes. Remove from the oven and allow to cool in the tin for a few minutes before turning out onto a wire rack to cool completely.

3 Whip the cream to firm peaks and stir in the rest of the sugar. Beat the mascarpone to soften it and mix into the whipped cream. Lightly crush half of the raspberries with a fork and add to the cream.

4 Cut the gateau into 2 rectangles and moisten them with the alcohol or the raspberry syrup, slightly diluted with water. Spread the raspberry cream on one of the rectangles, then cover with the whole raspberries, setting a few aside for the decoration. Place the other rectangle of gateau on top.

5 Sift a little icing sugar onto a work surface and roll out the almond paste to a thin sheet (the sugar makes it easier) to fit the top of the gateau. Place this on top of the gateau then refrigerate for several hours.

6 With a sharp knife, straighten the edges of the gateau at both ends then replace in the refrigerator until required. It will be at its best on the following day. Decorate with the remaining whole raspberries.

SERVES 4
PREPARATION TIME: 30 MINUTES
COOKING TIME: 25 MINUTES

RASPBERRY **MILLE-FEUILLE**

1 sheet pre-rolled butter puff pastry
100 g (3½ oz) caster sugar
100 g (3½ oz) icing sugar
200 ml (7 fl oz) double cream, chilled
200 g (7 oz) mascarpone
Few drops vanilla essence
250 g (8 oz) fresh raspberries

1 Preheat the oven to 230°C (450°F) Gas Mark 8. Unroll the pastry onto a baking sheet and sift over 75 g (3 oz) of the sugar. Put into the oven and immediately lower the temperature to 180°C (350°F) Gas Mark 4. After 10 minutes, place a second baking sheet on the pastry to prevent it from rising too much. Continue to bake for a further 8 minutes. Take the pastry out and increase the temperature to 240°C (475°F) Gas Mark 9.

2 Turn over the pastry, still within its baking sheets, and remove the top sheet. Sift 2 tablespoons of the icing sugar over the pastry surface and return to the oven, uncovered, for 5–8 minutes to caramelize. With a sharp knife and a ruler as a guide, cut the pastry into 3 equal rectangles.

3 Whip the cream with the remaining sugar. Stir the mascarpone to a smooth consistency, add the vanilla essence and mix into the whipped cream. Crush half the raspberries with a fork and add these to the cream.

4 Spread half the cream onto one piece of pastry, add a few whole raspberries and cover with a second piece of pastry. Repeat the process with the rest of the cream and some more whole raspberries, then place the third sheet of pastry on top. Sift over the remaining icing sugar and decorate with the remaining raspberries. Refrigerate and serve fairly soon to keep the pastry crisp.

SERVES 4
PREPARATION TIME: 15 MINUTES
COOKING TIME: 35 MINUTES

RASPBERRY **CRUMBLE**

500 g (1 lb) fresh raspberries
2 vanilla pods
150 g (5 oz) plain flour
125 g (4 oz) butter, cut into small pieces
3 tablespoons brown sugar
3 tablespoons flaked almonds

To serve: crème fraîche

1 Preheat the oven to 180°C (350°F) Gas Mark 4. Put the raspberries into an ovenproof dish with the vanilla pods, split in half and the seeds scraped out onto the raspberries.

2 Put the flour into a large bowl with the butter. Rub the butter into the flour until the mixture resembles fine breadcrumbs, then mix in the sugar.

3 Spread the crumble mixture over the fruit without pressing it down, scatter the almonds on top and bake just until the top is golden brown. Serve warm or chilled, with the crème fraîche.

SERVES 4
PREPARATION TIME: 25 MINUTES + RESTING TIME
COOKING TIME: 50 MINUTES

RASPBERRY **STRUDEL**

FOR THE PASTRY
125 ml (4 fl oz) milk
75 g (3 oz) butter + extra for greasing
1 tablespoon sugar
150 g (5 oz) plain flour
1 teaspoon baking powder
1 egg

FOR THE FILLING
75 g (3 oz) macaroons or amaretti biscuits, crushed
500 g (1 lb) fresh raspberries
20 g (¾ oz) butter
2 tablespoons caster sugar
1 or 2 tablespoons Grand Marnier

To serve: whipped cream or custard

1 To make the pastry: put the milk, butter and sugar into a small pan and heat gently to dissolve the sugar and melt the butter. Take off the heat and leave to cool. Sift the flour and baking powder into a large bowl. Make a well in the centre and break 1 egg into it, then add the cooled milk, reserving 1 tablespoon. Mix to a dough, knead for 5 minutes on a lightly floured work surface, then wrap in clingfilm and leave to rest for 15 minutes at room temperature.

2 Grease a baking sheet; preheat the oven to 180°C (350°F) Gas Mark 4. Roll out the pastry into a circle 5 mm (¼ inch) thick. Scatter over the crushed macaroons, then the raspberries, leaving a clear border all round. Cut the butter into tiny pieces and distribute them evenly, then sprinkle with the sugar. Sprinkle on the Grand Marnier, fold the edges of the pastry up over the raspberries, then roll up the whole thing in the form of a strudel.

3 Place on the baking sheet and brush with the reserved sweetened milk, then bake for 50 minutes. While the strudel is cooking, baste it with the juices that run from it. Serve with either whipped cream or fresh custard.

SERVES 4
PREPARATION TIME: 20 MINUTES
CHILLING TIME: MINIMUM 4 HOURS

KNICKERBOCKER GLORY

1 packet raspberry jelly
4–8 scoops vanilla ice cream or raspberry sorbet
   (or both)
250 g (8 oz) fresh raspberries
150 ml (¼ pint) double or whipping cream, chilled
Toasted flaked almonds

1 Prepare the jelly according to the instructions on the packet and leave to set in the refrigerator.

2 Process half of the raspberries in a blender or food processor and pass through a sieve to form a coulis. Whip the well-chilled cream.

3 In tall glasses, start with a basis of chopped jelly, then add some whole raspberries, a scoop of ice cream, more jelly and pour on some raspberry coulis. Add more whole raspberries and a second scoop of ice cream. Top with whipped cream and more raspberry coulis, decorate with a whole raspberry and a sprinkling of toasted flaked almonds and serve immediately.

SERVES 6
PREPARATION TIME: 20 MINUTES
CHILLING TIME: OVERNIGHT IF POSSIBLE

CHOCOLATE & RASPBERRY
SLICES

200 g (7 oz) thin almond biscuits
200 g (7 oz) softened butter + extra for greasing
200 g (7 oz) cocoa powder
200 g (7 oz) ground almonds
100 g (3½ oz) sugar
125 g (4 oz) fresh raspberries
1 egg

1 Break up the biscuits without reducing them to crumbs. Mix the butter with the cocoa powder and add the ground almonds.

2 Pour the sugar and 3 tablespoons of water into a small pan and dissolve over low heat. Remove from the heat and add to the butter, almond and cocoa mixture, then add the egg.

3 Gently mix in the broken biscuits and finally the raspberries.

4 Grease a 1-litre/2-lb loaf tin and pour in the mixture. Smooth the top level and cover with a piece of kitchen foil. Refrigerate – overnight if possible. Turn out carefully and cut into thin slices.

SERVES 4
PREPARATION TIME: 45 MINUTES
COOKING TIME: 30 MINUTES

RASPBERRY **RELIGIEUSES**

FOR THE CHOUX PASTRY
125 ml (4 fl oz) milk
125 ml (4 fl oz) water
100 g (3½ oz) unsalted butter, cut into small pieces,
   + extra for greasing
1 tablespoon granulated sugar
1 teaspoon salt
150 g (5 oz) plain flour
4 eggs

FOR THE FILLING
250 g (8 oz) raspberries + a few for decoration
100 ml (3½ fl oz) double cream, chilled
100 g (3½ oz) mascarpone
100 g (3½ oz) fromage frais
3 tablespoons caster sugar
6 tablespoons icing sugar + extra for dusting
75 g (3 oz) pink or white almond paste/marzipan

1 Grease a baking sheet or line it with baking parchment. Preheat the oven to 210°C (425°F) Gas Mark 7.

2 To make the choux pastry: heat the milk, water, butter, sugar and salt in a pan. Remove from the heat just before it boils, add the flour and stir vigorously with a spatula. When all the flour has been absorbed, return the pan to the heat. Stir until the paste comes away from the sides of the pan. Transfer the dough to a large bowl, beat the eggs and add them, a little at a time, to the dough, mixing in with a spatula. It should not be too soft. If the dough looks right (it will gently close up if you run your finger through it), do not add all the egg.

3 With a piping bag and a narrow nozzle, form very small balls of dough (choux) on the baking sheet. Next fit a larger nozzle and pipe the same number of larger choux. Put them into the oven and immediately reduce the temperature to 180°C (350°F) Gas Mark 4. Bake for 15–20 minutes so that they become nicely browned. Leave to cool on a wire rack.

4 For the filling: process 75 g (4 oz) of the raspberries in a blender or food processor and pass through a sieve to remove the seeds. Whip the chilled cream with the caster sugar, then stir the mascarpone until it is smooth and mix into the whipped cream. Set aside 5 tablespoons of the sieved raspberries and fold the rest into the cream, together with the remaining whole raspberries.

5 Sift a little icing sugar on a work surface and roll out the almond paste thinly. Make a hole in each of the large choux and fill them with the cream. Decorate them with a little circle of almond paste and stick the small choux on the top. Mix the remaining 5 tablespoons of raspberry coulis with the icing sugar, put a spoonful of this 'icing' over the small choux and sit a raspberry on the very top.

SERVES 4
PREPARATION TIME: 20 MINUTES
COOKING TIME: 30 MINUTES

BREAD & BUTTER PUDDING
WITH RASPBERRIES

8 thin slices of day-old brioche
2 tablespoons raspberry jam (optional)
Butter for spreading + extra for greasing
250 g (8 oz) fresh raspberries
2 eggs
150 ml (¼ pint) milk
150 ml (¼ pint) single cream
Dash of rum
Finely grated peel of ½ orange
4 tablespoons sugar
½ teaspoon ground cinnamon

1 Preheat the oven to 190°C (375°F) Gas Mark 5. Butter the brioche slices and spread with the jam. Cut each slice into two (triangles if the slices are square). Arrange them, as near vertically as possible, in a well-buttered, not too large ovenproof dish. Add the raspberries.

2 Beat the eggs with the milk, cream and rum. Add the peel of the orange, very finely grated. Pour this mixture over the brioche, sprinkle with sugar and cinnamon and bake for about 30 minutes: the time needed for the cream to set and the top to brown. This dish can also be prepared in little ramekins but the cooking time will need to be adjusted.

SERVES 4
PREPARATION TIME: 20 MINUTES
CHILLING TIME: MINIMUM 4 HOURS

RASPBERRY & STRAWBERRY
CHARLOTTE

3 leaves gelatine (about 6 g/¼ oz)
500 g (1 lb) fresh raspberries
500 g (1 lb) fresh strawberries
3–4 tablespoons caster sugar
Strawberry syrup
1 packet boudoir biscuits

To serve: vanilla ice cream or raspberry sorbet

1 Put the gelatine to soften in a little cold water. Process 375 g (12 oz) of the raspberries and strawberries with the sugar in a blender or food processor. Taste and add more sugar if necessary. Heat half of this purée. Squeeze out the gelatine and dissolve in the purée. Leave to cool a little, then add the remaining purée.

2 Cut the remaining strawberries into small pieces and add them with some of the whole raspberries to the cooled purée (reserve a few raspberries for decoration).

3 Dilute the syrup with a little water, and very briefly soak the biscuits in it (they go soggy quickly) before lining a charlotte mould with them. Pour in half the fruit mixture, add an intermediate layer of soaked biscuits, then pour in the last of the fruit mixture and add a layer of biscuits on the top. Put into the refrigerator to set.

4 Turn it out of the mould, decorate with the rest of the raspberries and serve with vanilla ice cream.

MAKES 12 MUFFINS
PREPARATION TIME: 20 MINUTES
COOKING TIME: 25 MINUTES

MUFFINS
WITH RASPBERRY JAM

300 g (10 oz) plain flour + extra for dusting
50 g (2 oz) unsalted butter + extra for greasing
50 g (2oz) caster sugar
1 tablespoon baking powder
2 eggs
125 g (4 oz) yogurt
50 ml (2 fl oz) milk
Vanilla essence
125 g (4 oz) fresh raspberries
8 tablespoons raspberry jam
Salt

1 Preheat the oven to 200°C (400°F) Gas Mark 6. Grease a 12-cup muffin tin and dust with flour.

2 Sift the flour, sugar and baking powder into a bowl and mix well, adding a good pinch of salt. Melt the butter. Whisk the eggs together with the yogurt, milk, melted butter and a few drops of vanilla essence. Pour onto the dry ingredients and mix quickly with a wooden spoon – the mixture should be slightly lumpy rather than smooth. Add the raspberries and stir in without over-mixing.

3 Fill the muffin cups to only two-thirds, put 2 teaspoons of jam on each muffin and bake for 20–25 minutes. Leave the muffins in the tray for about 20 minutes before turning them out onto a wire rack to cool.

SERVES 6–8
PREPARATION TIME: 30 MINUTES
COOKING TIME: 1¼ HOURS

REDCURRANT **CREAM TART**

1 sheet pre-rolled butter puff pastry
7–8 punnets redcurrants (about 1 kg/2 lb)
2 eggs
300 ml (½ pint) single cream
125 g (4 oz) caster sugar

1 Preheat the oven to 190°C (375°F) Gas Mark 5.

2 Roll out the pastry in a circle to line a tart tin 25 cm (10 inches) in diameter. Cover the base with a circle of nonstick baking paper, weight with dry beans or pie weights and bake for 15 minutes, then remove the paper and beans and return to the oven for a further 5 minutes (known as 'baking blind'). Remove from the oven and leave to cool. Lower the temperature of the oven to 160°C (325°F) Gas Mark 3.

3 Strip the currants from the stalks (the tines of a fork are useful here) then process the fruit in a blender or food processor and pass through a sieve to remove the seeds.

4 Whip the eggs with the fruit purée, cream and sugar. Pour this mixture into the prepared pastry case and bake for a scant hour. Be careful as the filling should not be completely set when it comes out of the oven. Leave to cool and set before serving.

SERVES 4
PREPARATION TIME: 15 MINUTES
COOKING TIME: 10 MINUTES

BLUEBERRY **PANCAKES**

150 g (5 oz) plain white flour
150 g (5 oz) wholemeal flour
1 tablespoon baking powder
½ teaspoon salt
75 g (3 oz) unsalted butter, cut into small pieces,
   + extra for greasing
1 egg
2 tablespoons honey
375 ml (12 fl oz) milk
200 g (7 oz) blueberries

To serve: butter, citrus juice, sugar

1 Mix the two kinds of flour with the baking powder and salt. Add the butter and rub in with the fingertips until the mixture resembles fine breadcrumbs.

2 Beat the egg with the honey and the milk and pour onto the dry ingredients. Add the blueberries and mix just sufficiently to incorporate all the ingredients.

3 Heat a heavy-based frying pan and grease it generously. Lower the heat to medium: the pan should be hot but the heat under it not excessive. Drop in small ladles of batter. Wait until bubbles form on the surface, then turn the pancakes over and cook the other side (about 1–2 minutes per side).

4 This recipe produces fairly thick pancakes. Serve with butter, lemon or orange juice, and sugar.

SERVES 4
PREPARATION TIME: 30 MINUTES + CHILLING TIME
COOKING TIME: 35 MINUTES

GOOSEBERRY **PIE**

FOR THE SHORTCRUST PASTRY
250 g (8 oz) flour
125 g (4 oz) butter, cut into small pieces
Salt

FOR THE FILLING
750 g (1½ lb) fresh gooseberries
1 egg, beaten
4–5 boudoir biscuits, crushed
3 tablespoons soft brown sugar

To serve: crème fraîche or vanilla ice cream

1 To prepare the pastry: sift the flour and salt into a bowl and add the butter. Rub the butter into the flour with the fingertips until the mixture resembles fine breadcrumbs. With a round-bladed knife, mix in only sufficient cold water to make a dough. Without over-working it, form the dough into a rough ball between the hands, adding a little more water if necessary, then put in a polythene bag and refrigerate for at least 1 hour.

2 Preheat the oven to 190°C (375°F) Gas Mark 5. Wash the gooseberries and top and tail them.

3 Roll out a little more than half of the pastry to a circle 18–20 cm (7–8 inches) in diameter. Brush with half the beaten egg, and scatter over the crushed biscuits. Pile the gooseberries onto the circle, leaving a clear border. Sprinkle on 2 tablespoons of the sugar then turn a 1-cm (½-inch) border of pastry up over the fruit.

4 Roll out the rest of the pastry into a circle slightly larger than the surface remaining of the fruit. Brush the edges lightly with water, place on the top and firmly seal the pastry edges. Brush with the rest of the beaten egg and cut a hole in the centre to allow the steam to escape. Bake for about 35 minutes, until the top is nicely browned. Serve with crème fraîche or vanilla ice cream.

SERVES 2–3
PREPARATION TIME: 15 MINUTES
COOKING TIME: 35 MINUTES

SMALL BUT SWEET
BLUEBERRY CRUMBLE

500 g (1 lb) blueberries
2 tablespoons granulated sugar
100 g (3½ oz) plain flour
75 g (3 oz) unsalted butter, cut into small pieces
Salt

To serve: crème fraîche

1 Preheat the oven to 180°C (350°F) Gas Mark 4.
2 Put the blueberries into a small ovenproof dish with 1 tablespoon of the sugar.
3 Sift the flour into a large bowl with a pinch of salt. Add the butter, and rub into the flour with the fingertips until the mixture resembles fine breadcrumbs. Add the remaining sugar.
4 Spread the mixture over the fruit without pressing it down and bake until the top is browned (30–35 minutes). Serve warm with crème fraîche.

SERVES 4
PREPARATION TIME: 20 MINUTES + CHILLING TIME
COOKING TIME: 5 MINUTES
CHILLING TIME: 3–4 HOURS

PAIN PERDU
WITH BERRY SOUP

500 g (1 lb) mixed berries, either fresh or frozen
   (blackcurrants, redcurrants, blackberries, raspberries, etc.)
3 tablespoons sugar
4 slices brioche
4 tablespoons mascarpone
4 tablespoons single cream

1 Put the fruit (frozen, or washed and stripped off any stalks) into a pan with 100 ml (3½ fl oz) of water and the sugar. Bring to the boil and cook for 2 minutes (a little longer for frozen fruit).

2 Spread the slices of brioche with mascarpone and use them to line ramekins, bowls or heatproof glasses. Divide the hot fruit soup between them.

3 May be eaten hot, or cooled and chilled for several hours. In either case, add a tablespoon of single cream to each before serving.

Cook's tip This is a fruity version of French toast.

SERVES 4–6
PREPARATION TIME: 20 MINUTES
COOKING TIME: 3 MINUTES
CHILLING TIME: MINIMUM 4 HOURS

PINK JELLY
WITH RED BERRIES

500 g (1 lb) mixed fresh red berries
   (strawberries, raspberries, redcurrants, etc.)
6 leaves gelatine (12 g/½ oz)
450 ml (¾ pint) sparkling rosé wine
1 lemon
4 tablespoons sugar

1 Prepare the fruit by washing and removing stalks. Put the gelatine to soften in a little cold water.

2 Heat 200 ml (7 fl oz) of the wine with 1 tablespoon of lemon juice and the sugar.

3 Squeeze out the gelatine and when the wine is very hot and the sugar dissolved, remove from the heat, completely dissolve the gelatine in it, and add the rest of the wine.

4 Divide the fruit between 4 or 6 glasses (depending on size) and pour over the liquid.

5 Leave to cool, then refrigerate for at least 4 hours.

SERVES 6
PREPARATION TIME: 35 MINUTES
COOKING TIME: 2–3 HOURS

BERRY **PAVLOVAS**

5 egg whites
350 g (11½ oz) caster sugar
Vanilla essence
750 g (1½ lb) mixed berries
100 ml (3½ fl oz) double cream, chilled
300 g (10 oz) fromage frais

1 Preheat the oven to 120°C (250°F) Gas Mark ½.

2 Prepare a large meringue or 6 small ones: whisk the egg whites until stiff, then slowly add 300 g (10 oz) of sugar followed by a few drops of vanilla essence; form into 1 large circle or 6 small ones on a baking sheet covered in nonstick baking paper. As a guide you can draw the circles round a small plate or saucer. Bake for 2–3 hours – the meringues need to dry out and the length of time this takes will depend on their size.

3 Wash the fruit and remove the stalks, then mix with the remaining sugar. Whip the cream; beat the fromage frais to make it smooth and fold it into the cream. Immediately before serving, spread the cream on the meringue (or meringues) and spoon the fruit over it.

Cook's tip To make a variation of Eton Mess: break up the meringue into fairly large pieces and mix all the ingredients roughly together, keeping their individual textures.

SERVES 4
PREPARATION TIME: 25 MINUTES
COOKING TIME: 10 MINUTES
CHILLING TIME: MINIMUM 4 HOURS

BLACKCURRANT **CREAM**

Butter, for greasing
1 sponge cake
700 g (1½ lb) blackcurrants
100 g (3½ oz) caster sugar
5 leaves gelatine (10 g/½ oz)
250 ml (8 fl oz) milk
4 egg yolks
Blackcurrant syrup
Crème de Cassis liqueur (optional)
250 ml (8 fl oz) double or whipping cream

1 Butter 4 small glasses, moulds or ramekins. Cut the sponge cake into circles to fit the containers and set them aside.

2 Wash the blackcurrants and remove the stalks. Reserve a few blackcurrants for decoration. Process the rest with 4 tablespoons of the sugar in a blender or food processor. Pass through a sieve to remove the seeds. Put the gelatine to soften in a little cold water.

3 Heat the milk. Whisk the egg yolks with the remaining sugar in a large bowl and continue to whisk while adding the hot (but not boiling) milk. Return the mixture to the pan and cook over low heat, stirring constantly until the custard thickens sufficiently to coat the back of the spoon.

4 Squeeze out the gelatine and completely dissolve it in the hot custard. Leave to cool slightly, then add the blackcurrant purée.

5 Whip the double cream and fold into the blackcurrant custard cream. Divide it between the glasses and cover each with a circle of sponge cake soaked in diluted blackcurrant syrup mixed with a little Crème de Cassis to taste, if using. Chill for at least 4 hours until set.

6 Dip each glass into hot water for just a second and loosen the edges with a knife to facilitate turning out the creams. Decorate with the reserved currants.

Cook's tip If you're in a hurry, you can put the blackcurrant-flavoured sponge cake in first, top with the blackcurrant cream, decorate, and serve in the glasses.

SERVES 6
PREPARATION TIME: 25 MINUTES
COOKING TIME: 45 MINUTES

FRUITY **MARBLE CAKE**

125 g (4 oz) softened unsalted butter + extra for greasing
200 g (7 oz) caster sugar
3 eggs
300 g (10 oz) plain flour + extra for dusting
2 teaspoons baking powder
Milk
300 g (10 oz) frozen mixed berries

1 Preheat the oven to 170°C (350°F) Gas Mark 4. Whisk the butter with 150 g (5 oz) of the sugar until light and fluffy. Beat in the eggs, one by one, then fold in the flour, sifted with the baking powder. The mixture should drop easily from a spoon, so add a little milk if necessary to reach this consistency.

2 Put the fruit with the remaining sugar and 100 ml (3½ fl oz) of water into a pan. Bring to the boil and cook just long enough to thaw out the fruit.

3 Pour the cake mixture into a greased cake tin dusted with flour. Add the fruit and form the marbling by swirling with a knife. Don't swirl too much otherwise the fruit will just get mixed in and the effect will be lost. Bake for 35–45 minutes, until a metal skewer plunged into the centre comes out quite clean.

SERVES 4
PREPARATION TIME: 35 MINUTES
COOKING TIME: 35 MINUTES
FREEZING TIME: 4 HOURS

COBBLER &
SOFT FRUIT ICE CREAM

1.5 kg (3 lb) mixed soft fruit
500 ml (17 fl oz) crème fraîche
Grenadine syrup
4 tablespoons sugar
225 g (8 oz) flour
2 teaspoons baking powder
1 vanilla pod
125 g (4 oz) butter, cut into small pieces
150 ml (¼ pint) fermented milk (available at supermarkets)
  (or 1 yogurt and 3 tablespoons milk)

To serve: crème fraîche

1 To make the ice cream: wash 1 kg (2 lb) of the fruit, remove all stalks, and process three-quarters of it in a blender or food processor. Add the grenadine to this purée and sweeten to taste. Mix with the crème fraîche and the rest of the prepared fruit and freeze in an ice-cream maker.

2 To make the cobbler: wash and prepare the remaining 500 g (1 lb) of fruit. Preheat the oven to 190°C (375°F) Gas Mark 5. Divide the fruit between 4 small ovenproof dishes and add ½ tablespoon of sugar to each. Sift the flour with the baking powder into a large bowl and add the remaining sugar. Split the vanilla pod and scrape the seeds into this mixture. Add the butter and rub in with the fingertips until the mixture resembles fine breadcrumbs. Add the fermented milk (or milk and yogurt) and stir lightly to obtain a fairly soft mixture.

3 Drop spoonfuls of the mixture over the fruit in the ramekins and bake for 30–35 minutes. Serve the cobbler warm with the fruit ice cream and crème fraîche.

English translation and adaptation: JMS Books LLP
Layout: cbdesign

First published in France in 2007 under the title
La Boîte à gâteau, by Hachette Livre (Marabout)
Copyright © 2007 Hachette Livre (Marabout)
Editorial: Catherine Berranger and Charlotte Müller-Buch

An Hachette Livre UK Company
www.hachettelivre.co.uk

First published in Great Britain in 2008 by
Hamlyn, a division of Octopus Publishing Group Ltd
2–4 Heron Quays, London E14 4JP
www.octopusbooks.co.uk

Copyright © English edition
Octopus Publishing Group Ltd 2008

Original French edition copyright
© HACHETTE LIVRE (Marabout) 2007

ISBN 978 0 600 61876 8

A CIP catalogue record for this book is available from
the British Library

Printed and bound in China

1 3 5 7 9 10 8 6 4 2

This book contains dishes that are made with raw or lightly cooked eggs.
These should be avoided by vulnerable people such as pregnant and
nursing mothers, invalids, the elderly, babies and young children.

STRAWBERRY
YOGURT

hamlyn

CONTENTS

SERVES 6
PREPARATION TIME: 25 MINUTES
COOKING TIME: 25 MINUTES

CRUMBLY CAKE
WITH STRAWBERRIES

225 g (7½ oz) plain flour
1 teaspoon baking powder
½ teaspoon salt
80 g (3 oz) caster sugar
80 g (3 oz) butter, cut in pieces
Finely grated rind of ½ orange
1 egg
60 ml (2¼ fl oz) milk
500 g (1 lb) strawberries
200 ml (7 fl oz) double/whipping cream
1 tablespoon icing sugar

1 Preheat the oven to 190°C (375°F) Gas Mark 5. Grease 2 cake tins 20 cm (8 inches) in diameter.

2 Sift together the flour and baking powder. Mix with the salt and sugar in a large bowl. Rub in the butter with your fingertips to the consistency of coarse breadcrumbs. Mix the grated rind into the dough. Add the egg and milk and mix in with a knife. Finish the dough by hand, without working it too much (it should be quite soft). Transfer to the cake tins.

3 Put in the oven and bake for 20–25 minutes. The top should be slightly golden. Turn out and cool on a wire rack.

4 Wash and hull the strawberries. Reserve a few for decoration and slice the remainder.

5 Whip the cream and spread it over one of the cakes. Arrange the strawberries on the cream and cover with the second cake. Dust with icing sugar and decorate with the remaining strawberries.

SERVES 6
PREPARATION TIME: 30 MINUTES
COOKING TIME: 45 MINUTES

BIG CHOUX PASTRY
WITH CREAM & STRAWBERRIES

FOR THE CHOUX PASTRY
150 ml (¼ pint) water
150 ml (¼ pint) milk
100 g (3½ oz) butter, cut into small pieces
150 g (5 oz) flour
3 eggs
Salt

FOR THE FILLING
300 ml (½ pint) double cream
40 g (1½ oz) icing sugar
500 g (1 lb) strawberries

1 Preheat the oven to 200°C (400°F) Gas Mark 6. Cover a baking sheet with nonstick baking paper.

2 To make the choux pastry: in a pan, heat the water, milk, butter and a pinch of salt. Remove from the heat just before it boils. Add all the flour at once and mix vigorously with a spatula. As soon as the flour has been thoroughly mixed in, put the pan back on the heat to dry out the mixture. Stir until the dough comes away from the sides of the pan, then transfer to a large bowl. Beat the eggs in another bowl and gradually add them to the dough, 'cutting' it with a spatula. The dough should not be too soft. If the dough looks right (it will gently close up if you run your finger through it), do not add all the egg.

3 Using a piping bag (medium nozzle), pipe a disc of choux pastry about 23 cm (9 inches) in diameter on the baking sheet (to make it easier, draw a circle using a cake tin as a guide). Pipe several layers of dough on top of one another to make the circle quite thick. If you don't have a piping bag, make the circle by piling up spoonfuls of dough in a ring. Put in the oven and bake for 10 minutes, then increase the oven temperature to 220°C (425°F) Gas Mark 7 and cook for a further 15–20 minutes, until golden. Set aside to cool on a wire rack.

4 For the filling: beat the chilled cream until stiff and add half the icing sugar. Wash and hull the strawberries, then cut half of them in biggish pieces and mix into the cream.

5 Divide the pastry disc into six segments and cut each portion in half horizontally. Spread the six bottom halves with strawberry cream and put the tops back on. Arrange the segments on a pretty plate so as to re-form the cake and pile the remaining strawberries in the middle. Dust with icing sugar immediately before serving.

SERVES 4
PREPARATION TIME: 15 MINUTES
CHILLING TIME: ABOUT 4 HOURS
(DEPENDING ON YOUR ICE-CREAM MAKER)

STRAWBERRY & CRÈME FRAÎCHE
ICE CREAM

1 kg (2 lb) full-flavoured strawberries
500 ml (17 fl oz) crème fraîche
Honey

1 Wash and hull the strawberries.

2 Put in a blender and whizz just to a purée. Add honey to taste. The quantity will depend on the flavour of the strawberries.

3 Mix with the crème fraîche and freeze in an ice-cream maker.

SERVES 4
PREPARATION TIME: 10 MINUTES
COOKING TIME: 10 MINUTES

STRAWBERRY **OMELETTE**

250 g (8 oz) strawberries
150 ml (¼ pint) single cream
2 eggs
50 g (2 oz) caster sugar
3 tablespoons breadcrumbs
30 g (1 oz) butter

1 Wash and hull the strawberries and cut in pieces. Beat together 100 ml (3½ fl oz) of the cream, the eggs, sugar (reserving 2 tablespoons) and breadcrumbs.

2 Preheat the grill.

3 Melt the butter in a small metal frying pan (not one with a plastic handle). Pour in the egg mixture and tip the pan to spread it well. Cook over medium to low heat for 5–6 minutes so the underside is golden.

4 Put the omelette under the grill just long enough for the top to set. Slide the omelette from the pan onto a warmed serving plate.

5 Decorate with the strawberries. Sprinkle with the remaining sugar and serve with the remaining cream.

SERVES 4
PREPARATION TIME: 30 MINUTES
COOKING TIME: 10 MINUTES

STRAWBERRY **MINI TARTLETS**

250 g (8 oz) strawberries
4 leaves gelatine (8 g)
300 ml (½ pint) milk
3 egg yolks
3 tablespoons caster sugar
100 ml (3½ fl oz) double or whipping cream
12 ready-made mini tartlets, shortcrust or rich shortcrust
Icing sugar for dusting

1 Reserve 12 strawberries (6 if they are large) and purée the remainder.

2 Soak the gelatine in a little cold water; squeeze out when ready to use.

3 Heat the milk, beat the egg yolks with the sugar and pour over the milk. Return the mixture to the pan and cook over low heat, stirring constantly until it has the consistency of custard. Completely dissolve the gelatine in the hot custard and set aside to cool.

4 Mix the strawberry purée with the custard. Whip the cream until firm peaks form and mix into the strawberry cream. Fill the tartlets and decorate each with a small strawberry or half a strawberry. Put to set in the refrigerator.

5 Dust with icing sugar before serving.

SERVES 6
PREPARATION TIME: 25 MINUTES
COOKING TIME: 3 MINUTES

BAKED **ALASKA**

500 g (1 lb) strawberries
2 tablespoons balsamic vinegar
100 g (3½ oz) caster sugar
500 ml (17 fl oz) vanilla ice cream
3 egg whites
1 ready-made sponge base, 20 cm (8 inches) in diameter
3 tablespoons orange juice

1 Wash, hull and slice the strawberries. Put them in a bowl with the balsamic vinegar and 2 tablespoons of the sugar. Set aside to soak.

2 Preheat the oven to 230°C (450°F) Gas Mark 8.

3 Take the ice cream out of the freezer. Beat the egg whites until stiff, add the remaining sugar and beat again.

4 Put the sponge on a heatproof serving dish and pour over the orange juice. Spread the strawberries over the top, leaving the edge uncovered. Put the slightly softened ice cream on top and shape it into a dome, then spread the meringue over the ice cream, covering it completely to make a seal. Bake in a very hot oven for about 3 minutes, just long enough for the meringue to turn golden in places. Serve immediately.

Cook's tip A dessert to make at the last minute!

SERVES 4
PREPARATION TIME: 25 MINUTES
CHILLING TIME: 4 HOURS

GRANITA WITH SHORTBREAD

500 g (1 lb) strawberries
150 g (5 oz) caster sugar
3 tablespoons lemon juice
150 ml (¼ pint) double cream
  (or 75 ml/3 fl oz double cream + 150 g /3½ fl oz fromage fra
4 shortbread biscuits (or 4 palets bretons,
  a type of buttery shortbread)

1 Wash and hull the strawberries and purée with the sugar, lemon juice and 500 ml (17 fl oz) of water. Pass this purée through a fine sieve. Pour into a freezerproof box and put in the freezer for 2 hours.

2 Take out the box and stir the half-frozen strawberries vigorously with a fork. Put them back in the freezer and repeat the procedure 1 hour later. Put back in the freezer for a further 1 hour.

3 Beat the chilled cream until firm peaks form and mix with the fromage frais, if appropriate.

4 Spoon the granita into glasses. Before serving, top with the cream and crumbled shortbread.

Cook's tip Granita is a type of Italian sorbet. It is half-frozen and can be served between courses in glass bowls.

SERVES 4
PREPARATION TIME: 40 MINUTES
COOKING TIME: 15 MINUTES
CHILLING TIME: MINIMUM 4 HOURS

TWO-TIER **CHARLOTTE**

750 g (1½ lb) strawberries
4 tablespoons caster sugar
5 leaves gelatine
500 ml (17 fl oz) milk
4 egg yolks
1 vanilla pod
200 ml (7 fl oz) double or whipping cream
A little butter for greasing
About 30 boudoir biscuits or sponge fingers
200 ml (7 fl oz) passion fruit juice (or orange juice)

1 Wash and hull the strawberries. Blend two thirds of them to a purée with 2 tablespoons of the sugar.

2 Cut the remaining strawberries in pieces. Soak the gelatine in cold water; squeeze out when ready to use.

3 Make an egg custard with the milk, egg yolks, the remaining sugar and the vanilla pod. Completely dissolve the softened gelatine in the hot custard and set aside to cool. Discard the vanilla pod.

4 Beat the chilled cream until firm peaks form. Mix together the strawberry purée, custard, whipped cream and half the remaining strawberry pieces.

5 Grease two fairly shallow charlotte moulds, one 15–20 cm (6–8 inches) in diameter and a second smaller one, and line both with boudoir biscuits briefly soaked in fruit juice.

6 Pour in the strawberry cream and top with a layer of boudoir biscuits to give the charlotte a little firmness. Cover and put in the refrigerator to set.

7 Turn out the bigger cake first and then the second on top. Decorate with the remaining strawberries or with fresh or crystallized flowers.

SERVES 6
PREPARATION TIME: 30 MINUTES
COOKING TIME: 1 HOUR

STRAWBERRY & RHUBARB **TART**

300 g (10 oz) frozen rhubarb or 3 sticks fresh rhubarb,
   washed and cut in 5-cm (2-inch) pieces
150 g (5 oz) caster sugar
500 g (1 lb) strawberries
1 roll pure butter puff pastry
2 tablespoons icing sugar
150 g (5 oz) mascarpone
150 g (5 oz) fromage frais
Seeds of 1 vanilla pod (or, more daringly, a piece of fresh ginger,
   very finely grated)

1 Preheat the oven to 190°C (375°F) Gas Mark 5. Line a baking sheet with nonstick baking paper.

2 Put the rhubarb in an ovenproof dish with 80 g (3 oz) of the caster sugar and cook for 35–40 minutes, or until the fruit is cooked but still holds its shape. Wash and hull the strawberries and cut in pieces. Mix half with the cooked rhubarb and reserve the remainder for decorating. Turn up the oven temperature to 230°C (450°F) Gas Mark 8.

3 Put the pastry on the lined baking sheet. Sift the remaining caster sugar over it. Put it in the oven and reduce the temperature to 180°C (350°F) Gas Mark 4. After 10 minutes, place a wire rack or metal cake tin on the pastry to prevent it from rising too much and bake for a further 8 minutes.

4 Take out the pastry and raise the oven temperature to maximum. Remove the wire rack or cake tin, place a sheet of nonstick baking paper on the pastry, cover with another baking sheet and turn it all upside down. Remove the first baking sheet and its baking paper. Sift over the icing sugar and put it in the oven to caramelize for 5–8 minutes, keeping a careful eye! Set aside to cool.

5 Stir together the mascarpone and fromage frais. Add the vanilla seeds or ginger. Spread this cream over the caramelized tart base. Cover with the strawberry and rhubarb compote. Decorate with the remaining pieces of strawberry.

SERVES 6
PREPARATION TIME: 30 MINUTES
COOKING TIME: 1 HOUR
CHILLING TIME: OVERNIGHT

TRIPLE STRAWBERRY
CHEESECAKE

1 kg (2 lb) strawberries
150 g (5 oz) caster sugar
200 g (7 oz) shortbread biscuits
50 g (2 oz) butter
900 g (1¾ lb) fromage frais, or Philadelphia
5 eggs
2 tablespoons plain flour
Finely grated rind of ½ lemon
1 teaspoon vanilla essence
125 g (4 oz) crème fraîche

1 Preheat the oven to 180°C (350°F) Gas Mark 4.

2 Wash and hull the strawberries. Purée two thirds of them with 2 tablespoons of the sugar.

3 Put the biscuits in a polythene bag and crush with a rolling pin. Melt the butter and mix with the biscuit crumbs. Line a springform cake tin 20–22 cm (8–9-inches) in diameter with nonstick baking paper, press the crumb mixture onto the base and bake for 10 minutes. Remove from the oven and reduce the temperature to 140°C (275°F) Gas Mark 1.

4 In a food processor or using an electric beater, stir the fromage frais (not more than 30 seconds), add the remaining sugar, the eggs one at a time, then the flour, the grated lemon rind, the vanilla essence, and finally the crème fraîche. Fold in half the strawberry purée, without trying to obtain an even mixture. Pour into the cake tin. Bake for 1 hour, then turn off the oven, leaving the cake in it with the door ajar, until it is completely cooled.

5 Turn out of the tin and store in the refrigerator until the next day. Slice the remaining strawberries. Cover the cheesecake with the remaining strawberry purée and add the sliced strawberries.

MAKES 12
PREPARATION TIME: 15 MINUTES
COOKING TIME: 30 MINUTES

PALESTINIAN **CAKES**

125 g (4 oz) ground almonds
125 g (4 oz) fine semolina
2 teaspoons baking powder
3 small plain yogurts
1 vanilla pod or a few drops of bitter almond extract
2 tablespoons flaked or chopped almonds
3 tablespoons honey
125 g (4 oz) caster sugar
15 g (½ oz) butter + extra for greasing
1 lemon
250 ml (8 fl oz) water

1 Preheat the oven to 170°C (340°F) Gas Mark 3–4. Grease a shallow square cake tin (as used for brownies), see step 3.

2 Mix together the ground almonds, semolina and baking powder. Add the yogurts and vanilla seeds scraped from the pod, or the almond extract.

3 Pour the mixture into the cake tin to no more than three-quarters full, because it swells during cooking. Smooth the surface. Sprinkle with the almonds, put in the oven and bake for 30 minutes.

4 In a small pan, heat the honey, sugar, butter, lemon juice to taste, and water. Stir to dissolve the sugar.

5 Turn out the cake and prick with a metal skewer. Pour over the hot syrup. To serve, cut in squares.

SERVES 4
PREPARATION TIME: 20 MINUTES
COOKING TIME: 40 MINUTES

RHUBARB & YOGURT
CREAM

500 g (1 lb) fresh rhubarb, washed
   and cut in 5-cm (2-inch) pieces, or frozen rhubarb
100 g (3½ oz) sugar
4 small Greek yogurts
2 tablespoons crème fraîche or mascarpone
Biscuits for serving (shortbread, amaretti)

1 Preheat the oven to 190°C (375°F) Gas Mark 5. Mix the rhubarb and sugar in an ovenproof dish and bake for 35–40 minutes.

2 When cooked, put in a sieve to drain well, then purée in a food processor. Mix half with the yogurts and pour into glasses.

3 Top with the remaining rhubarb purée and finish with a little crème fraîche or mascarpone. Refrigerate and serve lightly chilled with Scottish shortbread or amaretti.

SERVES 4
PREPARATION TIME: 15 MINUTES
COOKING TIME: 10 MINUTES
RESTING & CHILLING TIME: 6 HOURS

YOGURT & CARDAMOM
ICE CREAM

2 x 500 g (1 lb) pots good quality wholefat yogurt
Seeds of 4 cardamom pods
4 tablespoons caster sugar
250 ml (8 fl oz) water
100 g (3½ oz) sugar
1 teaspoon rosewater
Lightly tasted flaked almonds for serving

1 Put the yogurt in a sieve lined with a layer of muslin. Leave to drain for at least 3 hours (or overnight). This step is optional but it gives a creamier result.

2 Finely grind the cardamom seeds in a spice grinder (you can also crush them as much as possible in a mortar). Carefully mix the drained yogurt with the sugar and cardamom, transfer to a fairly shallow freezerproof container and put in the freezer.

3 When the yogurt is half frozen (reckon on about 1 hour), take it out and beat vigorously (by hand or with an electric beater). Put it back in the freezer. Repeat the process after 1 hour, then allow it to freeze.

4 Make a syrup by heating the water, sugar and rosewater in a pan. Stir to dissolve the sugar, then simmer to reduce the syrup. Take the ice cream out of the freezer and put it in the refrigerator 30 minutes before serving with the syrup and almonds. It is delicious with strawberries.

SERVES 4
PREPARATION TIME: 15 MINUTES
FREEZING TIME: 4 HOURS

YOGURT **GRANITA**

800 g (1¾ lb) thick yogurt (Greek style yogurt)
2–4 tablespoons barley malt syrup (or another flavour)
Fresh fruit for serving

1 Stir the yogurt with a spatula, tip into a shallow freezerproof box and place in the freezer or freezing compartment.
2 After 2 hours, take it out and stir vigorously with a fork.
3 Put back in the freezer for 1 hour, stir again and freeze again for 1 hour.
4 Serve with the syrup and fresh fruit.

SERVES 4
PREPARATION TIME: 20 MINUTES
COOKING TIME: 5 MINUTES
CHILLING TIME: MINIMUM 4 HOURS

ORANGE **PANNA COTTAS**

4 leaves gelatine
6 oranges, well scrubbed
1 lemon
50 g (2 oz) caster sugar
150 g (5 oz) yogurt
1 teaspoon orange flower water (optional)

1 Soak the gelatine in a little cold water; squeeze out when ready to use.

2 Peel 4 oranges and squeeze out the juice. Squeeze the lemon.

3 Measure 300 ml (½ pint) of orange juice (add a little water if necessary) and put in a small pan with the lemon juice, sugar and orange peel. Heat, stirring to dissolve the sugar. Drain the gelatine and dissolve completely in the hot liquid. Cover and leave to infuse for 10 minutes, then strain.

4 When the mixture is cold, stir in the yogurt and orange flower water, if using. Pour into little glass bowls or a single, pretty, moistened mould and put to set in the refrigerator for at least 4 hours before turning out.

5 Peel and slice the two remaining oranges and serve with the panna cottas.

SERVES 6
PREPARATION TIME: 25 MINUTES
COOKING TIME: 1 HOUR
RESTING TIME: 12 HOURS

MINI CHEESECAKES
WITH YOGURT TOPPING

150 g (5 oz) shortbread biscuits
50 g (2 oz) butter
300 g (10 oz) cream cheese (such as Philadelphia)
300 g (10 oz) fromage frais
100 g (3½ oz) caster sugar
3 eggs
Finely grated rind and juice of ½ lemon
4 small, or equivalent, wholefat yogurts (e.g. Greek yogurt)
100 g (3½ oz) lemon curd

1 Day one: Preheat the oven to 180°C (350°F) Gas Mark 4. Put the biscuits in a polythene bag and crush with a rolling pin. Melt the butter and mix with the crumbs. Press this mixture into the base of deep individual moulds (disposable foil moulds are very suitable). Bake for 10 minutes. Remove from the oven and reduce the temperature to 140°C (275°F) Gas Mark 1.

2 In a food processor or with an electric beater, stir the cheeses (no more than 30 seconds), add the sugar, the eggs one at a time, and the grated rind and juice of the half lemon. Pour into the moulds. Bake for 45 minutes, then turn off the oven, leaving the cakes in it with the door ajar to cool completely. Remove from the oven and store in the refrigerator until the next day.

3 Decant the yogurts in a large sieve lined with muslin over a big mixing bowl. Leave to drain overnight in the refrigerator.

4 Day two: Lightly mix the drained yogurt with the lemon curd, in a nice streaky pattern, and spread over the cheesecakes.

MAKES 12
PREPARATION TIME: 20 MINUTES + RESTING TIME
COOKING TIME: 25 MINUTES

YOGURT & BLUEBERRY
MUFFINS

300 g (10 oz) plain flour + extra for dusting
1 tablespoon baking powder
50 g (2 oz) caster sugar
50 g (2 oz) butter + extra for greasing
2 eggs
1 plain yogurt
50 ml (2 fl oz) milk
Finely grated rind of ½ lemon
1 vanilla pod
250 g (8 oz) fresh or frozen blueberries
Salt
1 tablespoon brown sugar
1 Greek yogurt for serving (optional)

1 Preheat the oven to 200°C (400°F) Gas Mark 6. Grease and flour a 12-cup muffin tin.

2 Sift the flour, baking powder and a good pinch of salt into a bowl and mix in the sugar.

3 Melt the butter.

4 Beat together the eggs, yogurt, milk, melted butter, grated lemon rind and vanilla seeds scraped from the pod. Pour over the dry ingredients, add the blueberries and mix briefly with a wooden spoon. Don't try to get a smooth mixture; there should be a few lumps left.

5 Fill the muffin cups three-quarters full. Sprinkle with the brown sugar, put in the oven and bake for 20–25 minutes. Leave to cool in the tins for about 20 minutes and then turn out. Eat warm, with Greek yogurt if using.

SERVES 4
PREPARATION TIME: 15 MINUTES + DRAINING TIME

CREAMY INDIAN-STYLE
YOGURT

12 small, or equivalent, wholefat plain yogurts
4–6 tablespoons caster sugar
Finely ground seeds of 4 cardamom pods
1 pinch saffron filaments (optional)
Rosewater
4 tablespoons chopped toasted almonds

1 Put the yogurt in two layers of muslin, tie a knot and suspend from a wooden spoon placed across a big, deep bowl. Leave to drain for 5 hours.

2 Beat the yogurt with the sugar, cardamom, saffron, if using, and a few drops of rosewater.

3 Serve the yogurt in glass bowls, sprinkled with the chopped toasted almonds.

SERVES 4
PREPARATION TIME: 15 MINUTES + DRAINING TIME

ORIENTAL YOGURT

12 small, or equivalent, wholefat plain yogurts
1 tablespoon tahini (sesame paste)
60 g (2¼ oz) halva (a kind of soft nougat with sesame)
Honey

1 Put the yogurt in two layers of muslin, tie a knot and suspend from a wooden spoon placed across a big, deep bowl. Leave to drain for 5 hours.

2 Beat the yogurt and mix with the tahini. Sweeten with honey, to taste. Crumble the halva and fold it gently into the yogurt (reserving a little for decoration).

3 Serve in glass bowls with a little halva sprinkled on top.

SERVES 4
PREPARATION TIME: 20 MINUTES
COOKING TIME: 30 MINUTES

LAYER CAKE
WITH YOGURT

Butter for greasing
1 small plain yogurt
250 g (8 oz) plain flour
1 teaspoon baking powder
125 g (4 oz) caster sugar
50 ml (2 fl oz) flavourless oil
3 eggs
4 tablespoons mascarpone + extra for serving
A few drops vanilla essence

TO SERVE
Mascarpone
Good quality strawberry or raspberry jam
Icing sugar for dusting

1 Preheat the oven to 200°C (400°F) Gas Mark 6. Grease a loaf tin.

2 Sift the flour and baking powder together into a bowl and mix in the sugar, oil, eggs, mascarpone and a few drops of vanilla essence.

3 Pour into the loaf tin, put in the oven and bake for 30 minutes. Allow to rest for 5 minutes then turn out onto a wire rack and leave to cool completely.

4 Cut the cake horizontally into three layers. Spread one layer thinly with jam and mascarpone and place the second layer on top. Spread this with jam and mascarpone, place the third layer on top and dust with icing sugar.

English translation and adaptation: JMS Books LLP
Layout: cbdesign

First published in France in 2007 under the title
La Boîte à gâteau, by Hachette Livre (Marabout)
Copyright © 2007 Hachette Livre (Marabout)
Editorial: Catherine Berranger and Charlotte Müller-Buch

An Hachette Livre UK Company
www.hachettelivre.co.uk

First published in Great Britain in 2008 by
Hamlyn, a division of Octopus Publishing Group Ltd
2–4 Heron Quays, London E14 4JP
www.octopusbooks.co.uk

Copyright © English edition
Octopus Publishing Group Ltd 2008

Original French edition copyright
© HACHETTE LIVRE (Marabout) 2007

ISBN 978 0 600 61876 8

A CIP catalogue record for this book is available from
the British Library

Printed and bound in China

1 3 5 7 9 10 8 6 4 2

This book contains dishes that are made with raw or lightly cooked eggs.
These should be avoided by vulnerable people such as pregnant and
nursing mothers, invalids, the elderly, babies and young children.

GREEN TEA
CHERRY

hamlyn

CONTENTS

PEAR & MATCHA CAKE **6**
CHOUX BUNS WITH GREEN TEA **8**
CHESTNUT & MATCHA TRIFLES **10**
MATCHA CHOUX SWANS **12**
CHESTNUT FILLED SPONGE CAKE **14**
ALMOND & GREEN TEA TRIANGLES **16**
GREEN TEA & ALMOND MILK
  CREAMS **18**
HOME-MADE ICE CREAM WITH
  MATCHA TEA **20**
CHOCOLATE & MATCHA LAYER CAKE **22**
EASY CREAM WITH LOTUS-FLAVOURED
  GREEN TEA **24**
CHERRY UPSIDE-DOWN CAKE **26**
CHERRY COBBLER **28**
PUFF PASTRY TARTLETS WITH CHERRIES
  & MASCARPONE **30**
TOASTED ALMOND ZABAGLIONE
  WITH CHERRIES **32**
BASQUE PIE **34**
CLASSIC CHERRY CAKE **36**
CHERRY & POPPY-SEED STREUSEL **38**
BLACK CHERRY TIRAMISU **40**
WHITE MOUSSE WITH MORELLO
  CHERRIES **42**
FROMAGE FRAIS & CHERRY ICE
  CREAM **44**

SERVES 4
PREPARATION TIME: 25 MINUTES
COOKING TIME: 1 HOUR

PEAR & MATCHA **CAKE**

5 perfectly ripe pears
125 g (4 oz) butter + extra for greasing
3 eggs
100 g (3½ oz) caster sugar
1 teaspoon matcha tea powder
125 g (4 oz) plain flour
Salt

1 Preheat the oven to 180°C (350°F) Gas Mark 4. Grease a tart tin.

2 Melt the butter gently in a pan. Beat together the eggs, sugar and tea. Add the melted butter, then the flour and a pinch of salt.

3 Peel and quarter the pears. Remove the core and pips.

4 Spoon a little of the mixture into the tart tin, arrange the pears on top, then cover with the remaining mixture. Bake for 45 minutes to 1 hour so the top browns nicely.

Cook's tip Matcha is a premium-quality green tea from Japan. It is bright green in colour and is used in the traditional Japanese tea ceremony. It is available at specialist Japanese delicatessens and by mail order via the internet. Store matcha tea powder in an airtight container in the freezer.

SERVES 4
PREPARATION TIME: 30 MINUTES
COOKING TIME: 30 MINUTES

CHOUX BUNS
WITH GREEN TEA

FOR THE FILLING
250 g (8 oz) mascarpone
200 g (7 oz) fromage frais or very thick yogurt
2 teaspoons matcha tea powder
2 tablespoons icing sugar

FOR THE CHOUX PASTRY
125 ml (4 fl oz) milk
125 ml (4 fl oz) water
100 g (3½ oz) butter, cut into small pieces,
   + a little for greasing
1 teaspoon salt
1 tablespoon caster sugar
150 g (5 oz) plain flour
4 eggs, beaten

1 Preheat the oven to 210°C (410°F) Gas Mark 6–7. Grease a baking sheet or line with nonstick baking paper.

2 To make the choux pastry: in a pan, heat the milk, water, butter, sugar and salt. Remove from the heat just before it boils. Add all the flour at once and mix vigorously with a spatula. As soon as the flour has been thoroughly mixed in, put the pan back on the heat to dry out the mixture. Stir until the dough comes away from the sides of the pan, then transfer to a large bowl. Beat the eggs in another bowl and gradually add them to the dough, 'cutting' it with a spatula. The dough should not be too soft. If it looks right (it will gently close up if you run your finger through it), do not add all the egg.

3 Using a small piping bag, pipe choux buns onto the baking sheet. Put them in the oven, bake for 10 minutes, then increase the oven temperature to 220°C (425°F) Gas Mark 7 and cook for a further 15–20 minutes. The choux buns should brown nicely. Leave to cool on a wire rack.

4 Beat the mascarpone and fromage frais, add 1 tablespoon of icing sugar and 1 teaspoon of the tea and beat again. Make a slit in the choux buns and fill with this mixture using a piping bag (or a spoon). Pile the buns on a serving dish and, using a sieve, dust with the remaining icing sugar and a little tea.

SERVES 6
PREPARATION TIME: 25 MINUTES
COOKING TIME: 15 MINUTES
CHILLING TIME: OVERNIGHT

CHESTNUT & MATCHA
TRIFLES

3 teaspoons good quality green tea leaves
350 ml (12 fl oz) milk
3 egg yolks
4 tablespoons caster sugar for the egg custard
2 tablespoons caster sugar for the whipped cream
4 slices ready-made sponge or about 15 boudoir biscuits
1 small glass muscat
4 tablespoons sweetened chestnut purée
2 punnets raspberries
2 teaspoons matcha tea powder
300 ml (½ pint) double or whipping cream

1 Heat the milk with the leaf tea. Remove from the heat just before it boils, cover and leave to infuse for 5 minutes, then filter.

2 Next make an egg custard with the tea-flavoured milk. Beat together the egg yolks and the 4 tablespoons of sugar in a heatproof bowl, then pour over the milk, stirring constantly. Return the mixture to the pan over low heat, stirring constantly until the custard thickens and coats the back of the spoon. Set aside to cool.

3 Put the sponge or boudoir biscuits in the bottom of 6 small dishes or 6 fairly large glasses. Drizzle with muscat.

4 Spread the chestnut purée over the cakes, then add the raspberries.

5 Whip the chilled cream with the caster sugar and 1 teaspoon of matcha tea. Cover the raspberries with the custard and top with the whipped cream. Dust with the remaining matcha. Refrigerate for several hours, if possible overnight.

SERVES 4
PREPARATION TIME: 30 MINUTES
COOKING TIME: 20 MINUTES

MATCHA **CHOUX SWANS**

300 ml (½ pint) double or whipping cream
1 teaspoon matcha tea powder
2–3 teaspoons icing sugar

FOR THE CHOUX PASTRY
125 ml (4 fl oz) milk
125 ml (4 fl oz) water
100 g (3½ oz) butter, cut into pieces,
   + a little for greasing
1 teaspoon salt
1 tablespoon caster sugar
150 g (5 oz) plain flour
4 eggs, beaten

1 Preheat the oven to 210°C (410°F) Gas Mark 6–7. Grease a baking sheet or line with nonstick baking paper.

2 To make the choux pastry: in a pan, heat the milk, water, butter, sugar and salt. Remove from the heat just before it boils. Add all the flour at once and mix vigorously with a spatula. As soon as the flour has been thoroughly mixed in, put the pan back on the heat to dry out the mixture. Stir until the dough comes away from the sides of the pan, then transfer to a large bowl. Beat the eggs in another bowl and gradually add them to the dough, 'cutting' it with a spatula. The dough should not be too soft. If it looks right (it will gently close up if you run your finger through it), do not add all the egg.

3 Preferably using a small piping bag, pipe ovals of choux dough about 6 cm (2½ inches) long on the baking sheet. Make swan necks as well, in fine 'S' shapes with one end more curved than the other (you will need a very small piping bag). Make twice as many ovals as necks. Put them in the oven, bake for 10 minutes, then increase the oven temperature to 220°C (425°F) Gas Mark 7 and cook for a further 10 minutes. The choux buns should brown nicely. Keep a check on the necks, which are thinner, and take them out earlier. Leave to cool on a wire rack.

4 Whip the cream to firm peaks. Add the tea and sugar and beat again.

5 To assemble the swans, start by cutting half the ovals in two. Top the whole ovals with cream and place a neck at one end and two half ovals at the sides to form the wings (cut them down if they are a bit too big). Place in the refrigerator and serve without too much delay.

SERVES 4
PREPARATION TIME: 20 MINUTES
COOKING TIME: 35 MINUTES

CHESTNUT FILLED
SPONGE CAKE

Butter for greasing
120 g (4 oz) sifted plain flour + extra for dusting
4 eggs
120 g (4 oz) caster sugar
2 teaspoons matcha tea powder + extra for dusting
3–4 tablespoons sweetened chestnut purée
4 tablespoons mascarpone

1 Preheat the oven to 180°C (350°F) Gas Mark 4. Grease and flour 2 cake tins 18–20 cm (7–8 inches) in diameter.

2 In a bowl over a pan of simmering water, beat together the eggs, sugar and tea. The mixture should become very light and frothy. Sift the flour into a bowl and stir into the mixture with a metal spoon.

3 Spoon into the cake tins, put into the oven and bake for about 20 minutes, reducing the temperature to 160°C (325°F) Gas Mark 3 after 15 minutes. Turn out and leave to cool on a wire rack.

4 Spread one of the sponge cakes with chestnut purée and mascarpone (without mixing them completely). Cover with the second sponge. Dust with a little tea powder, using a fine-mesh sieve.

MAKES 20–30 TRIANGLES
PREPARATION TIME: 1 HOUR
COOKING TIME: 15 MINUTES

ALMOND & GREEN TEA
TRIANGLES

FOR THE PASTRY
3 sheets filo pastry
150 g (5 oz) butter + extra for greasing
4 tablespoons icing sugar

FOR THE FILLING
30 g (1 oz) butter
300 g (10 oz) ground almonds
60 g (2½ oz) icing sugar
2 teaspoons matcha green tea powder
Juice of ½ orange

1 Make the filling first: melt the butter before mixing with the ground almonds, icing sugar, tea and orange juice.
2 Preheat the oven to 190°C (375°F) Gas Mark 5. Grease a baking sheet (or line with nonstick baking paper).
3 Melt the 150 g (5 oz) butter.
4 Take a sheet of filo pastry and brush with melted butter. Cut the sheet in half lengthways, then cut each half in four. Place a small dollop of filling on each rectangle then fold the pastry over into a triangle. Finish by rolling gently. Place on the baking sheet and brush again with butter. Repeat until all the filling and pastry have been used up.
5 Bake the triangles in the oven for 12–15 minutes. They should be nicely browned.

SERVES 6
PREPARATION TIME: 1 HOUR
COOKING TIME: 10 MINUTES
CHILLING TIME: MINIMUM 4 HOURS

GREEN TEA &
ALMOND MILK CREAMS

10 leaves gelatine (20 g)
250 ml (8 fl oz) almond milk (from a health food store)
120 g (4 oz) caster sugar
3 teaspoons matcha tea powder
250 ml (8 fl oz) double or whipping cream
Flavourless oil (such as groundnut), for brushing
2 tablespoons ground almonds, lightly toasted

1 Soak the gelatine in cold water; squeeze out when ready to use.

2 Heat the almond milk with the sugar and tea, stirring to dissolve the sugar. When the mixture is almost boiling, add the drained gelatine and stir to ensure it is completely dissolved. Leave to cool.

3 Whip the chilled cream and fold into the previous mixture (it should be really cold).

4 Spoon into 6 glasses or a large decorative mould, capacity 1 litre (1¾ pints), lightly greased with a flavourless oil. (There is no need to grease the glasses, because the dessert will be served in them.)

5 Refrigerate for at least 4 hours (overnight would be better). Dip the mould quickly in hot water and turn out, or serve in the glasses, if they look nice. Dust with ground almonds and serve with almond shortbread.

SERVES 4
PREPARATION TIME: 20 MINUTES
COOKING TIME: 10 MINUTES
FREEZING TIME: 5 HOURS

HOME-MADE ICE CREAM
WITH MATCHA TEA

500 ml (17 fl oz) milk
200 ml (7 fl oz) single cream
2 tablespoons matcha tea powder
3 whole eggs + 3 egg yolks
100 g (3½ oz) caster sugar
Salt
Small meringues for serving

1 Heat the milk and cream with the tea and a pinch of salt. Turn off the heat just before it boils, cover and leave to infuse for 10 minutes.

2 To make the egg custard, first beat the whole eggs and egg yolks with the sugar in a heatproof bowl. Pour in the hot milk, stirring constantly to prevent lumps forming. Pour into a clean pan and cook over low heat, stirring constantly, until the custard thickens and coats the back of the spoon. Set aside to cool.

3 Freeze for several hours in an ice-cream maker.

4 Serve with crumbled meringues. It's also delicious with a raspberry coulis.

SERVES 6
PREPARATION TIME: 45 MINUTES
COOKING TIME: 45 MINUTES

CHOCOLATE & MATCHA
LAYER CAKE

FOR THE SPONGE
50 g (2 oz) butter + extra for greasing
50 g (2 oz) plain flour + extra for dusting
6 eggs, separated
70 g (2¾ oz) caster sugar
55 g (2 oz) ground almonds
2 teaspoons matcha tea powder
Salt

FOR THE CHOCOLATE FILLING
200 g (7 oz) cream
200 g (7 oz) dark or milk chocolate, chopped

FOR THE SYRUP
200 ml (7 fl oz) green tea (prepared and cooled)
100 g (3½ oz) sugar

FOR THE ICING
150 g (5 oz) chocolate
30 g (1 oz) butter
30 g (1 oz) golden syrup

1 Preheat the oven to 180°C (350°F) Gas Mark 4. Grease and flour a cake tin.

2 To make the sponge: melt the butter and allow to cool. Beat the egg yolks with half the sugar. Add the ground almonds, then the flour sifted together with the matcha tea, and lastly the melted butter. Whisk the egg whites with the remaining sugar before folding them into the previous mixture. Fill the loaf tin three-quarters full with the mixture. Put in the oven, reducing the temperature immediately to 160°C (325°F) Gas Mark 3, and bake for about 35 minutes. To check that it is cooked, insert a metal skewer into the cake. It should come out clean. Leave in the tin for a few minutes before turning out to cool on a wire rack.

3 To make the filling: heat the cream, removing it from the heat as soon as it starts to boil. Add the chopped chocolate and stir thoroughly to melt it in the cream (the colour should be even all through). Leave to cool at room temperature, then put in the refrigerator to firm.

4 To make the syrup: heat the tea with the sugar, stirring to dissolve the sugar, and simmer for 5 minutes.

5 To assemble the cake: cut the sponge horizontally into three or four circles, then drizzle all of them with syrup before spreading all but one with the filling. Top with the last circle that has no filling on it.

6 Melt the ingredients for the icing in a bain-marie, or in a bowl set over a pan of barely simmering water, and stir well before spreading over the top of the cake. Leave to set.

SERVES 3
PREPARATION TIME: 10 MINUTES
COOKING TIME: 10 MINUTES
CHILLING TIME: MINIMUM 2 HOURS

EASY CREAM WITH
LOTUS-FLAVOURED GREEN TEA

500 ml (17 fl oz) milk (you could use soya milk)
3 teaspoons lotus-flavoured green tea leaves
   (or jasmine, if you can't get lotus)
2 tablespoons caster sugar
1 egg
50 g (2 oz) cornflour, Maizena if possible

To serve: langues de chat biscuits

1 Heat the milk. Remove from the heat just before it boils, stir in the tea leaves, cover and leave to infuse for 5 minutes.

2 In a slightly larger pan, beat together the sugar, egg and cornflour. Pour in the infused milk through a strainer, stirring constantly. Mix well and put back over fairly low heat. Bring to the boil, stirring constantly, then cook for 3 minutes over very low heat, while continuing to stir.

3 Take off the heat and pour into little glass bowls or moulds (lightly greased if you want to turn out the creams). Allow to cool before putting the creams in the refrigerator for at least 2 hours (turn them out first, if you don't want to serve them in their moulds).

4 Decorate with a few tea leaves and serve with langues de chat.

SERVES 4
PREPARATION TIME: 20 MINUTES
COOKING TIME: 55 MINUTES

CHERRY
UPSIDE-DOWN CAKE

100 g (3½ oz) soft butter + 50 g (2 oz) for greasing
75 g (3 oz) caster sugar + 2 tablespoons for dusting
500 g (1 lb) cherries, pitted
100 g (3½ oz) plain flour
1½ teaspoons baking powder
2 eggs
Bitter almond extract

1 Preheat the oven to 180°C (350°F) Gas Mark 4.

2 Put the 50 g (2 oz) of butter and the 2 tablespoons of sugar in a round or oval baking dish (about 21–23 cm/ 8–9 inches in diameter). Put over low heat and stir to melt the butter and dissolve the sugar. With a spatula, spread the mixture over the base and sides of the dish.

3 Arrange the cherries over the base.

4 Sift the flour and baking powder into a mixing bowl. Beat the eggs lightly before adding them, a few drops of the almond extract, and the remaining butter and sugar. Mix well.

5 Spoon the mixture over the cherries. Put into the oven and bake for 50 minutes. Wait 5 minutes before turning out onto a serving dish.

SERVES 4
PREPARATION TIME: 20 MINUTES
COOKING TIME: 35 MINUTES

CHERRY **COBBLER**

1 kg (2 lb) cherries
225 g (7½ oz) plain flour
2 teaspoons baking powder
2 tablespoons caster sugar
1 vanilla pod
50 g (2 oz) salted butter, cut into pieces
75 g (3 oz) unsalted butter, cut into pieces
1 small plain yogurt + 3 tablespoons milk

1 Preheat the oven to 190°C (375°F) Gas Mark 5.
2 Rinse and pit the cherries; put in a medium-sized oven-proof dish.
3 Sift the flour and baking powder into a mixing bowl. Add the sugar and the seeds scraped from the vanilla pod, then the butter. Rub in with the fingertips to give the consistency of coarse breadcrumbs. Then add the yogurt-milk mixture and mix (but not too much). You should get a fairly soft dough.
4 Drop spoonfuls of the dough over the cherries, put into the oven and bake for 30–35 minutes.
5 Serve warm with cream.

SERVES 6
PREPARATION TIME: 25 MINUTES
COOKING TIME: 25 MINUTES

PUFF PASTRY TARTLETS
WITH CHERRIES & MASCARPON

750 g (1½ lb) cherries
1 sheet pure butter puff pastry
75 g (3 oz) caster sugar
3 tablespoons icing sugar
150 ml (¼ pint) double cream
150 g (5 oz) mascarpone
2 tablespoons Marsala

1 Preheat the oven to 230 °C (450 °F) Gas Mark 8.

2 Pit the cherries and put in a mixing bowl with 1 tablespoon of Marsala and half the sugar.

3 Place the pastry on a greased baking sheet. Using a sieve, sprinkle with the remaining sugar and put in the oven. Reduce the temperature immediately to 180°C (350°F) Gas Mark 4. After 10 minutes, place a wire rack or metal mould on the pastry to prevent it from rising too much and bake for a further 8 minutes.

4 Take out the pastry and turn the oven temperature up to 240°C (475°F) Gas Mark 9. Remove the rack or mould, cover the pastry with a sheet of nonstick baking paper, put another baking sheet on top and turn the whole thing upside-down. Remove the first baking sheet and its baking paper. Sprinkle the pastry with 2 tablespoons of the icing sugar, again using a sieve. Return to the oven to caramelize for 5–8 minutes (keep a careful eye on it). Leave to cool.

5 With a pastry cutter or a sharp knife and using a glass as a guide, cut out discs of pastry 5–6 cm (2–2½ inches) in diameter.

6 Whip the chilled cream and stir in the mascarpone, then the remaining Marsala. Spread this cream over the discs of caramelized pastry. Top with cherries. Keep in a cool place, but serve without too much delay, dusted with the remaining icing sugar.

SERVES 4
PREPARATION TIME: 15 MINUTES
COOKING TIME: 10 MINUTES

TOASTED ALMOND ZABAGLIONE WITH CHERRIES

400 g (14 oz) cherries
4 very thin slices brioche
200 ml (7 fl oz) muscat
4 egg yolks
50 g (2 oz) caster sugar
1 tablespoon Amaretto (almond liqueur)
2 tablespoons flaked almonds

1 Pit the cherries.

2 Put the brioche into shallow heatproof ramekins. Drizzle with 3 tablespoons of the muscat and arrange the cherries on top.

3 In a bowl, whisk the egg yolks and sugar. Place the bowl over a pan of simmering water and whisk until the mixture begins to froth. Then add the remaining muscat and continue whisking to give a fairly firm cream. Lastly add the Amaretto.

4 Preheat the grill. Pour the zabaglione over the cherries, sprinkle with the almonds, grill briefly and serve immediately.

SERVES 6
PREPARATION TIME: 45 MINUTES
COOKING TIME: 50 MINUTES

BASQUE PIE

FOR THE FILLING
5–6 tablespoons good quality morello cherry jam
(or 400 g/14 oz fresh pitted cherries +
   4 Italian macaroons or amaretti)

FOR THE CONFECTIONER'S CUSTARD
500 ml (17 fl oz) milk
5 egg yolks
100 g (3½ oz) caster sugar
2 tablespoons plain flour
2 tablespoons cornflour, Maizena if possible
1 tablespoon rum

FOR THE PASTRY
200 g (7 oz) soft butter + extra for greasing
150 g (5 oz) caster sugar
4 eggs
1 vanilla pod
Finely grated rind of ½ lemon
280 g (9 oz) plain flour + extra for dusting
1 teaspoon baking powder

1 To make the confectioner's custard: first heat the milk. In a large bowl, beat together the egg yolks and sugar, add the flour and cornflour and beat again. Add a little milk that is just on the boil, beat, then gradually add the remaining milk, stirring constantly. Transfer the mixture to the pan and cook over medium to low heat, stirring constantly and scraping the bottom of the pan well. As soon as it comes to the boil, cook for a further 2–3 minutes, continuing to stir. Add the rum (without beating). Pour the cream into a bowl. Cover the surface with clingfilm to prevent a skin forming and leave to cool.

2 For the pastry: beat together the butter and sugar. Add 3 eggs, the grated lemon rind and the seeds from the vanilla pod, then the sifted flour and baking powder. Mix just enough to form a fairly soft dough. Wrap in clingfilm and put in the refrigerator.

3 Preheat the oven to 160°C (325°F) Gas Mark 3. Grease and flour a cake tin 20 cm (8 inches) in diameter.

4 Using a piping bag (medium nozzle), pipe the dough into the cake tin, making circles one on top of the other. Then cover the sides with dough (as thinly as possible). Spread the jam or pitted cherries on the dough and cover with confectioner's custard. Finish with a layer of dough, still piping in circles. Smooth the surface carefully with a spatula. You can make this without a piping bag – it just won't be quite as neat.

5 Beat the remaining egg and brush over the pastry. Put into the oven and bake for 40 minutes. Serve warm or cold.

SERVES 6
PREPARATION TIME: 40 MINUTES
COOKING TIME: 40 MINUTES

CLASSIC CHERRY **CAKE**

300 g (10 oz) butter + extra for greasing
300 g (10 oz) plain flour + extra for greasing
150 g (5 oz) glacé cherries
40 g (1¾ oz) ground almonds
5 eggs
300 g (10 oz) caster sugar
Vanilla essence or bitter almond extract
3 tablespoons flaked almonds

1 Preheat the oven to 190°C (375°F) Gas Mark 5. Grease and flour a large loaf tin.

2 Melt the butter. Cut the glacé cherries in two and mix with the ground almonds and 1 tablespoon of the flour. Sift the remaining flour into a bowl.

3 Beat together the eggs and sugar until the mixture turns pale and frothy. Carefully add the flour.

4 When mixing in the butter, put a little dough in the melted butter, then add all the melted butter to the dough.

5 Add a few drops of vanilla essence or almond extract, then the cherries with the ground almonds.

6 Fill the loaf tin three-quarters full. Top with flaked almonds. Put into the oven and turn down the temperature immediately to 170°C (325°F) Gas Mark 3. Bake for 35–40 minutes. Test by inserting a metal skewer into the cake, if it comes out clean it is ready.

SERVES 6
PREPARATION TIME: 35 MINUTES
COOKING TIME: 35 MINUTES

CHERRY & POPPY-SEED
STREUSEL

FOR THE PASTRY
1 roll of ready-made shortcrust pastry dough
1.5 kg (3 lb) pitted cherries
100 g (3½ oz) caster sugar
Butter for greasing

FOR THE POPPY-SEED CREAM
225 ml (8 fl oz) milk
50 g (2 oz) butter
150 g (5 oz) poppy seeds
3 tablespoons caster sugar
1 piece orange peel
1 vanilla pod
1 egg

FOR THE STREUSEL TOPPING
100 g (3½ oz) plain flour
75 g (3 oz) butter
3 tablespoons granulated sugar

1 To make the poppy-seed cream: in a pan heat the milk, butter, poppy seeds, sugar, orange peel and vanilla seeds scraped from the pod. Bring to the boil and cook for 20 minutes over very low heat. Run through a blender, leave to cool, then beat in the egg.

2 Make a syrup by dissolving 100 g (3½ oz) of sugar in 100 ml (3½ fl oz) of simmering water. Pit the cherries and poach for 7–8 minutes in this syrup, then drain.

3 Preheat the oven to 180°C (350°F) Gas Mark 4.

4 Roll out the dough and line a greased tart tin 8–9 inches in diameter.

5 Rub together the ingredients for the streusel with your fingertips to give the consistency of coarse breadcrumbs.

6 Spread the poppy-seed cream over the pastry base. Cover with the drained cherries. Sprinkle with streusel, put into the oven and bake for 30–35 minutes. Serve warm or cold.

Cook's tip Streusel is a crumbly topping for tarts and cakes, made of butter, flour, sugar and sometimes spices.

SERVES 4
PREPARATION TIME: 35 MINUTES
RESTING TIME: SEVERAL HOURS

BLACK CHERRY **TIRAMISU**

6 slices good quality chocolate cake (home-made or bought)
3 tablespoons good quality morello cherry jam
Cherry syrup or 1 glass cranberry juice
2 tablespoons cherry liqueur or Amaretto (optional)
500 g (1 lb) good quality cherries in syrup or fresh pitted
   black cherries (+ 6 fresh pitted cherries for decoration)
250 g (8 oz) mascarpone
2 very fresh eggs, separated
4 tablespoons caster sugar
Cocoa powder for dusting

1 Spread the slices of cake with the jam before placing them in the bottom of 6 fairly wide, not too deep glass dishes. Drizzle with diluted cherry syrup (or cranberry juice) and liqueur, if using. Arrange the cherries on top.

2 Beat the mascarpone with the egg yolks and sugar. Whisk the egg whites and fold into the mascarpone mixture. Spread this over the cherries. Stand in the refrigerator for several hours. To serve, dust with cocoa powder and decorate each dessert with a cherry.

SERVES 4
PREPARATION TIME: 20 MINUTES
CHILLING TIME: MINIMUM 4 HOURS

WHITE MOUSSE
WITH MORELLO CHERRIES

150 g (5 oz) shortbread biscuits
50 g (2 oz) butter, melted
3–4 leaves gelatine (8 g)
100 g (3½ oz) mascarpone
50 g (2 oz) caster sugar
200 ml (7 fl oz) double or whipping cream
2 egg whites
4 tablespoons good quality morello cherries in syrup

1 Roughly crush the biscuits (in a food processor or put them in a polythene bag and crush with a rolling pin). Melt the butter and mix with the crumbs. Spoon into individual glass bowls or ramekins.

2 Soak the gelatine in a little cold water for 5 minutes; squeeze out when ready to use. Put the drained gelatine into a pan over gentle heat with 3 tablespoons of water and stir until completely dissolved.

3 Whisk the mascarpone and the sugar into the gelatine. Whip the chilled cream and fold into the mascarpone. Whisk the egg whites stiff before gently folding them into the mixture.

4 Spoon into the serving dishes and leave to set for at least 4 hours in the refrigerator.

5 Decorate with cherries in syrup.

44

SERVES 4
PREPARATION TIME: 15 MINUTES
COOKING TIME: 10 MINUTES
FREEZING TIME: 4 HOURS (DEPENDING ON THE ICE-CREAM MAKER)

FROMAGE FRAIS & CHERRY
ICE CREAM

50 g (2 oz) almond shortbread biscuits
200 ml (7 fl oz) milk
4 tablespoons caster sugar
4 egg yolks
1 teaspoon cornflour, Maizena if possible
1 jar cherries in syrup
500 g (1 lb) well-drained fromage frais

1 Break the biscuits in not too small pieces.

2 Make an egg custard. Heat the milk. Beat together the sugar, egg yolks and cornflour in a heatproof bowl, then pour over the milk, stirring constantly. Pour the mixture back into the pan over low heat, stirring constantly until the custard thickens and coats the back of the spoon. Set aside to cool.

3 Stir the fromage frais with a whisk before mixing it into the custard. Freeze in an ice-cream maker.

4 Purée half the cherries. While the ice cream is still soft, stir in the purée, with the whole, pitted cherries and the broken biscuits. Serve immediately or keep in the freezer until 20 minutes before serving.

English translation and adaptation: JMS Books LLP
Layout: cbdesign

First published in France in 2007 under the title
La Boîte à gâteau, by Hachette Livre (Marabout)
Copyright © 2007 Hachette Livre (Marabout)
Editorial: Catherine Berranger and Charlotte Müller-Buch

An Hachette Livre UK Company
www.hachettelivre.co.uk

First published in Great Britain in 2008 by
Hamlyn, a division of Octopus Publishing Group Ltd
2–4 Heron Quays, London E14 4JP
www.octopusbooks.co.uk

ISBN 978 0 600 61876 8

A CIP catalogue record for this book is available from
the British Library

Printed and bound in China

1 3 5 7 9 10 8 6 4 2

This book contains dishes that are made with raw or lightly cooked eggs.
These should be avoided by vulnerable people such as pregnant and
nursing mothers, invalids, the elderly, babies and young children.

ORANGE
LEMON & LIME

hamlyn

CONTENTS

SERVES 6
PREPARATION TIME: 20 MINUTES
COOKING TIME: 1¼ HOURS

MARMALADE **GINGERBREAD**

100 g (3½ oz) unsalted butter, cut into small pieces,
   + extra for greasing
150 g (5 oz) liquid honey or golden syrup
250 g (8 oz) plain flour
2 teaspoons baking powder
2 teaspoons ground ginger or fresh ginger,
   peeled and finely grated
½ teaspoon ground cinnamon
½ teaspoon salt
250 g (8 oz) orange marmalade
1 egg

1 Preheat the oven to 180°C (350°F) Gas Mark 4. Grease a round or square cake tin and line with nonstick baking paper.

2 Melt the butter with the honey or golden syrup in a small pan.

3 Sift the flour, baking powder, ginger, cinnamon and salt into a large bowl. Make a well in the centre and pour in the butter and honey mixture. Begin by incorporating some of the flour then add the marmalade, the egg and 2 tablespoons of warm water. Mix thoroughly; if the dough is too stiff to drop off a spoon, add a little more water or milk.

4 Pour into the prepared tin, smooth off the top, put in the oven and bake for 1 hour. The cake should be browned and still quite soft in the centre (test it by inserting a skewer, which should come out clean). Leave to cool for 15 minutes before turning out onto a wire rack to cool.

SERVES 4–6
PREPARATION TIME: 25 MINUTES
COOKING TIME: 35 MINUTES

ALL-ORANGE **FAIRY CAKES**

80 g (3 oz) softened unsalted butter + extra for greasing
120 g (4 oz) plain flour + extra for dusting
2 oranges
6 tablespoons sugar
2 eggs, beaten
2 teaspoons baking powder

FOR THE CREAM
150 g (5 oz) mascarpone
150 g (5 oz) fromage frais
1 tablespoon caster sugar

1 Preheat the oven to 180°C (350°F) Gas Mark 4. Butter and flour 4 muffin cups or 6 smaller bun cups (ideally line with medium-sized paper cases).

2 Finely grate the rind of 1 orange and squeeze the juice. Beat the butter and sugar together and gradually add the eggs. Sift in the flour and baking powder and mix well, finally adding the rind and orange juice.

3 Pour into the cases, put in the oven and bake for about 25 minutes; cover with a sheet of foil in the course of baking to prevent the fairy cakes cooking too quickly.

4 Remove a thin layer of rind from the second orange and cut into fine strips for decorating. Squeeze the juice. Remove the cakes from the oven and pour over the juice.

5 Beat together the mascarpone, the fromage frais and the sugar. Ice the little cakes with this cream and decorate with the strips of orange rind.

SERVES 6
PREPARATION TIME: 30 MINUTES
COOKING TIME: 40 MINUTES

CARROT & ORANGE **GATEAU**

Butter for greasing
200 g (7 oz) caster sugar
2 eggs
2 oranges
200 g (7 oz) plain flour
1 teaspoon baking powder
1 teaspoon ground cinnamon
½ teaspoon ground ginger
pinch of nutmeg
150 ml (¼ pint) oil
200 g (7 oz) grated carrots
150 g (5 oz) raisins
1 lemon
200 g (7 oz) mascarpone
200 g (7 oz) fromage frais

1 Preheat the oven to 180°C (350°F) Gas Mark 4. Butter a cake tin 20–23 cm (8–9 inches) in diameter and line with nonstick baking paper.

2 Whisk the eggs with 125 g (4 oz) of the caster sugar. Grate the rind from one orange and squeeze the juice. Sift the flour with the spices and baking powder into a bowl.

3 Whisk the oil into the egg and sugar mixture and add the rind and orange juice. Gently fold in the flour, then the carrot and the raisins; do not over-mix.

4 Pour the mixture into the prepared tin, put in the oven and bake for about 40 minutes or until a metal skewer inserted into the centre emerges quite clean.

5 Meanwhile, grate the rind from the second orange and the lemon and squeeze the juice from both. Dissolve the remaining sugar in this juice. Beat the mascarpone and the fromage frais together until quite smooth, then add the grated rind and refrigerate.

6 Remove the cake from the oven, pierce all over with a skewer and pour over the orange and lemon syrup. Leave to cool completely, then spread the cream over the surface and decorate with the grated rind. Alternatively, slice the cake in half and fill it with the cream.

SERVES 4
PREPARATION TIME: 35 MINUTES + RESTING TIME
COOKING TIME: 1 HOUR

APFELSTRUDEL WITH ORANGE

FOR THE PASTRY
125 ml (4 fl oz) milk
75 g (3 oz) unsalted butter
1 tablespoon sugar
150 g (5 oz) plain flour
1 teaspoon baking powder
1 egg

FOR THE FILLING
5–6 cooking apples
3 oranges
2 lemons
2 tablespoons sugar
2 tablespoons orange marmalade
100 g (3½ oz) raisins
20 g (¾ oz) unsalted butter + extra for greasing

To serve: crème fraîche or custard

1 To make the pastry: put the milk in a small pan with the sugar and butter and heat gently until the sugar is dissolved and the butter melted, then take off the heat and leave to cool. Sift the flour with the baking powder into a large bowl, make a well in the centre and add the egg, together with the milk mixture, keeping a little of the mixture back to brush over the pastry before baking. Mix to form a dough, knead for 5 minutes on a lightly floured work surface, then wrap in clingfilm and leave to rest on the work surface for 15 minutes.

2 Peel the apples and cut into very thin slices. Peel the oranges with a sharp knife, removing all the white pith, then finely chop and put into a pan with the sugar and marmalade. Bring to the boil, stirring to dissolve the sugar, then lower the heat and leave until reduced to a syrupy consistency. Take off the heat and stir in the apple slices and the raisins.

3 Butter a baking sheet and preheat the oven to 180°C (350°F) Gas Mark 4. Roll out the pastry into a 5-mm (¼-inch) thick circle. Spread the orange and apple mixture on it, leaving a border about 2.5 cm (1 inch) wide all around. Cut the butter into tiny pieces and distribute them over the fruit. Fold the borders up over the fruit then roll up the pastry to form a strudel. Place the strudel on the prepared baking sheet and brush with the reserved egg and milk mixture.

4 Put in the oven and bake for 50 minutes, basting it from time to time with the juices that run from it. Serve with crème fraîche or custard.

SERVES 4
PREPARATION TIME: 30 MINUTES
COOKING TIME: 30 MINUTES

BLOOD ORANGE
CHIFFON TART

150 g (5 oz) shortbread biscuits
50 g (2 oz) unsalted butter
2 oranges
2 blood oranges
1 lemon
2 tablespoons cornflour
50 g (2 oz) caster sugar
2 eggs, separated

1 Preheat the oven to 200°C (400°F) Gas Mark 6.

2 Put the biscuits in a polythene bag and crush them with a rolling pin or reduce them to crumbs in a food processor. Melt the butter and mix with the biscuit crumbs. Press them into a tart tin 20 cm (8 inches) in diameter.

3 Finely grate the rind from the oranges and the lemon and squeeze the juice. Put in a measuring jug and add water if necessary to make 300 ml (½ pint).

4 Separate the eggs. Combine the cornflour with a little orange juice in a small pan, then stir in the sugar. Add the egg yolks, the grated orange rind and the rest of the juice. Place over gentle heat and stir constantly until the mixture thickens, then remove from the heat and leave to cool, stirring from time to time.

5 Whisk the egg whites until stiff and fold into the orange cream. Pour over the biscuit base, put in the oven and bake for 15 minutes. Leave to cool then refrigerate until ready to serve.

SERVES 4
PREPARATION TIME: 25 MINUTES
CHILLING TIME: MINIMUM 4 HOURS

ORANGE
MOUSSE POTS

150 g (5 oz) lemon-flavoured shortbread biscuits
40 g (2 oz) unsalted butter + extra for greasing
3 leaves gelatine (6 g/¼ oz)
250 g (8 oz) mascarpone
3 tablespoons caster sugar
200 ml (7 fl oz) single cream
4 oranges
2 egg whites

1 Roughly crush the biscuits in a polythene bag with a rolling pin or in a food processor. Melt the butter, mix with the crumbs and press into buttered ramekins or small pots.

2 Soften the gelatine in a little cold water. Beat the mascarpone with the sugar until smooth. Heat half of the cream, squeeze the gelatine and dissolve thoroughly in the cream, then mix into the mascarpone and add the rest of the cream. Finely grate the rind from 1 orange, squeeze the juice and add both these to the mixture. Beat the egg whites until stiff and gently fold in.

3 Pour the mixture onto the biscuit base in the ramekins and refrigerate for at least 4 hours or overnight if possible.

4 Before serving, peel the remaining oranges with a sharp knife to remove the white pith, then cut out each segment, discarding the membrane separating them. Either leave the mousses in the ramekins, or turn out onto a plate, having first passed a fine knife blade around the inside of the moulds. Serve together with the orange segments.

SERVES 4
PREPARATION TIME: 30 MINUTES
COOKING TIME: 5 MINUTES
FREEZING TIME: 4 HOURS

ORANGES GIVRÉES

6 oranges
150 g (5 oz) caster sugar
1 teaspoon orange flower water

To serve: Orange Viennese Shortbread Biscuits
   (see recipe on page 20)

1 Cut a small lid from 4 oranges and scoop out the flesh with a small knife and a spoon. Put the flesh into a sieve, press the juice out with a spatula and set aside.

2 Grate the rind from the remaining oranges and squeeze the juice. Put the grated rind into a pan with the sugar and orange flower water, bring to the boil and simmer for 4–5 minutes. (If the mixture gets too thick add a little of the orange juice.) Mix this syrup with the juice and freeze in an ice-cream maker, or in a tray in the freezer, stirring several times to remove the crystals.

3 Fill the hollowed-out orange skins and put in the freezer, removing about 15 minutes before serving to soften a little.

4 Serve with the orange-flavoured shortbread biscuits.

Cook's tip Oranges givrées means simply 'sorbet-filled oranges'.

MAKES 50 BISCUITS (MORE OR LESS, DEPENDING ON SIZE)
PREPARATION TIME: 40 MINUTES
COOKING TIME: 8 MINUTES PER BATCH

ORANGE VIENNESE
SHORTBREAD BISCUITS

230 g (8 oz) softened unsalted butter + extra for greasing
2 oranges
6 tablespoons icing sugar
1 vanilla pod, split in half lengthways
1 egg white
200 g (7 oz) plain flour
80 g (3 oz) ground almonds
Salt

1 Preheat the oven to 200°C (400°F) Gas Mark 6. Grease several baking sheets.

2 Finely grate the rind from the oranges. Using a balloon whisk or an electric hand beater, mix the butter, sugar, seeds scraped from the vanilla pod and the grated orange rind to obtain a fluffy mixture. Add the egg white and whisk again.

3 Sift the flour and ground almonds with a pinch of salt into a bowl then fold into the mixture with a large spoon.

4 Put the mixture into a piping bag fitted with a star-shaped nozzle and pipe the biscuits in little 'wave' shapes onto the baking sheets, leaving space for them to spread during baking. There will probably be enough for 2–3 batches.

5 Put in the oven and bake for 8 minutes; they should be lightly browned. Leave to set for a few minutes before transferring to wire racks to cool. Excellent companions for the Oranges Givrées on page 18, for example.

SERVES 6
PREPARATION TIME: 25 MINUTES
CHILLING TIME: 1 HOUR

LITTLE 'GREEN ORANGES'
FILLED WITH CANDIED ORANGE PEEL CREAM

Icing sugar for dusting and decoration
250 g (8 oz) almond paste/marzipan, coloured green
1 sponge cake base
2 tablespoons Grand Marnier or Bitter Orange Liqueur
300 g (10 oz) ricotta
100 g (3½ oz) mascarpone
1 orange
3 tablespoons caster sugar
75 g (3 oz) candied orange peel, finely chopped

1 Roll out the almond paste on a work surface dusted with icing sugar. Cut into circles with a 10-cm (4-inch) pastry cutter. Cut circles from the sponge cake with a 3-cm (1¼-inch) biscuit cutter, sprinkle with the liqueur and lay them in the centre of the almond paste circles.

2 Beat the ricotta with the mascarpone. Finely grate the rind from the orange and add it to the ricotta–mascarpone mixture along with the sugar. Finally add the candied peel.

3 Put a spoonful of this cream on each circle and gather up the almond paste around it like a pouch. Refrigerate for 1 hour then dredge with icing sugar and serve.

SERVES 6
PREPARATION TIME: 35 MINUTES
COOKING TIME: 30 MINUTES

ORANGE SCONES
WITH ORANGE CREAM

FOR THE CREAM
Finely grated rind and juice of 1 orange
1 lemon
2 eggs
40 g (2 oz) caster sugar
25 g (1 oz) unsalted butter, cut into small pieces

FOR THE SCONES
40 g (1½ oz) butter + extra for greasing
300 g (10 oz) plain flour + extra for dusting
1½ teaspoons baking powder
1 tablespoon sugar
½ teaspoon salt
Grated rind of 1 orange
50 g (2 oz) candied orange peel (optional)
1 egg
150 ml (¼ pint) milk
150 ml (¼ pint) whipping cream

1 To make the cream: in a large bowl, whisk the orange juice and finely grated rind, the juice of half the lemon, the eggs and the sugar. Add the butter and place the bowl over a pan of simmering water. Stir continuously until the cream thickens (10–15 minutes). Remove the bowl from the heat and leave to cool.

2 To make the scones: preheat the oven to 220°C (425°F) Gas Mark 7. Grease a baking sheet or line with nonstick baking paper. Mix the flour, baking powder, sugar, salt and the grated orange rind in a large bowl. Add the butter and rub into the flour with the fingertips. Add the candied peel, chopped small, then the egg and the milk. Mix together with a round-bladed knife. Form the dough into a rough ball by hand, without kneading it. It should be quite soft and pliable; add a little more milk or flour if necessary.

3 Put the dough on a floured work surface and flatten by hand to a thickness of at least 2.5 cm (1 inch). Cut into circles with a fluted 3-cm (1¼-inch) diameter biscuit cutter dipped in flour and lay them on the baking sheet. Put in the oven and bake for 12–15 minutes, then transfer to a wire rack to cool. Whip the well-chilled cream.

4 Serve as soon as possible, together with the orange cream, the whipped cream, and a cup of Earl Grey tea.

SERVES 4
PREPARATION TIME: 30 MINUTES
COOKING TIME: 1½ HOURS
CHILLING TIME: 1 HOUR

LEMON **MERINGUE PIE**

FOR THE SHORTCRUST PASTRY
200 g (7 oz) flour
100 g (3½ oz) unsalted butter, cut into small pieces
Salt

FOR THE FILLING
3 lemons
200 g (7 oz) caster sugar
35 g (1½ oz) cornflour
125 ml (4 fl oz) milk
25 g (1 oz) butter
2 eggs, separated

1 To make the shortcrust pastry: put the flour, butter and a pinch of salt into a large bowl. Rub in the butter with the fingertips until the mixture resembles fine breadcrumbs. Add 100 ml (3½ fl oz) of water and mix with a round-bladed knife. Finish it off by hand, adding a little water if necessary, and quickly form into a rough ball. Put into a polythene bag and refrigerate for at least 1 hour.

2 Preheat the oven to 180°C (350°F) Gas Mark 4. Roll out the pastry and use it to line a tart tin 20 cm (8 inches) in diameter. Cover the base with a circle of nonstick baking paper, weighted with dried beans or pie weights, put in the oven and bake for 20 minutes. Remove the beans and the paper and bake for a further 5 minutes.

3 Finely grate the rind from the 3 lemons and put into a small pan with 100 g (3½ oz) of the sugar, the cornflour and 50 ml (2 fl oz) water. Stir well then add 75 ml (3 fl oz) more water and the milk. Bring to the boil, stirring constantly, and cook for 1 minute, then remove from the heat and whisk in the butter. Squeeze the juice from 2 lemons and whisk 5 tablespoons of it into the cream. Whisk the yolks, one at a time, into the lemon cream. Leave to cool.

4 Preheat the oven to 140°C (275°F) Gas Mark 1. Pour the lemon cream into the cold pastry base and chill.

5 Whisk the egg whites, then add the remaining sugar once they have begun to froth and continue whisking until they form a stiff, shiny mixture. Spread the meringue over the tart, right to the edges, and bake for 50–60 minutes, when the meringue should be crisp. Leave to cool for at least 20 minutes before serving.

SERVES 6
PREPARATION TIME: 30 MINUTES
COOKING TIME: 50 MINUTES
CHILLING TIME: 1 HOUR

LEMON & BERGAMOT
TARTLETS

FOR THE SHORTBREAD PASTRY
125 g (4 oz) softened unsalted butter + extra for greasing
50 g (2 oz) caster sugar
1 egg
250 g (8 oz) plain flour
Salt

FOR THE FILLING
2 lemons
1 bergamot (if unavailable use 2 lemons or 3 limes)
125 g (4 oz) caster sugar
3 eggs
1 tablespoon cornflour
Icing sugar, for decorating

1 To make the shortbread pastry: mix the softened butter with the sugar. Add the egg and half a tablespoon of finely grated bergamot rind. Mix well then add the flour, previously sifted with the salt. Form the pastry into a ball, handling it as little as possible.

2 Preheat the oven to 180°C (350°F) Gas Mark 4 and grease 6 tartlet tins. Roll out the pastry and use it to line the buttered tartlet tins. Lay a circle of nonstick baking paper in each and weight with dried beans. Put in the oven and bake for 20 minutes. Remove the paper and beans and bake for a further 5–10 minutes.

3 Grate the rind of 2 lemons and half the bergamot. Squeeze the juice from all the fruit and use a little of it to mix with the cornflour. Heat the rest of the juice with the grated rind and the sugar until the sugar has dissolved. Add the cornflour, mixed with a little water, and the eggs. Cook over medium heat, stirring constantly, until the mixture thickens, then leave to cool.

4 Fill the pre-baked tartlets and return them to the oven for 10 minutes. Leave to cool and dredge with icing sugar before serving.

Cook's tip Bergamots are small, yellow, sour citrus fruits.

SERVES 4
PREPARATION TIME: 30 MINUTES
COOKING TIME: 45 MINUTES

MERINGUE-TOPPED
LIME BISCUITS

100 g (3½ oz) butter + extra for greasing
100 g (3½ oz) caster sugar
3 eggs, separated
Finely grated rind and juice of 1 lime
225 g (7½ oz) plain flour
1½ teaspoons baking powder
80 g (3 oz) chopped Brazil nuts or raw, unsalted pistachios
175 g (6 oz) icing sugar

1 Preheat the oven to 180°C (350°F) Gas mark 4. Grease a 20-cm (8-inch) square tin.

2 Beat together the butter and sugar until light and fluffy (using a food processor or electric whisk makes this easier). Whisk the yolks into the butter-sugar mixture, then add the lime rind and 1 tablespoon of lime juice.

3 Sift the flour with the baking powder and fold it gently into the mixture, which should be fairly firm. Put it into the prepared tin and tap gently on the work surface to level the top, then spread over the chopped nuts.

4 Whisk the egg whites until very stiff, adding the icing sugar a little at a time. Spread this meringue over the cake and form little peaks with a knife. Put in the oven and bake for 45 minutes, by which time the meringue peaks should have browned. Remove from the oven and leave to cool before cutting into rectangles.

SERVES 6
PREPARATION TIME: 30 MINUTES
COOKING TIME: 45 MINUTES

LIME & MANDARIN
SOUFFLÉS

100 g (3½ oz) butter + plus extra for greasing
200 g (7 oz) sugar
Finely grated rind and juice of 1 lime
Finely grated rind and juice of 1 mandarin orange
5 eggs, separated
75 g (3 oz) plain flour
1 teaspoon baking powder
500 ml (1 pint) milk

1 Preheat the oven to 180°C (350°F) Gas Mark 4. Butter 6 ramekins (200–250 ml/7–8 fl oz capacity).

2 Beat the butter and sugar together until light and fluffy then beat in the grated rind and the egg yolks, one at a time. Sift the flour with the baking powder and stir into the mixture. Add the milk, a little at a time, stirring just sufficiently to incorporate it into the other ingredients, then add the juice of the lime and mandarin orange. This should result in quite a runny mixture. Whisk the egg whites until stiff and gently fold them in with a large metal spoon.

3 Three-quarters fill the ramekins and place them in a roasting tin. Pour in enough hot water to come halfway up the moulds, put in the oven and bake for about 45 minutes. Serve warm.

SERVES 4
PREPARATION TIME: 25 MINUTES
CHILLING TIME: MINIMUM 4 HOURS

CHEAT'S LEMON
CHEESECAKE

180 g (6 oz) lemon-flavoured shortbread biscuits
60 g (2½ oz) butter
600 g (1¼ lb) fromage frais
200 g (7 oz) sweetened condensed milk
Finely grated rind and juice of 2 lemons

1 Crush the biscuits, melt the butter, and mix together. Press into the base of a cake tin 20 cm (8 inches) in diameter (preferably a springform).

2 Beat the fromage frais to make it smooth and mix with 4 tablespoons of condensed milk, the finely grated rind of the lemons and half their juice. Taste and adjust the sweetness-acid balance if necessary.

3 Pour onto the biscuit base and refrigerate for at least 4 hours. Release from the tin and decorate with grated lemon rind.

MAKES 3 JARS
PREPARATION TIME: 15 MINUTES
COOKING TIME: 15 MINUTES

LEMON **CURD**

4 eggs
300 g (10 oz) caster sugar
225 g (8 oz) softened butter, cut into small pieces
2 teaspoons cornflour
4 lemons (or 2 lemons and 3 limes)

1 Beat the eggs in an ovenproof bowl then add the sugar, the butter, the cornflour and the finely grated rind of the lemons (and limes if using).

2 Set the bowl over a pan of barely simmering water over medium to low heat and whisk the mixture until it thickens. Lower the heat to the minimum and continue to simmer, whisking constantly, for two more minutes, then pour into sterilized pots.

3 This lime curd will keep in the refrigerator for several weeks.

SERVES 6
PREPARATION TIME: 20 MINUTES
COOKING TIME: 1 HOUR

LEMON & ALMOND **TART**

150 g (5 oz) butter
1 sheet pre-rolled butter puff pastry
4 tablespoons lemon curd (see recipe page 36)
1 egg white
120 g (4 oz) caster sugar
4 egg yolks
50 g (2 oz) ground almonds

1 Preheat the oven to 200°C (400°F) Gas Mark 6. Melt the butter then leave it to cool completely.

2 Roll the pastry a little thinner and use it to line a tart tin 20–23 cm (8–9 inches) in diameter. Spread the lemon curd over the base.

3 Whisk together the egg white and the sugar until white and very frothy. Add the yolks and mix in thoroughly. Finally add the butter and the ground almonds. Pour this mixture over the lemon curd layer.

4 Put in the oven and bake for 1 hour, by which time the filling should be set, but do keep a close check – if the top begins to brown too quickly, cover with a sheet of kitchen foil.

5 Leave to cool for 15 minutes and serve warm. It may also be served cold. Individual tartlets make an attractive alternative.

SERVES 6
PREPARATION TIME: 40 MINUTES
COOKING TIME: 40 MINUTES

LEMON & LIME
WEEKEND CAKE

350 g (12 oz) butter + extra for greasing
350 g (12 oz) flour + extra for dusting
1 lemon + 2 limes
6 eggs
350 g (12 oz) granulated sugar
1 vanilla pod
100 g (3½ oz) caster sugar
50 g (2 oz) icing sugar

1 Preheat the oven to 190°C (375°F) Gas Mark 5. Grease and flour a large cake tin.

2 Melt the butter. With a potato peeler, remove the rind from half the lemon and 1 lime, avoiding the pith, and cut it into fine strips. Blanch these in boiling water for 2 minutes, rinse, repeat the process, then rinse and drain.

3 Finely grate the rind from the second lime and the remaining half lemon. Sift the flour into a bowl and add the grated rind.

4 Whisk the eggs with the granulated sugar until pale and frothy, then carefully fold in the flour and the vanilla seeds, scraped from the pod with a knife. Stir a little of this mixture into the melted butter, then add the melted butter to the mixture. Three-quarters fill the prepared cake tin, put into the oven, reduce the temperature to 180°C (350°F) Gas Mark 4 and bake for 35–40 minutes.

5 Heat the caster sugar and 100 ml (3½ fl oz) of water in a small pan until it begins to simmer and the sugar has dissolved. Add the blanched lemon and lime rind and leave to simmer gently for 10 minutes to crystallize, then drain.

6 Squeeze the lemon and limes and stir in the icing sugar to make a runny glaze. Take the cake out of the tin immediately it comes out of the oven and pour over the glaze. Increase the temperature to 200°C (400°F) Gas Mark 6 and return the cake to the oven, on a baking sheet. As soon as small bubbles begin to form, take it out and decorate with the crystallized peel.

SERVES 6
PREPARATION TIME: 20 MINUTES
CHILLING TIME: OVERNIGHT + ABOUT 2 HOURS

LEMONADE
WITH LEMON SORBET

8 lemons
170 g (6 oz) caster sugar
1 litre (1¾ pints) Perrier water
  (or other, less effervescent water)
500 ml (17 fl oz) ready-made lemon sorbet

1 Wash the lemons and peel with a potato peeler, taking care not to include any of the white pith.

2 Squeeze the lemons and put the juice, rind and sugar into a large bowl. Pour over 1.5 litres (2½ pints) of boiling water.

3 Leave overnight and next morning, filter, taste and add more sugar if necessary, then refrigerate.

4 Serve in tall glasses with a little Perrier and a scoop of lemon sorbet.

SERVES 4
PREPARATION TIME: 30 MINUTES
COOKING TIME: 40 MINUTES

LEMON **TURNOVERS**

1 sheet pre-rolled butter puff pastry
2 tablespoons softened unsalted butter
1 egg, beaten

FOR THE LEMON CREAM
Finely grated rind of 3 lemons + 100 ml (3½ fl oz) juice
3 egg yolks
100 g (3½ oz) caster sugar
30 g (1 oz) plain flour
2 tablespoons cornflour
300 ml (½ pint) milk

1 To prepare the lemon cream: in a heatproof bowl, whisk the egg yolks with 50 g (2 oz) of the sugar, add the flour, cornflour and the lemon rind and mix thoroughly with a whisk. Bring the milk almost to the boil in a medium pan and pour into the mixture, whisking constantly, then pour it all back into the pan. Bring to simmering point over gentle heat and cook for 2 minutes, stirring constantly. Add the lemon juice, a little at a time, stirring without whisking. Pour the cream into a cold bowl, cover with clingfilm and leave to cool.

2 Roll out the pastry a little more. Butter a baking sheet with the very soft butter, or line it with nonstick baking paper. Set aside 1–2 tablespoons of the remaining sugar and sprinkle the rest on the baking sheet.

3 Preheat the oven to 220°C (400°F) Gas Mark 6. Cut 4 x 10–12-cm (4–5-inch) diameter circles from the pastry, using a saucer as a template. Put a little of the cold lemon cream on one half, moisten the edges with cold water and fold the turnovers, pinching the borders to seal them. Arrange on the prepared baking sheet, brush over with the beaten egg, sprinkle with the remaining sugar and bake for about 25 minutes, until the turnovers are golden brown.

English translation and adaptation: JMS Books LLP
Layout: cbdesign

First published in France in 2007 under the title
La Boîte à gâteau, by Hachette Livre (Marabout)
Copyright © 2007 Hachette Livre (Marabout)
Editorial: Catherine Berranger and Charlotte Müller-Buch

An Hachette Livre UK Company
www.hachettelivre.co.uk

First published in Great Britain in 2008 by
Hamlyn, a division of Octopus Publishing Group Ltd
2–4 Heron Quays, London E14 4JP
www.octopusbooks.co.uk

Copyright © English edition
Octopus Publishing Group Ltd 2008

Original French edition copyright
© HACHETTE LIVRE (Marabout) 2007

ISBN 978 0 600 61876 8

A CIP catalogue record for this book is available from
the British Library

Printed and bound in China

1 3 5 7 9 10 8 6 4 2

This book contains dishes that are made with raw or lightly cooked eggs.
These should be avoided by vulnerable people such as pregnant and
nursing mothers, invalids, the elderly, babies and young children.

ROSE
LYCHEE

hamlyn

CONTENTS

SERVES 6
PREPARATION TIME: 30 MINUTES
COOKING TIME: 50 MINUTES

ROSE & REDCURRANT
MERINGUE PIE

150 g (5 oz) soft butter + extra for greasing
250 g (8 oz) caster sugar
4 eggs, separated
100 g (3½ oz) ground almonds
300 g (10 oz) plain flour
250 g (8 oz) redcurrants, without stalks
375 g (12 oz) raspberries
2 teaspoons rosewater

1 Preheat the oven to 190°C (375°F) Gas Mark 5. Grease a tart tin 23 cm (9 inches) in diameter.

2 In a mixing bowl, beat together the butter and half the sugar. Add the egg yolks, then the ground almonds, and sift in the flour. Line the tart tin with this pastry. Put in the oven and bake for about 30 minutes. Reduce the oven temperature to 150°C (300°F) Gas Mark 2.

3 Mix the redcurrants and raspberries with half the remaining sugar and the rosewater. Whisk the egg whites until stiff, add the remaining sugar and whisk again.

4 Spoon the redcurrant and raspberry mixture onto the cake base, leaving a 1.5-cm (½-inch) rim. Cover the fruit and the rim with meringue and draw a pattern in it with a spoon. Bake for 45 minutes–1 hour, until the meringue is pale golden and crisp on the outside.

SERVES 4
PREPARATION TIME: 45 MINUTES
COOKING TIME: 15 MINUTES

STRAWBERRY & ROSE
GAZELLE HORNS

FOR THE PASTRY
150 g (5 oz) plain flour
100 g (3½ oz) butter + extra for greasing
1 tablespoon caster sugar

FOR THE FILLING
250 g (8 oz) strawberries
A few untreated rose petals (optional)
50 g (2 oz) very soft butter
5 tablespoons icing sugar
150 g (5 oz) ground almonds
1 egg
3 tablespoons crème fraîche
1 teaspoon rosewater

TO FINISH
2 tablespoons flaked almonds
1 egg, beaten
Icing sugar

1 To make the pastry: melt the butter, then mix with the flour and sugar. Add 3 tablespoons of cold water. Knead for a few minutes. The dough should be firm but malleable. Set aside to rest at room temperature.

2 Wash and hull the strawberries and cut in very small pieces. If using, wash the rose petals thoroughly and chop very small. Mix the soft butter with the icing sugar, then add the ground almonds, egg and crème fraîche. Add the rosewater, then the strawberries and rose petals.

3 Preheat the oven to 180°C (350°F) Gas Mark 4. Grease a baking sheet.

4 Roll out half the dough to form a long rectangular strip 10 cm (4 inches) wide. Cut in squares. Roll each square out more. Put a small spoonful of filling in one corner. Fold the corner over the filling, roll up, then curl the ends round to form a crescent. Follow the same procedure with all the squares, then do the same with the other half of the dough.

5 Arrange the gazelle horns on the baking sheet, brush with beaten egg and sprinkle with flaked almonds. Put in the oven and bake for 15 minutes. Dust with icing sugar and serve with tea.

Cook's tip Gazelle horns are Moroccan pastries.

SERVES 6
PREPARATION TIME: 30 MINUTES + RESTING TIME
COOKING TIME: 2 HOURS

QUINCE & ROSE **TARTE TATIN**

FOR THE PASTRY
200 g (7 oz) plain flour
120 g (4 oz) butter, cut into pieces
2 tablespoons caster sugar
1 egg
Salt

FOR THE FILLING
2 quinces
5 apples
50 g (2 oz) butter, cut into pieces
3 tablespoons caster sugar
1–2 teaspoons rosewater
Crème fraîche or custard for serving

1 To make the pastry: put the flour sifted with a pinch of salt into a bowl, add the butter and rub the butter into the flour with your fingertips to the consistency of fine breadcrumbs. Stir in the sugar and mix in the egg with a palette knife to make a dough. Add a little cold water if necessary. Finish the dough by hand and form into a rough ball but do not work it too much. Put in a polythene bag in the refrigerator for 1 hour.

2 Preheat the oven to 190°C (375°F) Gas Mark 5. Peel and core the quinces, cut in quarters and arrange in an ovenproof dish. Bake in the oven for about 1 hour until tender. You can also bake them whole (washed but not peeled) and remove the skins after cooking.

3 Peel the apples and cut in quarters. Put the butter and sugar in a cake tin 23–25 cm (9–10 inches) in diameter, or a tatin tin if you have one. You could also use a frying pan as long as it is all metal and can go in the oven. Place directly over low heat and melt the butter with the sugar until it forms a golden caramel. Remove from the heat and add the apples and quinces to the caramel. Pour over the rosewater.

4 Roll out the pastry and cover the fruit with it, tucking the edges down between the fruit and the inside of the tin. Put in the oven and bake for about 45 minutes. The pastry should be golden. Take out of the oven, allow to rest for 10 minutes in the tin, then turn upside down onto a plate.

5 Serve with crème fraîche or an egg custard.

SERVES 4
PREPARATION TIME: 20 MINUTES
COOKING TIME: 20 MINUTES

ROSE, RASPBERRY & APRICOT
MADELEINES

60 g (2½ oz) butter + extra for greasing
50 g (2 oz) dried apricots
2 eggs
150 g (5 oz) caster sugar
1 small yogurt
Rosewater
180 g (6 oz) plain flour
2 teaspoons baking powder
1 handful raspberries
50 g (2 oz) icing sugar

1 Preheat the oven to 180°C (350°F) Gas Mark 4. Grease a madeleine tin(s) – you will need to bake two batches.

2 Chop the dried apricots. Melt the butter.

3 Beat the eggs together with half the sugar until the mixture turns pale. Add the yogurt, melted butter and 2 teaspoons of rosewater. Sift in the flour and baking powder and fold in carefully, without stirring too much. Lastly add the chopped apricots and the raspberries.

4 Fill the madeleine tins with the mixture. Put in the oven and bake for about 12–15 minutes. These madeleines may not rise very much! Turn out onto a wire rack to cool completely.

5 Melt the icing sugar over low heat with 2 tablespoons of water and one teaspoon of rosewater. Spread over the madeleines and allow to set before serving.

SERVES 6
PREPARATION TIME: 30 MINUTES
COOKING TIME: 20 MINUTES
CHILLING TIME: 1–2 HOURS

FEATHER-LIGHT SPONGE
WITH ROSE & RED BERRY CREAM

Butter for greasing
4 eggs, separated + 2 eggs, separated
120 g (4 oz) caster sugar + 2 tablespoons
Rosewater
120 g (4 oz) plain flour + extra for dusting
125 g (4 oz) mascarpone
375 g (12 oz) red berries
   (strawberries, raspberries or redcurrants, or a mixture)
75 g (3 oz) icing sugar
Red food colouring (optional)

1 Preheat the oven to 180°C (350°F) Gas Mark 4. Grease and flour 2 cake tins 18–20 cm (7–8 inches) in diameter.

2 In a bowl set over a pan of simmering water, beat 4 egg yolks and the 120 g (4 oz) of sugar with a few drops of rosewater. The mixture should become very light and frothy. Fold in the sifted flour with a big spoon.

3 Whisk the 4 egg whites until stiff and fold into the mixture. Spoon into the cake tins, put in the oven and bake for about 20 minutes, reducing the temperature to 160°C (325°F) Gas Mark 3 after 15 minutes. Turn out onto a wire rack to cool.

4 Beat the mascarpone in a large bowl to make it smooth. Add the 2 remaining egg yolks, a few drops of rosewater and the remaining 2 tablespoons of sugar and beat well. Whisk the 2 egg whites until stiff and fold into the mixture.

5 Wash the red fruits, remove the stalks and, if using strawberries, cut in pieces. Reserve a few whole berries for decoration.

6 Cover one round of sponge with fruit and the mascarpone cream. Put the second sponge on top and press lightly.

7 Mix the icing sugar with 3 tablespoons of water and a drop of colouring (to turn it pink). Ice the cake and decorate with the remaining berries. Refrigerate for 1–2 hours to allow the cream to set a little. Best eaten the same day.

SERVES 6
PREPARATION TIME: 1 HOUR
COOKING TIME: 45 MINUTES

SAINT-HONORÉS
WITH CRYSTALLIZED ROSE PETAL

FOR DECORATION
2 egg whites
300 g (10 oz) caster sugar
Petals from 3 roses not sprayed
    with insecticide or fertilizer

FOR THE SWEET PASTRY
250 g (8 oz) plain flour
150 g (5 oz) butter, cut into
    small pieces
75 g (3 oz) caster sugar
1 egg

FOR THE CHOUX PASTRY
125 ml (4 fl oz) milk
125 ml (4 fl oz) water
100 g (3½ oz) butter, cut into
    pieces
1 tablespoon caster sugar
1 teaspoon salt
150 g (5 oz) plain flour
4 eggs

FOR THE CARAMEL
200 g (7 oz) caster sugar

FOR THE CREAM
500 ml (17 fl oz) double or
    whipping cream
½ teaspoon rosewater
3 tablespoons icing sugar

1 For the decoration: put the egg whites in a bowl and the sugar on a plate. Quickly dip the petals in the egg white, then the sugar. Spread out on a wire rack to dry in a cool room.

2 To make the sweet pastry: sift the flour into a bowl and add the butter. Rub in with the fingertips to the consistency of coarse breadcrumbs. Stir in the sugar and egg with a palette knife. Knead the dough lightly by hand, adding a little water if necessary. Leave to rest for 1 hour in the refrigerator.

3 To make the choux pastry: heat the milk, water, butter, sugar and salt in a pan. Take off the heat just before it boils, put in all the flour and stir vigorously with a spatula. When the flour has all been absorbed, replace the pan on the heat to dry out the dough, stirring until it comes away from the sides of the pan, then transfer to a bowl.

4 Beat the eggs in a separate bowl and gradually add them to the mixture, beating them in with the spatula. It should not be too soft. If the dough looks right (it will gently close up if you run your finger through it), do not add all the egg.

5 Preheat the oven to 180°C (350°F) Gas Mark 4. Roll out the sweet pastry and with a 6-cm (2½-inch) biscuit cutter cut out 6 circles. Put on a baking sheet lined with nonstick baking paper. With a piping bag or a spoon, make a layer of choux pastry on top of each circle. Form 18–24 small choux buns on a second baking sheet. Put both trays into the oven and bake for about 20 minutes, removing the choux buns after 15 minutes, as they are likely to cook a little quicker.

6 Make a caramel with the remaining caster sugar and a little water. Dip both sides of each choux bun in it and divide the buns between the bases, sticking them at intervals round the edges. Beat the chilled cream with the rosewater and icing sugar until firm peaks form. Fill the centres of each cake with cream and decorate with crystallized rose petals.

SERVES 6
PREPARATION TIME: 5 MINUTES
COOKING TIME: 15 MINUTES

ROSE & MANDARIN
'LEMONADE'

Petals from 4 roses not sprayed with insecticide or fertilizer
150 g (5 oz) caster sugar
1 tablespoon rosewater
3 mandarins
Ice cubes
6 cans tonic water or sparkling water

1 Put the rose petals, sugar and 300 ml (½ pint) of water in a pan. Bring to the boil, stirring to dissolve the sugar. Simmer to achieve a light syrup. Allow to cool before adding the rosewater.

2 Squeeze the mandarins and add the juice to the rose-flavoured syrup.

3 Pour into glasses or a large carafe. Add ice cubes and dilute with the tonic water or sparkling water, to taste.

SERVES 4
PREPARATION TIME: 25 MINUTES
COOKING TIME: 15 MINUTES
FREEZING TIME: 4 HOURS

ROSE **MELBA**

150 ml (¼ pint) double or whipping cream
300 ml (½ pint) milk
60 g (2½ oz) caster sugar
1 teaspoon rosewater
Petals from 6 roses not sprayed with insecticide or fertilizer
4 egg yolks
1 tablespoon cornflour, Maizena if possible
4 ripe white peaches
Raspberry coulis (not too sweet, say, 250 g/8 oz raspberries
    mixed with a little sugar, to taste, and pressed through a sieve)

1 For the ice cream, whip the chilled cream and refrigerate. Heat the milk with the sugar, rosewater and chopped rose petals. Remove from the heat just before it boils, cover and leave to infuse 15 minutes.

2 In a bowl, beat together the egg yolks and cornflour. Pour over the milk, stirring constantly to prevent lumps forming, then pour back into the pan and simmer gently, stirring constantly, until it thickens and coats the back of the spoon. Pour into a bowl, allow to cool completely, then mix in the whipped cream. Freeze in an ice-cream maker or put in a freezerproof container in the freezer, stirring at hourly intervals 2 or 3 times to prevent crystals forming.

3 Peel the peaches and cut in quarters. Fill glasses with ice cream, peaches and raspberry coulis. You could decorate the melbas with crystallized rose petals (see the recipe for Saint-Honorés, page 16).

SERVES 6
PREPARATION TIME: 35 MINUTES + RESTING TIME
REFRIGERATION TIME: 30 MINUTES
COOKING TIME: 35 MINUTES

ROSE **LINZERTORTE**

FOR THE PASTRY
200 g (7 oz) plain flour
Salt
Cinnamon
60 g (2½ oz) ground almonds
3 tablespoons caster sugar
70 g (3 oz) butter, cut into pieces, + extra for greasing
1 egg

FOR THE FILLING
400 g (13 oz) raspberries (fresh or frozen)
200 g (7 oz) caster sugar
2 teaspoons rosewater
4 tablespoons redcurrant jelly
Whipped cream for serving

1 To make the pastry: sift together the flour with a pinch each of salt and cinnamon in a large bowl. Add the butter and rub in with the fingertips to the consistency of coarse breadcrumbs. Add the sugar and ground almonds. Mix in the lightly beaten egg and finish the dough by hand, working it as little as possible. This is a very soft dough. Wrap in clingfilm and stand in the refrigerator for at least 1 hour.

2 Put the raspberries in a pan with the sugar. Bring to the boil and simmer for 10–15 minutes over very low heat, stirring frequently, until it has the consistency of not too thick jam. Add the rosewater and allow to cool.

3 Preheat the oven to 190°C (375°F) Gas Mark 5. Set a quarter of the dough aside and line a greased tart tin 20 cm (8 inches) in diameter with the remainder; you can just press it with the palms of your hands. Stand in a cold place for 30 minutes.

4 Pour the raspberry jam over the tart base. Roll out the remaining dough and form strips, twisted if possible, to arrange in a grid on top of the raspberries. Seal the strips firmly to the edges of the tart.

5 Bake for 35 minutes and allow to cool. Heat the redcurrant jelly until liquid and brush the tart with it. Allow to cool and serve with whipped cream.

SERVES 4
PREPARATION TIME: 10 MINUTES

SWEET **LASSI**

500 g (1 lb 2 oz) plain yogurt
500 ml (17 fl oz) water
4 tablespoons caster sugar
4 teaspoons rosewater
1 teaspoon ground cardamom seeds

To serve: ice cubes

1 Put all the ingredients in a blender (or use a hand blender) and whizz to make a very frothy mixture.

2 Serve over ice cubes in attractive glasses. Lassi is a good accompaniment to gazelle horns (see page 8).

3 For a milkshake, make half the quantity of lassi and whizz in a blender with the ice cream from the recipe for Rose Melba (see page 20).

SERVES 4
PREPARATION TIME: 30 MINUTES
COOKING TIME: 10 MINUTES
CHILLING TIME : 4 HOURS

MINI TARTLETS WITH LYCHEES

ready-made shortcrust tartlet cases
24 lychees (preferably fresh)
300 ml (½ pint) milk
3 egg yolks
3 tablespoons caster sugar
100 ml (3½ fl oz) double or whipping cream
4 leaves gelatine (8 g)
Icing sugar

1 Set out the tartlets on a baking tray.

2 Peel and pit the lychees. Reserve 12 and purée the remainder. Soak the gelatine in a little cold water: squeeze out when ready to use.

3 Heat the milk to almost boiling point. Beat the egg yolks with the sugar, add the milk while stirring constantly, pour back into the pan and cook over low heat, stirring all the time until it is thick enough to coat the back of a spoon.

4 Completely dissolve the gelatine in the hot custard. Set aside to cool.

5 Mix the puréed lychees with the custard. Whip the chilled cream and fold into the lychee cream.

6 Fill the tartlets and decorate each with a lychee. Put in the refrigerator to set for about 4 hours. Dust with icing sugar before serving.

SERVES 4
PREPARATION TIME: 15 MINUTES
FREEZING TIME: 4 HOURS

LYCHEE **ICE CREAM**

500 g (1 lb) canned lychees in syrup (with the syrup)
2 limes
125 ml (4 fl oz) double cream
Fresh peeled and pitted lychees for serving

1 Drain the lychees, reserving the syrup, and purée with 3 tablespoons of lime juice and 200 ml (7 fl oz) of the reserved syrup.
2 Mix with the cream and churn in an ice-cream maker.
3 Serve with the fresh lychees.

SERVES 2
PREPARATION TIME: 10 MINUTES

LYCHEE & KIWI **SMOOTHIE**

4 kiwis
About 10 lychees (preferably fresh)
Vanilla essence
1 lime

1 Peel the kiwi fruits and peel and pit the lychees.
2 Pureé both fruits together with a little lime juice and a few drops of vanilla essence to achieve a very smooth, frothy mixture.
3 Serve immediately.

SERVES 6
PREPARATION TIME: 45 MINUTES
COOKING TIME: 30 MINUTES
RESTING TIME: 2 HOURS

LYCHEE **SAVARINS**

About 20 lychees
(preferably fresh)
Butter for greasing

FOR THE CONFECTIONER'S
CUSTARD
500 ml (17 fl oz) milk
5 egg yolks
100 g (3½ oz) caster sugar
2 tablespoons plain flour
2 tablespoons cornflour,
  Maizena if possible
2 teaspoons rum

FOR THE SAVARIN DOUGH
4 tablespoons milk
1½ teaspoons dried yeast
1 tablespoon sugar
150 g (5 oz) plain flour
1 egg
80 g (3 oz) fairly soft butter

FOR THE SYRUP
150 ml (¼ pint) water
100 g (3½ oz) caster sugar
Juice of 1 lemon
1–2 tablespoons lychee liqueur

1 To make the confectioner's custard: heat the milk. In a heatproof bowl, beat together the egg yolks and sugar; add the flour and cornflour and beat again. When the milk is about to boil, pour in a little and beat, then gradually add the remaining milk, stirring constantly. Pour the mixture back into the pan and cook over medium to low heat, stirring constantly and scraping the bottom of the pan well. Bring to the boil, then cook for a further 2–3 minutes, continuing to stir, until the custard coats the back of the spoon. Add the rum (without beating). Pour the custard into a bowl. Cover the surface with clingfilm and leave to cool.

2 To make the savarin dough: warm the milk. Mix the yeast with the sugar, then stir it into the warm milk in a mixing bowl. Add the flour and the egg and beat immediately (preferably with an electric whisk). Cut the butter in pieces and beat it into the mixture. Continue beating for 2–3 minutes. Cover the bowl with clingfilm and set aside for about 1½ hours for the dough to rise, if possible in a warm place. It should double in volume.

3 For the syrup, heat the water, sugar and lemon juice in a small pan. Stir to dissolve the sugar, then simmer and reduce to a slightly syrupy consistency. Add the lychee liqueur.

4 Grease small savarin moulds or ramekins (or use disposable aluminium moulds). Fill no more than half full with small balls of dough. Leave to rise for a further 30 minutes.

5 Preheat the oven to 180°C (350°F) Gas Mark 4. Bake for about 15 minutes. The savarins should have risen and turned golden. Pour the syrup over the savarins, then top with cream and peeled, pitted lychees.

Cook's tip You can use whipped cream instead of confectioner's custard.

SERVES 6
PREPARATION TIME: 25 MINUTES
COOKING TIME: 1 HOUR

LYCHEE **GATEAU**

300 g (10 oz) canned lychees in syrup
250 g (8 oz) butter + extra for greasing
200 g (7 oz) caster sugar
1 teaspoon vanilla essence
4 eggs
330 g (11 oz) plain flour
2 teaspoons baking powder
250 ml (8 fl oz) milk

1 Preheat the oven to 180°C (350°F) Gas Mark 4. Grease a cake tin.

2 Drain the lychees, reserving the syrup, and cut in four.

3 Beat together the butter, sugar and vanilla essence until the mixture becomes very fluffy. Beat in the eggs one at a time. Sift the flour and baking powder together and mix carefully into the batter. Add the milk and the lychee quarters.

4 Scoop into the cake tin, put into the oven and bake for about 1 hour. Check with an inserted metal skewer and, if ready, turn out onto a wire rack to cool.

5 If desired, you can drizzle the cake with some of the reserved lychee syrup.

SERVES 4
PREPARATION TIME: 20 MINUTES
COOKING TIME: 35 MINUTES
CHILLING TIME: OVERNIGHT IF POSSIBLE

CAKE WITH LYCHEE FILLING

Butter for greasing
120 g (4 oz) plain flour + extra for dusting
4 eggs, separated
120 g (4 oz) caster sugar
120 g (4 oz) mascarpone
120 ml (4 fl oz) double cream
3–4 tablespoons caster sugar
2 cans lychees
Rum or lychee liqueur
125 g (4 oz) pink or white almond paste
Icing sugar for dusting

1 Preheat the oven to 180°C (350°F) Gas Mark 4. Grease and flour a baking tray with raised sides (no bigger than 30 cm x 20 cm/12 x 10 inches). You could also use a rectangular cake tin. The cake will be a bit thicker, but that will be fine.

2 Beat the egg yolks with the 120 g (4 oz) of sugar. The mixture should become very light and airy. Sift the flour and fold into the beaten yolks with a large spoon. Whisk the egg whites until stiff, then fold them carefully into the mixture.

3 Transfer the mixture to the baking tray or cake tin, put in the oven and bake for about 15–20 minutes. Turn out onto a wire rack and leave to cool.

4 Beat the mascarpone to make it smooth. Whip the chilled cream with the 3–4 tablespoons of sugar, to taste, then mix with the mascarpone. Drain the lychees, reserving the syrup, purée half of them, and fold the purée into the cream.

5 Cut the cake into two equal rectangles. Drizzle with some of the lychee syrup mixed with a little rum or lychee liqueur. Spread three-quarters of the cream on one of the rectangles, add the whole lychees, cover with the remaining cream and place the other rectangle of cake on top. Dust the work surface with icing sugar, roll out the almond paste and cover the cake with it.

6 Stand in the refrigerator several hours. With a sharp knife, cut off both ends of the cake to neaten it. The cake will be even better the next day.

SERVES 6
PREPARATION TIME: 25 MINUTES
COOKING TIME: 2 MINUTES

SHORTBREAD TARTLETS
WITH LYCHEES

125 g (4 oz) shortbread biscuits (or palets bretons if available)
30 g (1 oz) butter
200 g (7 oz) mascarpone
200 g (7 oz) Greek yogurt
Finely ground seeds from 4 cardamom pods
Rosewater
Golden syrup
About 20 fresh lychees, pitted
1 lime
Small dried roses for decoration

1 Crush the biscuits to crumbs. Melt the butter and mix with the crumbs. Spoon this mixture into 6 small tartlet tins (or individual disposable aluminium moulds). Put into the refrigerator for 2 hours.

2 Stir the mascarpone and yogurt until smooth and mix with the cardamom and a few drops of rosewater. Sweeten to taste with golden syrup.

3 Fill the tartlets and top with lychees. Coat with golden syrup mixed with a little lime juice. Decorate with small rose petals.

SERVES 6
PREPARATION TIME: 20 MINUTES
COOKING TIME: 3 MINUTES
CHILLING TIME: MINIMUM 4 HOURS

LYCHEE **JELLY**

6 leaves gelatine (12 g)
450 ml (¾ pint) sparkling wine (such as Clairette de Die)
1 lime
4 tablespoons caster sugar
500 g (1 lb) peeled and pitted lychees (preferably fresh)

1 Cut the lychees in two. Soften the gelatine in a little cold water; squeeze out when ready to use.

2 Heat 200 ml (7 fl oz) of wine, then add 1 teaspoon of lime juice, or to taste, and the sugar. Remove the hot wine from the heat, add the gelatine and stir well to dissolve completely. Add the remaining wine.

3 Divide the lychees into 6 glasses and pour over the jelly. Refrigerate for at least 4 hours to set.

SERVES 6
PREPARATION TIME: 15 MINUTES
(+ PREPARATION TIME FOR ICE CREAM AND JELLY)

LYCHEE **VERRINES**

Home-made lychee ice cream (see page 28)
Home-made lychee jelly (see page 40)
   (made in a large bowl, then chopped)
About 20 fresh lychees, peeled, pitted and halved
Raspberry coulis
Finely grated rind of 2 limes
300 g (10 oz) fromage frais
4 tablespoons flaked almonds, lightly toasted

1 In individual glasses, put successive layers of chopped jelly, lychees, ice cream, coulis and fromage frais.
2 Sprinkle with the grated lime rind and the toasted flaked almonds.
3 Serve immediately.

Cook's tip Verrines are layered starters or desserts served in small glasses to display the different colours and textures. Art in a glass!

SERVES 6
PREPARATION TIME: 20 MINUTES + SOAKING AND RESTING TIME
COOKING TIME: 25 MINUTES

GLUTINOUS RICE
WITH LYCHEES

400 g (13 oz) glutinous rice
400 ml (14 fl oz) coconut milk
100 g (3½ oz) granulated sugar
Salt
About 20 lychees, peeled and pitted

1 Rinse the rice in a sieve under running water and drain. Soak for at least 1 hour (or overnight) in a pan with 500 ml (17 fl oz) of cold water.

2 Bring the pan of rice to the boil. Stir once, boil for 5 minutes, then reduce the heat to minimum. Cover tightly and simmer for 20 minutes. Remove from the heat and set aside to rest, still covered, for 10 minutes.

3 In another pan, mix the coconut milk, sugar and a pinch of salt. Bring to the boil and then simmer, stirring almost constantly, until the liquid has been reduced by about one third. Transfer to a large bowl (reserve a little coconut milk for serving) and add the rice. Mix carefully.

4 Serve spoonfuls of rice in small bowls, with the lychees and the remaining coconut milk.

English translation and adaptation: JMS Books LLP
Layout: cbdesign

First published in France in 2007 under the title
La Boîte à gâteau, by Hachette Livre (Marabout)
Copyright © 2007 Hachette Livre (Marabout)
Editorial: Catherine Berranger and Charlotte Müller-Buch

An Hachette Livre UK Company
www.hachettelivre.co.uk

First published in Great Britain in 2008 by
Hamlyn, a division of Octopus Publishing Group Ltd
2–4 Heron Quays, London E14 4JP
www.octopusbooks.co.uk

Copyright © English edition
Octopus Publishing Group Ltd 2008

Original French edition copyright
© HACHETTE LIVRE (Marabout) 2007

ISBN 978 0 600 61876 8

A CIP catalogue record for this book is available from
the British Library

Printed and bound in China

1 3 5 7 9 10 8 6 4 2

This book contains dishes that are made with raw or lightly cooked eggs.
These should be avoided by vulnerable people such as pregnant and
nursing mothers, invalids, the elderly, babies and young children.

ORANGE FLOWER WATER
VIOLET

CONTENTS

SERVES 6
PREPARATION TIME: 20 MINUTES + CHILLING TIME
COOKING TIME: 25 MINUTES

CANTUCCINI

200 g (7 oz) whole almonds
2 eggs + 1 yolk
200 g (7 oz) caster sugar
2 tablespoons orange flower water
Finely grated rind of 1 orange
200 g (7 oz) plain flour
1 teaspoon baking powder
Butter, for greasing

1 Preheat the oven to 190°C (370° F) Gas Mark 5. Spread the almonds on a baking sheet and place in the top of the oven for about 5 minutes to toast, but check frequently as they can burn very quickly.

2 Whisk together 1 egg, the yolk and the sugar. Add the orange flower water and orange rind. Sift the flour together with the baking powder and add to the mixture. Finally stir in the toasted almonds. Refrigerate for 20 minutes to stiffen.

3 Form 2 long, fairly thick 'sausages' (4–5 cm/1½–2 inches in diameter) from the dough and place them, spaced well apart, on a greased baking sheet. Beat the remaining egg and brush over the dough. Bake for about 15 minutes, after which the dough should be set but only lightly browned.

4 Remove the cantuccini from the oven, but don't switch off the heat, and slide them onto a cutting board. Cut into diagonal slices about 1.5 cm/¾ inch thick. Place the cantuccini on the baking sheet and return to the oven for a further 10 minutes.

5 Remove from the oven and place on a wire rack to cool. They should become very hard.

Cook's tip These crisp biscuits originate from Italy and are delicious dunked in coffee or in a sweet wine, such as Vino Santo or Muscat.

SERVES 4
PREPARATION TIME: 25 MINUTES
COOKING TIME: 45 MINUTES

ANGEL CAKE

50 g (2 oz) icing sugar
50 g (2 oz) plain flour
6 egg whites
50 g (2 oz) granulated sugar
1 tablespoon orange flower water
Salt

1 Preheat the oven to 180°C (350°F) Gas Mark 4.

2 Sift the icing sugar and flour together with a pinch of salt into a bowl.

3 Whisk the egg whites in another bowl until stiff. Add the granulated sugar and whisk again, then stir in the orange flower water. Fold in the dry ingredients one tablespoonful at a time.

4 Pour the mixture carefully into an ungreased nonstick cake tin, filling to no more than two-thirds from the top, and bake for 40–45 minutes. Run a spatula between the cake and the sides of the tin and turn out onto a wire rack to cool.

Cook's tip Serve this feather-light cake with seasonal fruit and cream.

SERVES 6
PREPARATION TIME: 25 MINUTES
COOKING TIME: 40 MINUTES

TORTA DELLA NONNA

2 sheets pre-rolled rich shortcrust pastry
4 egg yolks
4 tablespoons sugar
Finely grated rind of 1 lemon
1 tablespoon cornflour
350 ml (12 fl oz) milk
3 tablespoons plain flour
1 tablespoon orange flower water
75 g (3 oz) pine nuts
Icing sugar, for dusting

1 Preheat the oven to 180°C (350°F) Gas Mark 4.

2 Roll the pastry a little thinner and use half of it to line a 20–23 cm (8–9 inch) tart tin.

3 Whisk together the egg yolks, sugar and lemon rind in a heatproof bowl and set aside.

4 Mix the cornflour with a little of the cold milk then pour into a pan and mix in the flour, orange flower water and the remaining milk. Bring to boiling point and pour over the egg mixture, stirring constantly. Return the mixture to the pan and stir constantly over low heat until it just begins to simmer. Continue to stir over the heat for 2 more minutes then transfer to a clean bowl, cover the surface with clingfilm to prevent skin forming, and leave to cool.

5 When the cream has cooled completely, pour it into the pastry case. Make a lid with the other half of the pastry and seal the edges well. Scatter over the pine nuts. Put in the oven and bake for 30–40 minutes until the top is nicely browned. Leave to cool. This tart is best eaten the next day.

Cook's tip Torta della Nonna is an Italian-style cream pie with pine nuts, just like Grandma used to make!

MAKES ABOUT 24
PREPARATION TIME: 20 MINUTES + CHILLING TIME
COOKING TIME: 15 MINUTES

MADELEINES
WITH ORANGE FLOWER WATER

200 g (7 oz) melted butter + extra for greasing
4 eggs
150 g (5 oz) caster sugar
1 tablespoon orange flower honey
1 tablespoon orange flower water
180 g (6 oz) plain flour + extra for dusting
1 teaspoon baking powder
Salt

1 Melt the butter and leave to cool. Whisk the eggs and sugar together until the mixture is light and frothy. Stir in the honey and the orange flower water.

2 Sift the flour together with the baking powder and a pinch of salt and add to the mixture. Finally, carefully mix in the melted butter. Refrigerate for 20–30 minutes if possible.

3 Preheat the oven to 200°C (400°F) Gas Mark 6. Grease 2 x 12-space madeleine trays with the extra melted butter and dust with flour.

4 Take the mixture out of the refrigerator and stir with a spatula to eliminate any bubbles. Fill the indents no more than two-thirds full, preferably with a piping bag fitted with a fairly large, plain nozzle.

5 Put in the oven but as soon as the edges of the madeleines are set (after about 5 minutes), lower the temperature to 180°C (350°F) Gas Mark 4. Bake until the madeleines have risen and browned (12–15 minutes in total). Leave to cool in the trays for a few minutes and then turn out onto a wire rack to cool completely.

Cook's tip A madeleine is a small cake shaped like a shell.

SERVES 6
PREPARATION TIME: 30 MINUTES + PROVING TIME
COOKING TIME: 20 MINUTES

AIGUES-MORTES
FOUGASSE

500 g (1 lb) strong white flour
75 g (3 oz) caster sugar
1 teaspoon salt
12 g (½ oz) fresh yeast (or equivalent dried yeast,
  see manufacturer's instructions)
100 ml (3½ fl oz) milk
2 eggs
1 tablespoon orange flower water
4 tablespoons olive oil
Finely grated rind and juice of 1 orange

1 Sift the flour, 2 tablespoons of the sugar and the salt into a large bowl. Make a well in the centre.

2 (If using dried yeast follow the maker's instructions.) Warm the milk and dissolve the fresh yeast. Be careful not to overheat it; a finger dipped into it should be able to remain there comfortably for a count of 10. Pour the dissolved yeast into the well, together with the eggs, orange flower water, 3 tablespoons of the olive oil, the orange juice and half the orange rind. Gradually incorporate the dry ingredients into the liquid to form a supple dough.

3 Knead the dough for 5 minutes by hand or for 2 minutes in a food processor. Cover with oiled clingfilm and leave for 90 minutes, when it should have doubled in volume.

4 Roll out the risen dough to form a flat disc, brush with the remaining oil and sprinkle with the remaining sugar. Leave to rise for a further 30 minutes.

5 Preheat the oven to 220°C (425°F) Gas Mark 7. Bake for 20–25 minutes. The top should be only slightly browned and the fougasse should sound hollow when the base is tapped.

Cook's tip Aigues-Mortes fougasses are rustic flatbreads from southern France.

SERVES 6
PREPARATION TIME: 25 MINUTES
COOKING TIME: 45 MINUTES

MARBLE CAKE
WITH ORANGE FLOWER WATER

125 g (4 oz) butter, softened, + extra for greasing
150 g (5 oz) caster sugar
1 tablespoon orange flower water
3 eggs
300 g (10 oz) plain flour + extra for dusting
2 teaspoons baking powder
4 tablespoons cocoa powder
100 ml (3½ fl oz) milk

To serve:
Buttermilk
2 tablespoons sugar
2 teaspoons orange flower water

1 Preheat the oven to 180°C (350°F) Gas Mark 4.

2 Whisk the butter and sugar together until light and fluffy. Add the orange flower water then beat in the eggs, one at a time. Sift the flour with the baking powder and add to the mixture. Mix the cocoa powder with a little of the milk then stir a little of the cake mixture into it. Add as much of the remaining milk as is needed to make a thin batter that will run gently from a tilted spoon.

3 Pour the cake mixture into a carefully greased cake tin, dusted with flour. Cover with the cocoa and milk batter and use a knife to form the marbling.

4 Put in the oven and bake for 35–45 minutes. The cake is ready when a metal skewer inserted into the centre emerges quite clean.

5 Serve with glasses of ice-cold buttermilk, flavoured with the orange flower water and sugar and frothed up in a blender or shaken vigorously in a bottle.

SERVES 6
PREPARATION TIME: 30 MINUTES
COOKING TIME: 45 MINUTES

LEMON & ORANGE FLOWER WATER **SOUFFLÉS**

100 g (3½ oz) butter + extra for greasing
200 g (7 oz) caster sugar
Finely grated rind of 2 lemons + the juice
5 eggs
75 g (3 oz) plain flour
1 teaspoon baking powder
500 ml (17 fl oz) milk
1 tablespoon orange flower water

To serve: single cream

1 Preheat the oven to 180°C (350°F) Gas Mark 4. Grease 6 small ovenproof dishes or ramekins (200–250 ml/ 7–8 fl oz).

2 Cream the butter and sugar together until light and fluffy. Add the grated lemon rind and juice. Separate the eggs and vigorously beat the yolks into the mixture, one by one.

3 Sift the flour with the baking powder and incorporate into the mixture a little at a time, then stir in the milk, being careful not to over-mix. Finally add the orange flower water.

4 Whisk the egg whites until stiff and gently fold into the mixture with a metal spoon.

5 Three-quarters fill the dishes or ramekins, place them in a roasting tin and pour in enough hot water to reach halfway up the sides. Put in the oven for about 45 minutes. Serve warm with a little single cream.

SERVES 6
PREPARATION TIME: 20 MINUTES
RESTING TIME: OVERNIGHT

ORANGES & LEMONS

5 lemons
2 oranges
170 g (6 oz) granulated sugar
2 tablespoons orange flower water
1 litre (1¾ pints) carbonated water (optional)

1 Scrub the lemons thoroughly and remove the outer rind with a potato peeler or zester, being very careful not to include any of the white pith. Squeeze the juice from the lemons and oranges.

2 Put the juice and rind into a large bowl and add the sugar and 1.5 litres (2½ pints) of boiling water. Leave overnight.

3 Next morning, strain and add the orange flower water. Taste and add more sugar if required, then refrigerate.

4 Serve the lemonade as it comes or diluted with some carbonated water.

SERVES 4–6
PREPARATION TIME: 50 MINUTES
COOKING TIME: 30 MINUTES

ORANGE
CROQUEMBOUCHE

FOR THE CONFECTIONER'S CUSTARD
5 egg yolks
100 g (3½ oz) caster sugar
2 tablespoons plain flour
2 tablespoons cornflour
500 ml (17 fl oz) milk
1 tablespoon orange flower water
Finely grated rind of 1 orange

FOR THE CHOUX PASTRY
150 ml (¼ pint) water
½ teaspoon salt
50 g (2 oz) unsalted butter, cut into small pieces
65 g (2½ oz) flour
2 eggs, beaten

FOR THE CARAMEL
200 g (7 oz) granulated sugar

1 To make the custard: whisk the egg yolks and sugar in a large bowl, add the flour and cornflour and whisk again. Bring the milk to just below boiling point, whisk a little of it into the mixture, then gradually add the rest of the milk, stirring constantly. Return to the pan and cook over a gentle heat, stirring constantly and taking care to scrape the base of the pan. When it reaches the boil, simmer for a further 2–3 minutes, stirring. Add the orange flower water and the grated orange rind. Pour the custard into a bowl, lay clingfilm on the surface to prevent skin forming, and leave to cool.

2 To make the choux pastry: heat the water, salt and butter in a pan and remove from the heat just before it comes to the boil. Add the flour all at once and beat vigorously with a spatula. Once the flour is fully incorporated, put the pan back on the heat, stirring until the dough comes away from the sides of the pan. Transfer to a large bowl and add the eggs one by one, mixing them in with the spatula. If the dough looks right (it will gently close up if you run your finger through it), do not add all the egg.

3 Preheat the oven to 200°C (400°F) Gas Mark 6. Grease and line a baking sheet with nonstick baking paper. Using a piping bag with a small nozzle, form 20–24 little balls on the baking sheet, leaving space for them to expand. Bake at for 10 minutes, then increase the oven temperature to 220°C (425°F) Gas Mark 7 and cook for a further 15–20 minutes. Remove from the oven and leave to cool on a wire rack. Fill with the custard, using a piping bag with a fine nozzle.

4 To prepare the caramel: put the sugar into a pan with 100 ml/3½ fl oz of water and boil until the mixture turns a golden colour, then plunge the base of the pan into cold water to stop it cooking further. Dip the choux buns into the caramel and pile them up in a cone. Pour over any remaining caramel.

SERVES 4
PREPARATION TIME: 30 MINUTES
COOKING TIME: 30 MINUTES

PASTRY SLICE
WITH ORANGE CREAM

2 egg yolks
3 tablespoons granulated sugar
Finely grated rind of 1 lemon
2 tablespoons cornflour
250 ml (8 fl oz) milk
2 tablespoons plain flour
1 tablespoon orange flower water
75 g (3 oz) butter + extra for greasing
200 g (7 oz) ricotta
75 g (3 oz) finely chopped candied peel (optional)
4 sheets of filo pastry

To serve: icing sugar

1 Whisk the egg yolks, sugar and finely grated lemon peel together in a heatproof bowl. In a pan, mix the cornflour with a little of the milk then add the flour, orange flower water and the remaining milk and bring to boiling point. Stirring constantly, pour onto the egg mixture, return it to the pan, then bring back to a simmer and cook for 2 minutes, still stirring constantly. Remove from the heat and transfer to a clean, dry bowl, cover the surface with clingfilm to prevent a skin forming and leave to cool.

2 Preheat the oven to 190°C (375°F) Gas Mark 5; grease and line a baking sheet with nonstick baking paper

3 Melt the butter. Mix the prepared custard with the ricotta and the candied peel, if using.

4 Cut the sheets of filo pastry in half and lay 4 half-sheets side by side on the baking sheet, each sheet brushed with melted butter. Spread with the custard and cover with the remaining half pastry sheets. Brush over with melted butter. Put in the oven for about 20 minutes or until the pastry is nicely browned. Serve warm or cold, dredged with a little icing sugar.

26

SERVES 6
PREPARATION TIME: 25 MINUTES
COOKING TIME: 10 MINUTES
CHILLING TIME: MINIMUM OF 4 HOURS

MARSHMALLOW

10 leaves of gelatine, weighing about 36 g/1¼ oz
Flavourless oil (such as groundnut)
4 tablespoons icing sugar
4 tablespoons cornflour
400 g (13 oz) caster sugar
3 egg whites
2 tablespoons violet syrup

1 Put the gelatine to soften in a little cold water. Oil a shallow square or rectangular mould. Mix the icing sugar with the cornflour and use half of this to dust evenly inside the mould, tapping out any excess. Reserve the remaining half.

2 Put the sugar in a pan with 200 ml (7 fl oz) of water over gentle heat. Whisk the egg whites until stiff.

3 Heat the violet syrup, diluted in 100 ml (3½ fl oz) of water. Squeeze out the gelatine. Remove the syrup from the heat and add the gelatine, making sure it dissolves completely.

4 Increase the heat under the sugar and boil to the soft ball stage (after boiling for about 5 minutes, drop a small quantity of the syrup into a bowl of cold water; if it forms a malleable soft ball it has reached the correct stage). Pour the violet and gelatine mixture into the sugar syrup then pour the whole of this syrup quickly into the whisked egg white, continuing to whisk constantly until the mixture has completely cooled.

5 Pour into the mould and leave in the refrigerator for a minimum of 4 hours. When ready to serve, remove from the mould, cut into rectangles, and dust with the remaining icing sugar and cornflour mixture. Make sure that all the sides are coated and shake gently to remove any excess.

SERVES 4
PREPARATION TIME: 20 MINUTES + RESTING OVERNIGHT
COOKING TIME: 10 MINUTES

WAFFLES WITH VIOLET CREAM

125 g (4 oz) unsalted butter
600 ml (1 pint) milk
15 g (½ oz) fresh yeast, or equivalent dried yeast
   (see manufacturer's instructions)
1 teaspoon salt
1 teaspoon granulated sugar
200 g (7 oz) plain flour
100 g (3½ oz) chestnut flour
2 eggs
200 ml (7 fl oz) double or whipping cream, chilled
2 tablespoons violet syrup

To decorate: crystallized violets

1 Start preparing the recipe the day before it is to be served. Melt the butter and warm the milk. In a large bowl, dissolve the yeast in a little warm milk then add the rest of the milk, together with the melted butter, salt, sugar and both kinds of flour. (If using dried yeast, follow the maker's instructions.) Beat vigorously for several minutes then leave to rest overnight.

2 Next day, add the eggs to the batter and beat vigorously once more.

3 Make sure the cream is well chilled, flavour it with the violet syrup and whisk until firm peaks form.

4 Cook the waffles in a preheated waffle iron for 3–4 minutes and serve with the violet cream, decorated with the crystallized violets.

SERVES 6
PREPARATION TIME: 15 MINUTES
COOKING TIME: 10 MINUTES
FREEZING TIME: MINIMUM OF 4 HOURS

VIOLET **ICE CREAM**

300 ml (½ pint) milk
4 egg yolks
2 teaspoons cornflour
2 tablespoons sugar
200 g (7 oz) mascarpone
2 tablespoons violet syrup

1 To make the egg custard: heat the milk. Whisk the egg yolks with the sugar and cornflour in a bowl, pour on the hot milk, stirring constantly, then return the mixture to the pan. Cook gently, stirring constantly, until the custard coats the back of the spoon. Leave to cool.

2 Whisk the mascarpone with the violet syrup until it is smooth, then incorporate it into the custard.

3 Freeze in an ice-cream maker. An alternative method is to freeze the mixture in a freezerproof container, uncovered, until it begins to set around the edges. Turn the mixture into a bowl and beat until smooth, then return to the freezer.

SERVES 6
PREPARATION TIME: 1 HOUR + RESTING TIME
COOKING TIME: 1 HOUR

VIOLET-FLAVOURED
PUITS D'AMOUR

FOR THE SHORTCRUST PASTRY
200 g (7 oz) plain flour
125 g (4 oz) unsalted butter,
  cut into small pieces, + extra
  for greasing
75 g (3 oz) caster sugar
1 vanilla pod
1 egg

FOR THE FILLING
500 ml (17 fl oz) milk
5 egg yolks
4 tablespoons sugar
2 tablespoons cornflour
2 tablespoons plain flour
3 tablespoons violet syrup

FOR THE CHOUX PASTRY
4 tablespoons milk
4 tablespoons water
50 g (2 oz) unsalted butter
½ teaspoon salt
1 teaspoon sugar
75 g (3 oz) plain flour
2 eggs

FOR THE CARAMEL
50 g (5 oz) granulated sugar
1 tablespoon violet syrup

1 To make the sweet shortcrust pastry: sift the flour with the sugar, add the butter and rub into the dry ingredients with the tips of the fingers until the mixture resembles fine breadcrumbs. Add the egg and mix together with a round-bladed knife. Form the pastry into a ball by hand, adding a little water if necessary. Refrigerate for 1 hour.

2 To prepare the filling: whisk the egg yolks and sugar in a large bowl with the seeds scraped from the vanilla pod, add the flour and the cornflour and carry on whisking. Heat the milk. As it is coming to the boil, pour a little into the egg and sugar mixture and continue to whisk as you gradually add the rest of the milk. Return the mixture to the pan and cook over moderate heat, stirring continuously and scraping the base of the pan with the spatula. Cook for a further 2–3 minutes after it comes to the boil, still stirring constantly. Transfer the cream to a bowl and add the violet syrup. Lay a sheet of clingfilm directly on the surface and leave to cool.

3 To make the choux pastry, see recipe page 23.

4 Preheat the oven to 180°C (350°F) Gas Mark 4.

5 Roll out the shortcrust pastry and use to line greased tartlet tins. Prick the base all over with a fork, pipe a circle of choux pastry along the inside edge of each case and bake for about 20 minutes, then leave to cool.

6 Fill the tartlets with the prepared filling and smooth the top. Make some caramel with the sugar, 200 ml (7 fl oz) of water (see page 22) and the violet syrup. Pour over the filling.

Cook's tip Puits d'amour is made of two rounds of pastry filled with pastry cream. ·

SERVES 6
PREPARATION TIME: 1 HOUR
COOKING TIME: 10 MINUTES
CHILLING TIME: MINIMUM OF 4 HOURS

VIOLET **BLANCMANGE**

6 leaves gelatine weighing about 20 g (¾ oz)
450 ml (¾ pint) almond milk (made with equal quantities
    almonds, sugar and water, pounded and rubbed through
    a fine sieve)
4 tablespoons sugar
2 tablespoons violet syrup + extra for serving
250 ml (8 fl oz) single cream
Flavourless oil (such as groundnut)

To serve: red soft fruit coulis

1 Soften the gelatine in a little cold water and squeeze out when ready to use.

2 Heat the almond milk with the sugar, stirring to dissolve the sugar. When the mixture is almost boiling, add the gelatine, and stir well to dissolve it. Add the violet syrup and leave to cool. Finally add the single cream.

3 Pour the mixture into a decorative, lightly oiled 1-litre (1¾-pint) mould. The blancmange may also be served in individual glasses, which need not be oiled. Refrigerate for at least 4 hours.

4 Dip the mould very briefly into hot water and turn out the blancmange. Serve with a little violet syrup and a coulis of red soft fruit.

SERVES 4
PREPARATION TIME: 20 MINUTES
COOKING TIME: 40 MINUTES
CHILLING TIME: 3–4 HOURS

VIOLET **RHUBARB CREAM**

500 g (1 lb) fresh rhubarb, washed and cut into short pieces,
   or frozen rhubarb
4 tablespoons sugar
500 g (1 lb) Greek yogurt
2 tablespoons crème fraîche or mascarpone
3 tablespoons violet syrup

1 Preheat the oven to 190°C (375°F) Gas Mark 5. Put the rhubarb with the sugar in an ovenproof dish and put in the oven for 35–40 minutes.

2 When the rhubarb is cooked, either rub it through a sieve, or drain and purée in a food processor. Mix half of the purée with the yogurt in the processor and divide it between the serving bowls or glasses.

3 Top this with the rest of the rhubarb purée, finish with a little crème fraîche or mascarpone and sprinkle with the violet syrup. Refrigerate and serve very cold.

SERVES 4
PREPARATION TIME: 15 MINUTES
FREEZING TIME: 4 HOURS

VIOLET **YOGURT GRANITA**

750 g (1½ lb) thick, Greek-style yogurt
2–4 tablespoons violet syrup

To serve: fresh fruit

1 Put the yogurt into a fairly deep plastic container and place in the freezing compartment of the refrigerator, or the freezer. Remove after 2 hours and stir it vigorously with a fork.

2 Return to the freezer for a further hour then stir again. Return to the freezer for one more hour.

3 Serve with violet syrup and fresh fruit.

Cook's tip Granita is a type of Italian sorbet. It is half-frozen and can be served between courses in glass bowls.

MAKES 12 MUFFINS
PREPARATION TIME: 20 MINUTES
COOKING TIME: 25 MINUTES

BLUEBERRY & VIOLET **MUFFINS**

300 g (10 oz) plain flour + extra for dusting
50 g (2 oz) unsalted butter + extra for greasing
50 g (2 oz) caster sugar
1 tablespoon baking powder
Salt
2 eggs
125 g (4 oz) yogurt
50 ml (2 fl oz) milk
Finely grated rind and juice of ½ lemon
4 tablespoons violet syrup
1 vanilla pod
250 g (8 oz) fresh or frozen blueberries
Icing sugar

1 Preheat the oven to 200°C (400°F) Gas Mark 6. Grease a 12-cup muffin tin and dust with flour.

2 Sift the flour with the sugar, baking powder and a good pinch of salt into a bowl

3 Melt the butter. Beat the eggs with the yogurt, melted butter, milk, lemon rind, 2 tablespoons of violet syrup and the seeds from the vanilla pod (split the pod and scrape out the inside with a small knife). Pour onto the dry ingredients, add the blueberries and mix briefly with a wooden spoon – the mixture should remain slightly lumpy rather than smooth.

4 Fill the muffin cups no more than three-quarters full and bake for 20 minutes.

5 Add icing sugar to taste to the remaining violet syrup and a little of the lemon juice and stir to obtain a runny mixture. When the muffins are ready, remove from the oven, pour this mixture over them and return to the oven for 3–4 minutes. Allow them to cool for 20 minutes in the tins before turning them out onto a wire rack to cool completely.

SERVES 4
PREPARATION TIME: 30 MINUTES
COOKING TIME: 15 MINUTES
CHILLING TIME: OVERNIGHT

TRIFLE

3 egg yolks
5 tablespoons sugar
350 ml (12 fl oz) milk
1 vanilla pod
4 slices of light sponge, or trifle sponges
4–5 amaretti (Italian macaroons)
1 small glass Muscat
4 tablespoons violet syrup
2 punnets of raspberries
300 ml (½ pint) double or whipping cream, chilled

To serve: crystallized violets for decoration
   (real ones if possible – they are so much better)

1 To make the custard: in a small pan, heat the milk with the seeds from the vanilla pod almost to boiling point. Meanwhile, whisk the egg yolks with 4 tablespoons of the sugar in a heatproof bowl. Continue to whisk while pouring on the almost boiling milk. Return to the pan, lower the heat and stir constantly until the custard thickens. Leave to cool.

2 Put the sponge cakes and the amaretti in the bottom of a serving bowl and sprinkle with the Muscat and 3 tablespoons of the violet syrup, lightly diluted with water.

3 Keeping a few raspberries aside for decoration, crush the remaining raspberries and sugar together with a fork, then spread over the cake.

4 Whip the cream to firm peaks and whisk in the remaining violet syrup. Mix one-third of the whipped cream into the custard and spread it over the raspberries. Top with the rest of the whipped cream.

5 Refrigerate until the following day and decorate with raspberries and violets before serving.

SERVES 6
PREPARATION TIME: 30 MINUTES
COOKING TIME: 1¼ HOURS

BLACKCURRANT & VIOLET **TART**

1 sheet pre-rolled butter puff pastry
7–8 punnets blackcurrants (about 1 kg/2 lb)
2 eggs
300 ml (7 fl oz) single cream
½ teaspoon salt
3 tablespoons violet syrup
6 tablespoons caster sugar

1 Preheat the oven to 190°C (375°F) Gas Mark 5. Line a tart tin 25 cm (10 inches) in diameter with the pastry. Cover with a circle of nonstick baking paper, weight it with dried beans or pie weights, and bake for 20 minutes. Remove the paper and beans and return to the oven for a further 5 minutes. Leave to cool.

2 Lower the oven temperature to 160°C (325°F) Gas Mark 3.

3 Strip the blackcurrants from the stalks, then rinse and top and tail them. Purée the fruit in a food processor, then push through a fine sieve to remove the seeds.

4 Beat the eggs, cream, salt, violet syrup and the sugar into the blackcurrant purée, then pour into the pastry case and cook for a scant hour – the filling should tremble slightly as it comes out of the oven. Leave to cool and set before serving.

English translation and adaptation: JMS Books LLP
Layout: cbdesign

First published in France in 2007 under the title
La Boîte à gâteau, by Hachette Livre (Marabout)
Copyright © 2007 Hachette Livre (Marabout)
Editorial: Catherine Berranger and Charlotte Müller-Buch

An Hachette Livre UK Company
www.hachettelivre.co.uk

First published in Great Britain in 2008 by
Hamlyn, a division of Octopus Publishing Group Ltd
2–4 Heron Quays, London E14 4JP
www.octopusbooks.co.uk

Copyright © English edition
Octopus Publishing Group Ltd 2008

Original French edition copyright
© HACHETTE LIVRE (Marabout) 2007

ISBN 978 0 600 61876 8

A CIP catalogue record for this book is available from
the British Library

Printed and bound in China

1 3 5 7 9 10 8 6 4 2

This book contains dishes that are made with raw or lightly cooked eggs.
These should be avoided by vulnerable people such as pregnant and
nursing mothers, invalids, the elderly, babies and young children.

CHESTNUT
WHITE CHOCOLATE

hamlyn

CONTENTS

SERVES 6
PREPARATION TIME: 30 MINUTES
COOKING TIME: 40 MINUTES

CHESTNUT & GREEN TEA
VACHERIN

Butter for greasing
4 egg whites
200 g (7 oz) caster sugar
½ teaspoon vanilla essence
150 g (5 oz) ground hazelnuts
200 g (7 oz) chestnut purée (available in delicatessens
   and some supermarkets)
80 g (3 oz) icing sugar
300 ml (½ pint) double/whipping cream
1 teaspoon matcha tea

1 Preheat the oven to 180°C (350°F) Gas Mark 4. Grease 2 cake tins 18–20 cm (7–8 inches) in diameter. Line with greased nonstick baking paper.

2 Whisk the egg whites until stiff, add the sugar and beat again, then carefully add the vanilla and 100 g (3½ oz) of the ground hazelnuts. Spoon the mixture into the two cake tins and smooth the tops. Bake for 35–40 minutes. Turn out, remove the paper and put on a wire rack to cool.

3 Beat the chestnut purée with the sifted icing sugar (reserving 2 tablespoons). Whip the chilled cream and mix half with the chestnut purée. Add the matcha tea powder and 1 tablespoon of icing sugar to the remaining whipped cream. Place one round of meringue on a serving dish and spread with chestnut purée, then with matcha cream. Cover with the second meringue round. Sprinkle with the remaining hazelnuts and icing sugar. You can make individual vacherins instead, if you prefer.

Cook's tip Vacherin is a dessert made of rounds of meringue layered with cream or ice cream, so-called because it resembles Vacherin cheese in colour and shape.

SERVES 6
PREPARATION TIME: 35 MINUTES
REFRIGERATION TIME: SEVERAL HOURS

CHARLOTTE-STYLE
YULE LOG

5 leaves gelatine (10 g)
500 ml (17 fl oz) milk
1 vanilla pod
4 egg yolks
2 tablespoons caster sugar
200 ml (7 fl oz) double cream
125 g (4 oz) sweetened chestnut purée
6 marrons glacés (or pieces are fine) + 6 more for decoration
About 30 boudoir biscuits, or sponge fingers
Red fruit syrup
5 tablespoons redcurrant jelly

1 Soak the gelatine in cold water; squeeze out when ready to use.

2 To make the egg custard: heat the milk with the split vanilla pod (scrape the seeds into the pan with a small knife) almost to boiling point. Beat together the egg yolks and sugar, pour over the nearly boiling milk, stirring constantly, pour back into the pan and cook over low heat, stirring until it thickens and coats the back of the spoon. Completely dissolve the softened gelatine in the hot custard then leave to cool.

3 Whip the chilled cream. Mix together the chestnut purée, custard and whipped cream. Add the chestnut pieces.

4 Line a loaf tin with clingfilm. Line with boudoir biscuits soaked briefly in the diluted fruit syrup.

5 Heat the jelly gently and spread half over the boudoir biscuits. Pour in half the cream, add a layer of boudoir biscuits, spread with the remaining jelly and the last of the cream and cover with soaked boudoirs.

6 Cover and refrigerate to set. Turn out and decorate with crumbled marrons glacés.

SERVES 6
PREPARATION TIME: 20 MINUTES
COOKING TIME: 30 MINUTES

CHESTNUT CREAM
CAKES

100 g (3½ oz) unsalted butter + extra for greasing
500 g (1 lb) sweetened chestnut purée
4 eggs, separated
2 tablespoons plain flour
Icing sugar for decoration

To serve: crème fraîche or vanilla ice cream

1 Preheat the oven to 180°C (350°F) Gas Mark 4. Grease 6 small moulds.
2 Melt the butter, then mix with the chestnut purée and egg yolks. Sift in the flour.
3 Whisk the egg whites until firm and fold in carefully.
4 Divide between the moulds, put in the oven and bake for 30 minutes.
5 Dust with icing sugar and serve warm with crème fraîche or a scoop of vanilla ice cream.

SERVES 6
PREPARATION TIME: 25 MINUTES

ETON MESS
WITH CHESTNUTS

1 large white meringue (or several small ones)
150 ml (½ pint) double cream
6 generous tablespoons sweetened chestnut purée
1 kg (2 lb) fromage frais, drained
1 punnet raspberries
4–6 marrons glacés

1 Crumble the meringue, but not into too small pieces.
2 Whip the chilled cream to make firm peaks.
3 Mix together all the ingredients (apart from the marrons)into an appetizing 'mess'.
4 To serve, spoon into bowls or glasses and decorate with the crumbled marrons.

Cook's Tip Eton Mess is a mixture of meringue pieces, whipped cream and fruit (traditionally strawberries).

SERVES 4
PREPARATION TIME: 20 MINUTES + OVERNIGHT
COOKING TIME: 10 MINUTES

CHESTNUT CREAM **WAFFLES**

125 g (4 oz) butter
600 ml (1 pint) milk
15 g (½ oz) fresh yeast (or equivalent dried yeast)
1 teaspoon salt
1 teaspoon caster sugar
200 g (7 oz) plain flour
100 g (3½ oz) chestnut flour
2 eggs
Sweetened chestnut purée
Mascarpone
Flaked almonds

1 Melt the butter. Warm the milk. Mix the yeast in a little milk in a large mixing bowl. Add the remaining milk, melted butter, salt, sugar and both kinds of flour. Beat vigorously for several minutes. Leave overnight to rest.

2 The next day beat in the eggs. Cook the waffles in a preheated waffle iron for 3–4 minutes. Serve with the chestnut purée, mascarpone and lightly toasted almonds.

SERVES 4
PREPARATION TIME: 30 MINUTES
COOKING TIME: 1 HOUR
CHILLING TIME: 1 HOUR

CHESTNUT **FLAN**

FOR THE PASTRY
200 g (7 oz) plain flour
100 g (3½ oz) butter from the freezer + extra for greasing
Salt

FOR THE FILLING
200 ml (7 fl oz) milk
200 ml (7 fl oz) crème fraîche
4 eggs
50 g (2 oz) cornflour, Maizena if possible
4 tablespoons sweetened chestnut purée
Salt
200 g (7 oz) pack whole cooked chestnuts

1 To make the pastry: put the flour and a pinch of salt in a mixing bowl. Take the butter out of the freezer and grate it into the flour using a grater with large holes. Add 4 tablespoons of cold water and mix the dough with a palette knife (using 'cutting' movements). Add more water if necessary. Form into a ball and put in the refrigerator to rest.

2 Preheat the oven to 200°C (400°F) Gas Mark 6. Line a greased flan tin with the dough, cover with a sheet of nonstick baking paper and fill with dried beans. Pre-bake the tart base for 10 minutes.

3 Beat together the milk, crème fraîche, eggs, cornflour and chestnut purée.

4 Cover the tart base with the cooked chestnuts, pour over the mixture, put in the oven and bake for 40 minutes. The cream should be set and the top should be well risen and golden.

SERVES 6
PREPARATION TIME: 15 MINUTES
COOKING TIME: 20 MINUTES

CHESTNUT **BREAD**

500 g (1 lb) chestnut flour
4 tablespoons olive oil
3 tablespoons caster sugar
1 egg
Milk
100 g (3½ oz) chopped green walnuts (freshly shelled)
2 sprigs rosemary
Salt

1 Preheat the oven to 180°C (350°F) Gas Mark 4. Mix together the flour, 2 tablespoons of the oil, the sugar and a pinch of salt. Add the egg and mix in. This should give a soft dough (but not at all runny). Add milk if necessary.
2 Grease a baking sheet with the remaining oil. Cover with the dough and sprinkle with rosemary leaves and chopped walnuts, pushing them down a little into the dough. Put into the oven and bake for 20 minutes. Cut in squares and eat cold.

Cook's tip This bread is known as 'Castagnaccio' and comes from Corsica. It is a thick batter or dough made with chestnut flour, also used to make fritters or thick waffles.

SERVES 4
PREPARATION TIME: 15 MINUTES
FREEZING TIME: 4 HOURS

MILKY GRANITA
WITH CHESTNUTS

800 g (1¾ lb) thick, Greek-style yogurt
2 tablespoons barley malt syrup or a syrup of your choice
4 marrons glacés
4 tablespoons sweetened chestnut purée

1 Put the yogurt in a shallow freezerproof box and place in the freezer.

2 Take out after 2 hours and stir vigorously with a fork. Put back in the freezer for 1 hour, stir again, and freeze for a further 1 hour.

3 Spoon the granita into glasses, pour over a little syrup, then add the chestnut purée and the marrons.

Cook's tip Granita is a type of Italian sorbet. It is half-frozen and can be served between courses in glass bowls.

SERVES 6
PREPARATION TIME: 30 MINUTES
COOKING TIME: 15 MINUTES
CHILLING TIME: SEVERAL HOURS

CHESTNUT & APPLE **TRIFLE**

4–5 apples (a tart variety, such as Braeburn or Cox's)
25 g (1 oz) butter
4 tablespoons caster sugar
1 sponge base
Apple juice
200 g (7 oz) vanilla-flavoured chestnut purée
250 g (8 oz) mascarpone
2 eggs, separated
Flaked almonds, lightly toasted

1 Peel and quarter the apples. Melt the butter in a frying pan, skim the froth that has formed on the surface and add the quartered apples. Fry on one side until golden, turn over, sprinkle with 2 tablespoons of the sugar and brown on the other side until the sugar is slightly caramelized.

2 Cut the sponge in pieces and place in the bottom of a not too deep dish (transparent if possible). Drizzle with apple juice. Spread the chestnut cream over the soaked sponge. Cover with the cooked apples.

3 Beat the mascarpone with the egg yolks and the remaining sugar. Whisk the egg whites until stiff and fold into the mixture. Spread over the apples.

4 Place in the refrigerator for several hours if possible. Decorate with the almonds before serving.

SERVES 4
PREPARATION TIME: 20 MINUTES
COOKING TIME: 30 MINUTES

SUGARED CHESTNUTS

500 g (1 lb) fresh chestnuts
Milk
Caster sugar
Crème fraîche or fromage frais (or both)
1 cinnamon stick
Powdered cinnamon

1 Preheat the oven to 200°C (400°F) Gas Mark 6. Slit the skins of the chestnuts and roast in the oven for about 15 minutes. Peel and finish cooking by simmering in the milk with the cinnamon stick until tender.

2 To serve, crush the chestnuts with a fork in bowls with a little sugar, crème fraîche and/or fromage frais, and a pinch or two of ground cinnamon.

SERVES 8
PREPARATION TIME: 30 MINUTES
COOKING TIME: 45 MINUTES

PANFORTE
WITH WHITE CHOCOLATE

Butter for greasing
50 g (2 oz) hazelnuts
50 g (2 oz) whole almonds
50 g (2 oz) white chocolate
175 g (6 oz) candied peel (orange, lemon or grapefruit)
25 g (1 oz) grated coconut (good quality)
50 g (2 oz) plain flour
¼ teaspoon ground cinnamon
125 g (4 oz) caster sugar
125 g (4 oz) runny honey
Butter for greasing

FOR DECORATION
2 tablespoons icing sugar
1 teaspoon cinnamon

1 Preheat the oven to 190°C (375°F) Gas Mark 5. Grease a flan tin 20 cm (8 inches) in diameter and line with a circle of nonstick baking paper.

2 Spread the hazelnuts out on a baking sheet and toast for 5–6 minutes. Rub in a cloth to detach the skins. Roughly chop the hazelnuts, almonds and chocolate. Chop the candied peel a little more finely. Mix with the coconut, flour and cinnamon. Reduce the oven temperature to 150°C (150°F) Gas Mark 2.

3 In a small pan, melt the sugar and honey over low heat. Allow to simmer very gently until the mixture thickens. Test by plunging ½ teaspoon of this syrup in a bowl of cold water. It should form a ball. Remove from the heat, pour over the fruit and nuts and mix well.

4 Press this mixture into the tin to a thickness of 1 cm (½ inch). Put in the oven and bake for 30–35 minutes. Turn out onto a wire rack and leave to cool.

5 Remove the baking paper, put on a plate and, using a fine-mesh sieve, sift over the icing sugar mixed with the cinnamon. Serve cut in very thin slices, with strong coffee.

MAKES 16
PREPARATION TIME: 30 MINUTES
COOKING TIME: 40 MINUTES

BLONDIES

80 g (3 oz) butter + extra for greasing
50 g (2 oz) Brazil nuts (or whole, skinned hazelnuts)
500 g (1 lb) white chocolate
3 eggs
125 g (4 oz) caster sugar
175 g (6 oz) plain flour
1 teaspoon baking powder
1 teaspoon natural vanilla essence
Salt

1 Preheat the oven to 180°C (350°F) Gas Mark 4. Grease a shallow square cake tin (about 25 cm/10 inches square).
2 Chop the nuts and the white chocolate.
3 Put 125 g (4 oz) of the chocolate and the butter in a heatproof bowl over a pan of simmering water, off the heat. Melt and mix well to make it smooth. While the chocolate is cooling, beat together the eggs and sugar, until the mixture turns pale. Add the melted chocolate.
4 Sift the flour, baking powder and a pinch of salt together over the previous mixture; mix gently.
5 Lastly add the nuts, the remaining chocolate and the vanilla essence, stirring just enough to mix them in. Spoon into the tin and bake for 30 minutes. Allow to cool, then cut in squares.

SERVES 6
PREPARATION TIME: 25 MINUTES
COOKING TIME: 10 MINUTES

WHITE CHOCOLATE
& CRANBERRY ROLL

30 g (1 oz) butter + extra for greasing
4 eggs, separated
125 g (4 oz) caster sugar
125 g (4 oz) plain flour
100 g (3½ oz) white chocolate
100 ml (3½ fl oz) double or whipping cream
100 g (3½ oz) dried cranberries
1 lemon
1 lime
1 orange

1 Preheat the oven to 200°C (400°F) Gas Mark 6. Generously grease a Swiss roll tin, or line a baking sheet with buttered nonstick baking paper.

2 Melt the butter. Beat together the egg yolks and sugar to give a very pale, frothy mixture. Whisk the egg whites until stiff. Sift the flour and mix in, then add the egg whites, then the melted butter.

3 Pour into the well-greased Swiss roll tin or baking tray, put in the oven and bake for 10 minutes, just long enough for the cake to begin to turn golden. Detach the cake from the paper, place on a damp tea towel and leave to cool.

4 Break the white chocolate in pieces and melt in a bain-marie or in a heatproof bowl over a pan of barely simmering water. Whip the chilled cream. Fold in the chocolate, then the cranberries.

5 Squeeze the juice from the lemon, lime and orange and drizzle over the cake. Spread with cream, then roll up the cake with the help of the cloth. Trim the ends and place on a serving dish.

SERVES 4
PREPARATION TIME: 20 MINUTES + RESTING TIME
COOKING TIME: 35 MINUTES

WHITE PEACH &
WHITE CHOCOLATE TART

FOR THE PASTRY
200 g (7 oz) plain flour
100 g (3½ oz) unsalted butter,
   cut into pieces, + extra for greasing
1 teaspoon salt

FOR THE FILLING
100 g (3½ oz) white chocolate
5 ripe white peaches
125 ml (4 fl oz) double cream
1 egg
4 tablespoons caster sugar

1 To make the pastry: put the flour, salt and butter in a large bowl. Rub with the fingertips to the consistency of coarse breadcrumbs. Add 100 ml (3½ fl oz) of cold water and mix in with a palette knife. The dough will come together. Finish the dough by hand (adding a little water if necessary), and form into a rough ball without working too much. Wrap in clingfilm and put in the refrigerator to rest for at least 1 hour.

2 Preheat the oven to 190°C (375°F) Gas Mark 5. Grease a tart tin and sprinkle with 2 tablespoons of sugar.

3 Roll out the pastry dough and line the tin.

4 Chop the white chocolate and sprinkle over the pastry base.

5 Peel the peaches and slice thinly. Arrange in a rose pattern on top of the chocolate.

6 Beat together the cream, egg and 1 tablespoon of the sugar and pour over the chocolate and peaches. Put into the oven and bake for 30–35 minutes.

7 Sprinkle with the remaining sugar and put under a very hot grill to caramelize the top, or use a kitchen blowtorch.

SERVES 6
PREPARATION TIME: 35 MINUTES
COOKING TIME: 1¼ HOURS

WHITE CHOCOLATE,
HAZELNUT & APRICOT CAKE

250 g (8 oz) soft butter + extra for greasing
250 g (8 oz) plain flour + extra for dusting
250 g (8 oz) caster sugar
4 eggs
1 cup very strong espresso (optional)
2 teaspoons baking powder
200 g (7 oz) white chocolate, chopped
75 g (3 oz) hazelnuts, chopped very fine, almost to powder
75 g (3 oz) dried apricots, chopped

1 Preheat the oven to 180 °C (350 °F) Gas Mark 4. Grease and flour a 1-kg/2-lb capacity loaf tin or line with nonstick baking paper.

2 Beat together the butter and sugar until the mixture becomes very fluffy (it's easier with an electric beater). Beat in the eggs one at a time. Add the coffee, if using.

3 Sift the flour and baking powder together and fold carefully into the batter using a large metal spoon, 'cutting' the mixture.

4 Add the white chocolate (reserving a little for decoration), hazelnuts and apricots. Stir just enough to combine everything.

5 Spoon into the loaf tin. Put the remaining chocolate in the centre of the top. Put into the oven and bake for about 1¼ hours. Test by inserting a metal skewer into the cake. It should come out clean. Leave to rest for 15 minutes before turning out onto a wire rack to cool.

SERVES 6
PREPARATION TIME: 30 MINUTES + RESTING TIME
COOKING TIME: 50 MINUTES

LIME & WHITE CHOCOLATE
TARTLETS

FOR THE SHORTCRUST PASTRY
250 g (8 oz) plain flour
125 g (4 oz) soft butter, cut into pieces,
   + extra for greasing
50 g (2 oz) caster sugar
1 egg
1 pinch salt

FOR THE FILLING
4 limes
125 g (4 oz) caster sugar
1 tablespoon cornflour, Maizena if possible
3 eggs, beaten
100 g (3½ oz) white chocolate
Icing sugar

1 To make the shortcrust pastry: sift the flour together with a pinch of salt into a large bowl. Add the butter and rub in with your fingertips to the consistency of coarse breadcrumbs. Add the sugar and the egg, mix well, and bring the dough together without working too much. Wrap in clingfilm and put in the refrigerator for at least 1 hour.

2 Preheat the oven to 180 °C (350 °F) Gas Mark 4. Roll out the dough and line greased tartlet tins with it. Put a piece of nonstick baking paper and a handful of dried beans into each, put in the oven and bake for 20 minutes, then remove the paper and beans and bake for a further 5–10 minutes.

3 Finely grate the rind of 2 limes and squeeze the juice from all 4 limes. Mix the cornflour in a little of the juice. Heat the remaining juice with the grated lime rind and sugar, stirring to dissolve the sugar. Add the cornflour and allow to cool a little, then add the beaten eggs. Cook over medium to low heat, stirring until the mixture thickens. Set aside to cool.

4 Chop the chocolate and spread over the base of the tartlets. Cover with the lime cream. Bake in the oven for 10 minutes. Allow to cool. Dust with a little icing sugar before serving.

MAKES 12
PREPARATION TIME: 20 MINUTES
COOKING TIME: 25 MINUTES

WHITE CHOCOLATE
MUFFINS

50 g (2 oz) butter + extra for greasing
300 g (10 oz) plain flour + extra for dusting
1 tablespoon baking powder
50 g (2 oz) caster sugar
200 g (7 oz) white chocolate
2 eggs
125 g plain yogurt + 50 ml/2 fl oz milk
Finely grated rind of ½ lemon
Vanilla essence
1 punnet raspberries
75 g (3 oz) chopped walnuts
Salt

1 Preheat the oven to 200°C (400°F) Gas Mark 6. Grease and flour a 12-cup muffin tin.
2 Sift together the flour, baking powder and a good pinch of salt into a bowl and stir in the sugar.
3 Chop the chocolate. Melt the butter.
4 Beat together the eggs, yogurt and milk, melted butter, grated lemon rind and a few drops of vanilla essence, to taste. Pour over the dry ingredients.
5 Mix very briefly with a wooden spoon. Do not attempt to make a smooth mixture; there should be lumps in it. Add the chopped chocolate and the raspberries, without stirring too much.
6 Three-quarters fill the muffin cups. Put into the oven and bake for 20–25 minutes. Leave to cool in the tin for about 20 minutes before turning out.

SERVES 8
PREPARATION TIME: 15 MINUTES
COOKING TIME: 20 MINUTES

WHITE CHOCOLATE & PEAR
TURNOVERS

1 sheet all butter ready-rolled puff pastry
1 35-g white Toblerone
4 perfectly ripe or poached pears
1 egg yolk

1 Preheat the oven to 220°C (425°F) Gas Mark 7.
2 Cut circles of pastry 5–6 cm (2–2½ inches) in diameter.
3 On each circle put a triangle of Toblerone and a piece of pear of the same size. Fold over to make a turnover and seal well by moistening the edges with water. Continue until all the ingredients have been used up.
4 Make a slit in the top of each turnover, place them on a baking sheet, put into the oven and bake for about 20 minutes until golden. Eat warm.

42

SERVES 6
PREPARATION TIME: 30 MINUTES
COOKING TIME: 1 HOUR
CHILLING TIME: OVERNIGHT

RED FRUIT **CHEESECAKE**

150 g (5 oz) petit-beurre biscuits
50 g (2 oz) butter
100 g (3½ oz) white chocolate
750 g (1½ lb) fromage frais
4 eggs
2 tablespoons plain flour
Finely grated rind of 1 lemon
125 ml (4 fl oz) crème fraîche
500 g red fruits, fresh or frozen
50 g (2 oz) caster sugar

1 Preheat the oven to 180°C (350°F) Gas Mark 4.

2 Put the biscuits in a polythene bag and crush with a rolling pin. Melt the butter and mix with the biscuit crumbs. Press this mixture into a cake tin 20–23 cm (8–9 inches) in diameter, lined with nonstick baking paper. Put in the oven and bake for 10 minutes. Remove from the oven and reduce the temperature to 140°C (275°F) Gas Mark 1.

3 Chop the chocolate in pieces and melt in a bain-marie or in a bowl set over barely simmering water. Stir the fromage frais in a food processor or with an electric beater (no longer than 30 seconds). Add the eggs one at a time, then the flour and grated lemon rind, then the crème fraîche and finally the melted chocolate. Tip into the cake tin and bake for 1 hour.

4 Put the fruits in a pan with the sugar and 1 tablespoon of water. Bring to the boil and simmer for 2 minutes. Set aside to cool. When the cake is ready, leave to cool completely in the oven with the door ajar. Remove from the oven and spoon the fruit over the top. Put in the refrigerator and do not eat until the next day.

SERVES 4
PREPARATION TIME: 10 MINUTES

DARK CHOCOLATE SORBET
WITH WHITE CHOCOLATE SAUCE

200 g (7 oz) white chocolate
50 ml (2 fl oz) double cream
4 scoops dark chocolate sorbet
White chocolate shavings

1 Melt the chocolate in a bain-marie or in a heatproof bowl set over a pan of barely simmering water.

2 Heat the cream and add to the chocolate.

3 Serve the sauce hot over the sorbet, decorated with shavings of white chocolate.

English translation and adaptation: JMS Books LLP
Layout: cbdesign

First published in France in 2007 under the title
La Boîte à gâteau, by Hachette Livre (Marabout)
Copyright © 2007 Hachette Livre (Marabout)
Editorial: Catherine Berranger and Charlotte Müller-Buch

An Hachette Livre UK Company
www.hachettelivre.co.uk

First published in Great Britain in 2008 by
Hamlyn, a division of Octopus Publishing Group Ltd
2–4 Heron Quays, London E14 4JP
www.octopusbooks.co.uk

Copyright © English edition
Octopus Publishing Group Ltd 2008

Original French edition copyright
© HACHETTE LIVRE (Marabout) 2007

ISBN 978 0 600 61876 8

A CIP catalogue record for this book is available from
the British Library

Printed and bound in China

1 3 5 7 9 10 8 6 4 2

This book contains dishes that are made with raw or lightly cooked eggs.
These should be avoided by vulnerable people such as pregnant and
nursing mothers, invalids, the elderly, babies and young children.

CARAMEL
SALTED BUTTER

hamlyn

CONTENTS

CARAMEL SHORTBREAD **6**
BRAZIL NUT NOUGATINE **8**
APPLE & CARAMEL SUNDAE **10**
MARBLED CARAMEL CHEESECAKE **12**
LITTLE POTS OF DULCE DE LECHE **14**
FUDGE **16**
EASY CRÈME BRÛLÉE **18**
CARAMEL SAUCE **20**
ROUDOUDOUS **22**
UPSIDE-DOWN CREAM **24**
QUINCE & BUTTER SPONGE **26**
APPLE CRUMBLE **28**
MILLEFEUILLE **30**
BREAD & BUTTER PUDDING **32**
BUTTERED RICE PUDDING **34**
PINE NUT & ALMOND TUILES
    WITH SALTED BUTTER **36**
CHOCOLATE & SALTED BUTTER
    FONDANT **38**
CUPCAKES WITH SPICED SALTED
    BUTTER ICING **40**
PARIS-BREST WITH SALTED BUTTER **42**
KOURABIEDES **44**

MAKES ABOUT 16
PREPARATION TIME: 25 MINUTES
COOKING TIME: 50 MINUTES
RESTING TIME: 1½ HOURS IN TOTAL

CARAMEL **SHORTBREAD**

150 g (5 oz) softened butter
80 g (3 oz) caster sugar
200 g (7 oz) plain flour
Salt

FOR THE TOPPING
30 g (1 oz) butter
30 g (1 oz) soft light brown sugar
125 ml (4 fl oz) sweetened evaporated milk
200 g (7 oz) good quality milk chocolate

1 Preheat the oven to 150°C (300°F) Gas Mark 2. Grease a shallow, round or rectangular metal cake tin (ideally a springform tin).

2 Beat together the butter and sugar until the mixture becomes almost frothy (this is easier with a food processor or an electric mixer). Sift the flour and a pinch of salt onto the mixture and fold in by 'cutting' the dough with a knife (if using a food processor, just give it a few turns of the blades at minimum speed). Scoop the dough together with one hand, taking care not to work it too much, and use the palm of your hand to spread a layer of dough 1.5 cm (¾ inch) thick over the base of the tin. Flatten the surface by pressing, with a small board if possible. Prick with a fork.

3 Put in the oven and bake for 40 minutes (the pastry should remain very pale). Remove from the oven and turn out of the tin, as soon as possible, onto to a wire rack to cool.

4 To make the topping: put the butter, sugar and evaporated milk in a small pan. Melt over low heat, stirring constantly. Allow to thicken for a few minutes, while continuing to stir. Spread over the cooled biscuit and leave to set for about 30 minutes. Melt the chocolate in a heatproof bowl over barely simmering water or in a microwave and spread it on top of the caramel. Allow to set for about an hour, then cut in squares to serve.

SERVES 6
PREPARATION TIME: 10 MINUTES
COOKING TIME: 10 MINUTES
RESTING TIME: 20 MINUTES

BRAZIL NUT **NOUGATINE**

150 g (5 oz) Brazil nuts
150 g (5 oz) granulated sugar

1 Line a baking sheet with nonstick baking paper (or use a silicone sheet).

2 Put the sugar in a pan with 100 ml (3½ fl oz) of water. Bring to the boil and leave on the heat until it forms a nice light caramel.

3 Remove from the heat, mix in the Brazil nuts and pour immediately onto the baking paper.

4 Leave to harden then break in pieces. Delicious when chopped in small pieces and sprinkled on Greek yogurt.

SERVES 4
PREPARATION TIME: 15 MINUTES
COOKING TIME: 50 MINUTES

APPLE & CARAMEL **SUNDAE**

4 russet apples (or Reinette 'Queen of Pippins'
   apples from France, if available)
150 g (5 oz) butter toffees
250 g (8 oz) Greek yogurt
Ice cream made with fromage frais

1 Preheat the oven to 190°C (375°F) Gas Mark 5.

2 Wash and core the apples but do not peel. Bake in the oven for about 40 minutes (the flesh should more or less fall apart).

3 Melt the toffees in a small pan over very low heat. Remove from the heat and add the yogurt.

4 Remove the apple skins and serve in bowls with the ice cream and the caramel sauce.

SERVES 6
PREPARATION TIME: 35 MINUTES
COOKING TIME: 1¼ HOURS
RESTING TIME: OVERNIGHT

MARBLED CARAMEL
CHEESECAKE

FOR THE BASE
200 g (7 oz) sablé biscuits, or digestives
50 g (2 oz) butter

FOR THE CREAM
About 150 g (5 oz) butter toffees
50 ml (2 fl oz) single cream or milk, or more if necessary
750 g (1½ lb) fromage frais
150 g (5 oz) caster sugar
3 eggs + 2 egg yolks
2 tablespoons plain flour
1 teaspoon vanilla essence
125 g (4 oz) thick crème fraîche

1 Preheat the oven to 190°C (375°F) Gas Mark 5. Melt the butter. Crumble the biscuits in a food processor (or put them in a tightly closed freezer bag and crush with a rolling pin) and mix with the melted butter. Press this crumb base into a springform cake tin 20 cm (8 inches) in diameter. Put in the oven for 10 minutes. Lower the temperature to 140°C (275°F) Gas Mark 1.

2 Melt the toffees very gently in a pan. Add sufficient cream or milk to make this sauce quite runny. Set aside to cool.

3 Beat the fromage frais with an electric whisk for about 30 seconds. Add first the sugar, then the eggs and yolks one at a time, beating continuously, then the vanilla essence and lastly the flour and the crème fraîche.

4 Pour into the cake tin and smooth over the surface. Pour over the caramel sauce in a thin stream, drawing several concentric circles. Then, with a knife, draw the marbling by 'cutting' across the circles. Put in the oven and bake for about 1 hour. The cream should be just set around the edges but still a little quivery at the centre of the cake. Leave the cheesecake in the oven with the door ajar for a further 1 hour. Cool completely outside the oven before turning out and storing in the refrigerator, if possible until the next day.

SERVES 6
PREPARATION TIME: 10 MINUTES
COOKING TIME: 2 HOURS

LITTLE POTS
OF DULCE DE LECHE

1 litre (1¾ pints) milk
150 g (5 oz) caster sugar
1 vanilla pod
8 egg yolks

1 In a pan put half the milk, the sugar and the split vanilla pod (scrape the seeds out over the milk). Bring slowly to the boil, then simmer over very low heat for about 1½ hours, stirring regularly. The milk should reduce to half to make a kind of caramel: this is 'dulce de leche'. Allow to cool, then remove the vanilla pod.

2 Preheat the oven to 160°C (325°F) Gas Mark 3. Beat the egg yolks with the remaining milk. Add the dulce de leche. Pour into ramekins and place them in a roasting tin. Slide the tin into the oven and fill it with warm water to halfway up the ramekins. Bake for about 35 minutes, long enough for the creams to set. Allow to cool, refrigerate and eat cold.

SERVES 6
PREPARATION TIME: 10 MINUTES
COOKING TIME: 35 MINUTES
RESTING TIME: 2 HOURS

FUDGE

300 ml (½ pint) milk
500 g (1 lb) brown sugar
60 g (2¼ oz) butter
Vanilla essence

1 Grease a 15-cm (6-inch) square mould. Heat the milk, sugar and butter in a pan over low heat. Bring the mixture to the boil, stirring constantly, and simmer gently for about 30 minutes.

2 Drop a spot of caramel into a bowl of cold water. If it forms a little ball, it's done. If not, continue cooking and repeat the test.

3 Remove the pan from the heat, add a few drops of vanilla essence to taste and beat the mixture. It should form a thick cream. Pour into the tin and allow to set before cutting in squares.

SERVES 6
PREPARATION TIME: 20 MINUTES
COOKING TIME: 1 HOUR
RESTING TIME: 15 MINUTES

EASY **CRÈME BRÛLÉE**

500 ml (17 fl oz) single cream
500 ml (17 fl oz) milk
1 vanilla pod
8 egg yolks
225 g (7–8 oz) caster sugar (or more, according to taste)
3 passion fruits

1 Preheat the oven to 120°C (250°F) Gas Mark ½.

2 Heat the cream and milk with the split vanilla pod (scrape the seeds out over the milk). Remove from the heat just before it boils, cover and leave to infuse for 15 minutes.

3 Beat the egg yolks together with 125 g (4 oz) of the sugar, until the mixture turns pale. Remove the vanilla pod from the cream, pour the cream over the egg mixture, and blend in without making it frothy. Pour into ramekins, put in the oven and bake for about 40 minutes, just long enough for the cream to set.

4 Cover a baking sheet with nonstick baking paper. Put the remaining sugar in a pan with 4 tablespoons of water. Boil the sugar and water until you get a nice caramel. Pour immediately onto the sheet of baking paper, allow to set, then break in pieces.

5 Allow the creams to cool, then store in the refrigerator. Scoop out the flesh of the passion fruits. Just before serving, scatter splinters of caramel over the creams and decorate with passion fruit flesh.

20

SERVES 4
COOKING TIME: 5 MINUTES

CARAMEL **SAUCE**

60 g (2¼ oz) butter (salted is best)
100 g (3½ oz) brown sugar
120 ml (4 fl oz) single cream

1 Melt the butter and sugar in a small pan over low heat, stirring to dissolve the sugar.

2 Add the cream, bring to the boil and simmer for 3 minutes over fairly low heat until the sauce thickens.

3 Allow to cool a little and pour over your chosen dessert.

Cook's tip Caramel sauce is a delicious accompaniment to ice cream, apple tarts, etc.

SERVES 4
PREPARATION TIME: 10 MINUTES
COOKING TIME: 10 MINUTES
RESTING TIME: 1 HOUR

ROUDOUDOUS
(CANDY IN A SHELL)

Seashells (limpets, cockles…very thoroughly washed)
30 g (1 oz) butter
150 g (5 oz) granulated sugar
2 tablespoons orange juice

1 Put the butter, sugar and 1 tablespoon of orange juice in a pan and boil until you get a golden caramel.

2 Mix in the second tablespoonful of juice and pour into the shells.

3 Leave to cool for at least 1 hour.

Cook's tip French children lick these bonbons straight from the shell. An ideal little treat to make during a wet day on a seaside holiday.

SERVES 4
PREPARATION TIME: 20 MINUTES
COOKING TIME: 1 HOUR
RESTING TIME: OVERNIGHT

UPSIDE-DOWN **CREAM**

200 g (7oz) sugar
1 litre (1¾ pints) milk
2 vanilla pods
2 clementines, well scrubbed
6 eggs

1 Preheat the oven to 150°C (300°F) Gas Mark 2. Squeeze the clementines and retain the peel with the flesh removed.
2 In a small pan, heat 150 g (5 oz) of the sugar with 4 tablespoons of clementine juice until you get a nice caramel. Pour it into a mould and tip in all directions to spread the caramel over the bottom and sides.
3 Bring the milk to the boil with the split vanilla pods and the clementine peel. Remove from the heat, cover and set aside to infuse for 10 minutes. Beat together the eggs and the remaining sugar. Pour the milk in a thin stream through a sieve, stirring very gently to avoid creating froth.
4 Pour the cream into the mould and place the mould in an ovenproof dish. Fill the dish with warm water to halfway up the mould and put in the oven for 50 minutes. Allow to cool, then chill in the refrigerator overnight. Turn out of the mould to serve.

SERVES 4
PREPARATION TIME: 20 MINUTES
COOKING TIME: 35 MINUTES

QUINCE & BUTTER **SPONGE**

4 eggs, separated
120 g (4 oz) caster sugar
120 g (4 oz) plain flour + extra for dusting
Quince jelly
Soft salted butter for spreading + extra for greasing

1 Preheat the oven to 180°C (350°F) Gas Mark 4. Grease and flour 2 cake tins 18–20 cm (7–8 inches) in diameter.

2 In a bowl, beat together the egg yolks and sugar. The mixture should become very frothy. Sift the flour and blend into the mixture with a metal spoon. Whisk the egg whites until stiff and gently fold into the mixture.

4 Pour into the cake tins, put in the oven and bake for about 20–25 minutes. Turn out and cool on a wire rack.

5 Spread one of the sponges with a thin layer of salted butter and quince jelly. Place the second sponge on top. Serve with coffee.

SERVES 4
PREPARATION TIME: 20 MINUTES
COOKING TIME: 1¼ HOURS

APPLE **CRUMBLE**

6–7 cooking apples
150 g (5 oz) plain flour
100 g (3½ oz) salted butter, cut into pieces
2–3 tablespoons sugar

To serve: crème fraîche

1 Preheat the oven to 200°C (400°F) Gas Mark 6.

2 Wash and core the apples. Put in a medium-size ovenproof dish and bake until the flesh collapses and the skins come away, but do not let it cook to a purée.

3 In a mixing bowl, rub the flour into the butter with the fingertips to give the consistency of crumbs. Add 2 tablespoons of the sugar.

4 Reduce the oven temperature to 180°C (350°F) Gas Mark 4. Remove the apple skins, leaving the flesh in the dish, mix in the remaining sugar and smooth the top with a fork. Cover with the crumble and bake for about 35 minutes. Serve with the crème fraîche.

SERVES 4
PREPARATION TIME: 45 MINUTES
COOKING TIME: 35 MINUTES

MILLEFEUILLE

FOR THE DOUGH
200 g (7 oz) plain flour
100 g (3½ oz) salted butter from the freezer
75 g (3 oz) caster sugar
2 tablespoons icing sugar + extra for decoration

FOR THE CONFECTIONER'S CUSTARD
500 ml (17 fl oz) milk
1 vanilla pod
5 egg yolks
100 g (3½ oz) caster sugar
2 tablespoons flour
2 tablespoons cornflour (Maizena if possible)

1 To make the pastry: put the flour in a mixing bowl and grate the very hard butter over it using a grater with large holes. Add 3–4 tablespoons of cold water. Use a palette knife to mix the dough. Form into a ball (without working it too much) and place in the refrigerator.

2 To make the cream: heat the milk with the split vanilla pod. In a heatproof bowl, whisk together the egg yolks and sugar, add the flour and the cornflour and beat well. Add a little boiling milk, beat again, then gradually add the remaining milk, whisking constantly. Pour the mixture back into the pan and cook over medium to low heat, beating continuously and scraping the bottom of the pan well. Cook for 2–3 minutes after the first bubbles appear, while continuing to stir. Pour the cream into a bowl. Cover closely with clingfilm and allow to cool.

3 Preheat the oven to 230°C (450°F) Gas Mark 8. Line a baking sheet with nonstick baking paper or a silicone sheet. Roll the dough into a rectangle and place on the baking sheet. Sieve 75 g (3 oz) of sugar over the dough. Put in the oven and reduce the temperature to 180°C (350°F) Gas Mark 4. After 10 minutes, place a light nonstick baking sheet on the rectangle of dough to prevent it from rising too much and bake for a further 8 minutes.

4 Take out the pastry and turn up the heat to maximum. Turn the baking sheets upside down and remove the top one. Sieve the 2 tablespoons of icing sugar over it and return to the now very hot oven to caramelize for 5–8 minutes, keeping a careful eye on it. Set aside to cool. With a good sharp knife, cut the pastry into three rectangles of equal size. Spread the caramelized side with cream, put a second rectangle on top, spread this with cream and top with the final rectangle. Dust with icing sugar.

SERVES 4
PREPARATION TIME: 20 MINUTES
COOKING TIME: 30 MINUTES

BREAD & BUTTER **PUDDING**

Finely grated rind of 1 lemon
8 slices stale bread or brioche
Unsalted butter for spreading + extra for greasing
100 g (3½ oz) raisins
150 ml (¼ pint) milk
150 ml (¼ pint) single cream
2 eggs
4 tablespoons brown sugar

1 Preheat the oven to 190°C (375°F) Gas Mark 5. Grease a medium-size ovenproof dish with butter.

2 Spread the bread generously with butter. Cut the slices in half, diagonally if the slices are square. Arrange as near vertically as possible in the ovenproof dish. Add the raisins.

3 Beat together the milk, cream, eggs and grated lemon rind. Pour into the dish and sprinkle with sugar. Put in the oven and bake for about 30 minutes, so the cream sets and the top turns golden.

34

SERVES 4
PREPARATION TIME: 5 MINUTES
COOKING TIME: 30 MINUTES

BUTTERED **RICE PUDDING**

1 litre (1¾ pints) milk
1 cinnamon stick
1 vanilla pod
150 g (5 oz) short-grain rice
4–5 tablespoons sugar
30 g (1 oz) unsalted butter

1 In a large pan heat the milk, cinnamon stick and the split vanilla pod (scrape the seeds into the pan). Bring gradually to the boil.

2 Sprinkle in the rice. Stir, reduce the heat and simmer gently, stirring frequently. The rice should take about 25 minutes to cook but check regularly as the grains should retain their shape.

3 Add the sugar and then the butter, mixing carefully. Discard the cinnamon stick and vanilla pod. Serve warm.

36

MAKES ABOUT 20
PREPARATION TIME: 25 MINUTES
COOKING TIME: 17 MINUTES PER BATCH
CHILLING TIME: 1 HOUR

PINE NUT & ALMOND TUILES
WITH SALTED BUTTER

125 g (4 oz) caster sugar
1 whole egg + 2 egg whites
40 g (1½ oz) plain flour
Finely grated rind of 1 lemon
1 vanilla pod
100 g (3½ oz) flaked almonds
50 g (2 oz) pine nuts
75 g (3 oz) salted butter + a little for greasing

1 Mix together sugar and the whole egg, then add the egg whites. Sift the flour and add with the finely grated peel of the lemon. Split open the vanilla pod and scrape the seeds into the mixture. Mix in the almonds and pine nuts with a spatula, taking care not to break them. Refrigerate for 1 hour.

2 Preheat the oven to 240°C (475°F) Gas Mark 9. Grease several baking sheets generously with butter. Using a teaspoon, place small amounts of dough on the baking sheet, spaced well apart, and gently flatten each one with a fork dipped in cold water. Put in the oven and bake for 4 minutes but watch very carefully as the tuiles are ready when their edges are golden brown, while the centres remain very pale. You will have to bake several batches.

3 Have some small glasses ready for use beside the oven. When the tuiles begin to turn golden, take them out and slip them one at a time onto the glasses (to give them their curved shape). When they have hardened, put them on a wire rack to cool.

Cook's tip Tuiles – meaning 'tiles' – are named for their curved shape, which resembles roof tiles.

SERVES 6
PREPARATION TIME: 25 MINUTES
COOKING TIME: 25 MINUTES

CHOCOLATE & SALTED BUTTER
FONDANT

125 g (4 oz) dark chocolate, chopped
125 g (4 oz) salted butter + a little for greasing
100 g (3½ oz) sugar
3 eggs
8 tablespoons cocoa powder

1 Preheat the oven to 180°C (350°F) Gas Mark 4. Grease a sponge tin 20 cm (8 inches) in diameter.

2 Melt the chocolate and butter in a heatproof bowl over barely simmering water; make sure the bowl does not touch the water.

3 Add the sugar, then the eggs, and then the sifted cocoa (reserve a little for decoration). Mix well and pour into the tin. Put in the oven and bake for 25 minutes.

4 Leave to rest for 5 minutes before turning out to cool. Dust with cocoa.

MAKES 12
PREPARATION TIME: 30 MINUTES
COOKING TIME: 35 MINUTES

CUP CAKES WITH
SPICED SALTED BUTTER ICING

100 (3½ oz) soft unsalted butter
80 g (3 oz) soft salted butter
80 g (3 oz) sugar
Vanilla essence
3 eggs
225 g (7½ oz) plain flour
2 teaspoons baking powder
Ground cinnamon
Nutmeg
Ground ginger

FOR THE TOPPING
100 g (3½ oz) salted butter
300 g (10 oz) icing sugar
1 teaspoon vanilla essence
½ teaspoon ground cinnamon
Ground ginger
Salt
Milk

1 Preheat the oven to 160°C (325°F) Gas Mark 3. Line a 12-cup muffin tin with paper cases or grease well.

2 Beat both kinds of butter, the sugar and a few drops of vanilla essence until very fluffy. Add the eggs one at a time. Sift together the flour, baking powder and a pinch each of the spices and mix in carefully.

3 Fill the cases with the mixture, leaving space at the top for the topping. Put in the oven and bake for 35 minutes; test by inserting a metal skewer, which should come out clean. Remove from the oven and leave to cool on a wire rack.

4 To make the topping: mix together the first 4 ingredients, then add a good pinch of the ground ginger and a small pinch of salt. Add a little milk if necessary to make the mixture workable but firm.

5 When the cakes have cooled, decorate generously with the topping.

SERVES 6
PREPARATION TIME: 45 MINUTES
COOKING TIME: 30 MINUTES

PARIS-BREST
WITH SALTED BUTTER

FOR THE CHOUX PASTRY
125 ml (4 fl oz) milk
125 ml (4 fl oz) water
1 teaspoon salt
1 tablespoon caster sugar
100 g (3½ oz) butter, cut in pieces
150 g (5 oz) plain flour
4 eggs, beaten

FOR THE MOUSSELINE CREAM
500 ml (17 fl oz) milk
1 vanilla pod
5 egg yolks
100 g (3½ oz) caster sugar
2 tablespoons plain flour
2 tablespoons cornflour, Maizena if possible
150 g (5 oz) soft unsalted butter
150 g (5 oz) soft salted butter
125 g (4 oz) ground praline
   (from a specialist bakery or confectioner's)

1 To make the cream: heat the milk with the split vanilla pod. In a mixing bowl, beat together the egg yolks and sugar; add the flour and cornflour and beat again. Add a little boiling milk, beat again, then gradually add the remaining milk, stirring constantly. Pour the mixture back into the pan and cook over medium to low heat, stirring constantly and scraping the bottom of the pan well. When the first bubbles appear, cook and stir constantly for a further 2–3 minutes. Pour the cream into a bowl, cover closely with clingfilm and set aside to cool.

2 Stir the cold mousseline before mixing in the praline (reserving 2 tablespoons) and the unsalted and salted butter mashed together.

3 Preheat the oven to 200°C (400°F) Gas Mark 6. Grease a baking sheet or line with nonstick baking paper.

4 To make the choux pastry: in a pan, heat the milk, water, salt, sugar and butter. Remove from the heat just before it boils. Add all the flour at once and mix vigorously with a spatula. As soon as the flour has been thoroughly mixed in, put the pan back on the heat to dry out the mixture. Transfer to a large bowl and gradually add the beaten eggs, 'cutting' the dough with a spatula. If the dough looks right (it will close up if you run your finger through it), do not add all the egg.

5 Using a piping bag (small nozzle), pipe a disc of choux pastry on the baking sheet. Pipe several layers to make the disc quite thick. Sprinkle with the remaining praline. Bake for 10 minutes, then increase the oven temperature to 220°C (425°F) Gas Mark 7 and cook for a further 15–20 minutes, until golden brown. Leave to cool on a wire rack.

6 Cut the choux pastry in half horizontally, spread one half with the cream and place the other half on top.

MAKES ABOUT 20
PREPARATION TIME: 20 MINUTES
COOKING TIME: 20 MINUTES
CHILLING TIME: 30 MINUTES

KOURABIEDES

120 g (4 oz) soft salted butter + extra for greasing
Nutmeg
2 teaspoons orange flower water
50 g (2 oz) icing sugar, sifted
90 g (3¼ oz) plain flour
120 g (4 oz) ground almonds

1 Using a spatula, mash the butter in a large bowl. Add a pinch of freshly ground nutmeg, the orange flower water and the icing sugar (reserving 2 tablespoons for dusting). Lastly, sift in the flour and add the ground almonds. Form into a dough, taking care not to work it too much.

2 Put in the refrigerator for 30 minutes to firm.

3 Preheat the oven to 160°C (325°F) Gas Mark 3.

4 Spread the dough by hand in a greased rectangular baking tin, put in the oven and bake for 20 minutes. The dough should be firm but pale. Allow to cool for 5 minutes, cut into squares and dust with icing sugar.

Cook's tip Kourabiedes are melt-in-the-mouth Greek cookies.

English translation and adaptation: JMS Books LLP
Layout: cbdesign

First published in France in 2007 under the title
La Boîte à gâteau, by Hachette Livre (Marabout)
Copyright © 2007 Hachette Livre (Marabout)
Editorial: Catherine Berranger and Charlotte Müller-Buch

An Hachette Livre UK Company
www.hachettelivre.co.uk

First published in Great Britain in 2008 by
Hamlyn, a division of Octopus Publishing Group Ltd
2–4 Heron Quays, London E14 4JP
www.octopusbooks.co.uk

ISBN 978 0 600 61876 8

A CIP catalogue record for this book is available from
the British Library

Printed and bound in China

1 3 5 7 9 10 8 6 4 2

This book contains dishes that are made with raw or lightly cooked eggs.
These should be avoided by vulnerable people such as pregnant and
nursing mothers, invalids, the elderly, babies and young children.

MINT
LIQUORICE

hamlyn

CONTENTS

SERVES 4
PREPARATION TIME: 20 MINUTES

MINT & POMEGRANATE
TARTLETS

12 small tartlet cases made from 1 sheet ready-made
  butter shortcrust pastry, already baked
250 g (8 oz) mascarpone
2 pomegranates
12 small mint leaves

1 Beat the mascarpone until smooth with a spatula, then divide it between the tartlet cases.
2 To serve, scatter a few pomegranate seeds on each tartlet and add a mint leaf to each.

SERVES 6
PREPARATION TIME: 20 MINUTES
COOKING TIME: 10 MINUTES
CHILLING TIME: MINIMUM 4 HOURS

MINT **PANNA COTTA**

450 ml (¾ pint) milk
450 ml (¾ pint) single cream
3 tablespoons caster sugar
3 sprigs mint
6 leaves gelatine (12 g/½ oz)
Mint syrup
Flavourless oil (such as groundnut)

1 Lightly oil 6 small moulds. Heat the milk and cream together with the sugar and the mint leaves (reserve a few for decoration) to just below boiling point. Stir to dissolve the sugar, remove from the heat, cover and leave to infuse for 15–20 minutes, then discard the mint. Meanwhile put the gelatine to soak in a little water.

2 Squeeze out the gelatine. Reheat the milk and cream sufficiently to dissolve the gelatine. Stir well, then pour into the oiled moulds and leave to set in the refrigerator for at least 4 hours.

3 Turn out of the moulds and serve with a little mint syrup, decorated with the reserved mint leaves. The panna cottas may also be served with a chocolate sauce or soft fruit.

SERVES 4
PREPARATION TIME: 20 MINUTES + COOLING TIME
COOKING TIME: 5 MINUTES
CHILLING TIME: MINIMUM 2 HOURS

MINT & ORANGE
YOGURT JELLIES

4 leaves gelatine (8 g/$\frac{1}{3}$ oz)
6 oranges
1 lemon
4 sprigs mint
50 g (2 oz) caster sugar
150 g (5 oz) yogurt
1 teaspoon orange flower water (optional)

1 Soften the gelatine in a little cold water. Finely grate the peel from 4 of the oranges; squeeze the juice from the 4 oranges and the lemon. Measure 300 ml (½ pint) of orange juice (top up with water if necessary) and put into a pan with the grated peel, the lemon juice, mint and sugar. Stir over medium heat until the sugar has dissolved. Squeeze out the gelatine and add, stirring in to dissolve. Take off the heat, cover and leave to infuse for 10 minutes, then strain and leave to cool.

2 Mix this liquid with the yogurt. Divide between 4 small moulds or use one decorative mould, rinsed out with water to facilitate turning out the jellies. Put in the refrigerator to set for at least 2 hours.

3 Peel and slice the remaining oranges and serve with the jellies.

SERVES 4–6
PREPARATION TIME: 20 MINUTES
COOKING TIME: 3 MINUTES
CHILLING TIME: MINIMUM 4 HOURS

MINT, STRAWBERRY & RASPBERRY **JELLY**

500 g (1 lb) mixed fresh strawberries and raspberries
6 sprigs mint
6 leaves gelatine (12 g/½ oz)
2 tablespoons rum, preferably white
3–4 tablespoons cane sugar syrup
Juice from 1 lime
250 ml (8 fl oz) Perrier water

1 Rinse the fruit, hull the strawberries and cut any large ones in half. Rinse and dry the mint and strip off the leaves. Put the gelatine to soften in a little cold water; squeeze out when ready to use.

2 Heat 200 ml (7 fl oz) of water with the rum, the syrup and 1 tablespoon of lime juice. Remove from the heat, add the gelatine and stir to dissolve completely. Add the Perrier water.

3 Divide the fruit between 4–6 glasses and add the most attractive of the mint leaves. Pour the liquid over the fruit and leave to set for at least 4 hours in the refrigerator.

SERVES 6
PREPARATION TIME: 35 MINUTES

ETON MESS WITH MINT

1 ready-made meringue base
500 g (1 lb) redcurrants
50 g (2 oz) caster sugar
100 ml (3½ fl oz) whipping cream
300 g (10 oz) fromage frais
4 sprigs mint
1–2 tablespoons mint syrup

1 Break the meringue into pieces. Rinse the redcurrants and remove the stalks – through the tines of a fork is a quick way. Mix the fruit with the sugar.

2 Whip the cream. Beat the fromage frais to soften it. Wash the mint and strip off the leaves.

3 Roughly stir together all the ingredients into an attractive 'mess'. Pile into decorative glasses and serve.

Cook's Tip Eton Mess is a mixture of meringue pieces, whipped cream and fruit (traditionally strawberries).

SERVES 6
PREPARATION TIME: 15 MINUTES + 3 HOURS MACERATION
COOKING TIME: 1 HOUR 45 MINUTES
RESTING TIME: 3 HOURS

FRUIT CAKE WITH MINT TEA

450 g (15 oz) chopped dried fruit (raisins, apricots, etc.)
275 ml (9 fl oz) cold mint tea (preferably made with fresh mint)
200 g (7 oz) light soft brown sugar
Butter for greasing
2 eggs
250 (8 oz) plain flour
2 teaspoons baking powder
1 teaspoon four spice (failing that, cinnamon)
Salt

1 Put the fruit to macerate for at least 3 hours in the tea, mixed with the sugar.

2 Preheat the oven to 180°C (350°F) Gas Mark 4. Grease a cake tin and line with nonstick baking paper.

3 Beat the eggs. Sift the flour with the baking powder and the spice, mix with the beaten egg, then add the fruit, together with the tea they were macerated in.

4 Pour into the cake tin, put in the oven and bake for 1½–1¾ hours. Check a metal skewer inserted in the centre emerges quite clean.

5 Leave in the tin for 5–10 minutes before turning out onto a wire rack to cool completely. Store the fruit cake wrapped in foil to keep it moist.

SERVES 6
PREPARATION TIME: 25 MINUTES
COOKING TIME: 40 MINUTES
RESTING TIME: OVERNIGHT IF POSSIBLE

GRANDMA'S MINT TART

2 sheets pre-rolled sweetened shortcrust pastry
350 ml (12 fl oz) milk
1 tablespoon cornflour
3 tablespoons plain flour
5 sprigs mint
4 tablespoons caster sugar
4 egg yolks
Juice of 1 lemon
75 g (3 oz) pine nuts
Icing sugar for dredging

1 Roll the pastry a little thinner and use one sheet to line a tart tin 20–23 cm (8–9 inches) in diameter.

2 Mix the cornflour with a little cold milk, then add the flour. Heat the rest of the milk with the mint leaves. Remove from the heat the moment it comes to the boil, cover and leave to infuse for 15 minutes, then strain and discard the mint.

3 In a heatproof bowl, beat the egg yolks with the sugar and the juice of the lemon. Pour the milk slowly onto the flour and cornflour mixture, stirring constantly until smooth. Return this mixture to the pan and bring back to the boil.

4 Pour the milk and flour mixture onto the egg and sugar mixture, stirring constantly, then return to the pan over gentle heat, stirring constantly for about 2 minutes until the mixture thickens to coat the back of the spoon. Pour into a clean, dry bowl to cool.

5 Preheat the oven to 180°C (350°F) Gas Mark 4. When the cream has set, spread it on the pastry base. Cut another circle of pastry to form the lid and moisten the border to make a good seal. Scatter over the pine nuts, put in the oven and bake for 35–40 minutes, allowing the top to become nicely browned. Leave to cool. This tart is best eaten the next day.

MAKES ABOUT 30
PREPARATION TIME: 45 MINUTES
COOKING TIME: 10 MINUTES
CHILLING TIME: OVERNIGHT

CHOCOLATE MINT **TRUFFLES**

200 g (7 oz) plain chocolate
4 sprigs mint
150 ml (¼ pint) single cream
Cocoa powder

1 Chop the chocolate into very small pieces and place in a heatproof bowl. Wash and dry the mint and strip off the leaves.

2 Put the cream in a small pan with the mint and bring to the boil. Remove from the heat, cover and leave to infuse for 10 minutes, then strain and discard the mint.

3 Pour the cream onto the chocolate and stir until the chocolate has melted. Leave to cool, then refrigerate overnight to allow it to set.

4 Next day, form the chocolate mint ganache into little balls, roll them in cocoa powder and arrange on a plate.

SERVES 4
PREPARATION TIME: 10 MINUTES
COOKING TIME: 10 MINUTES
CHILLING TIME: 2 HOURS

MINT **LASSI**

6 sprigs mint + extra for decoration
600 ml (1 pint) milk
300 ml (½ pint) yogurt mixed with 300 ml (½ pint) milk
Caster sugar

To serve: shortbread biscuits or Cornes de gazelle

1 Wash and dry the mint.

2 Pour the milk into a pan and add the mint. Bring almost to the boil, remove from the heat, cover and leave to infuse for 10–15 minutes before discarding the mint.

3 Transfer the milk to a jug or bowl, leave to cool, then refrigerate for an hour or two until thoroughly chilled.

4 Whisk the chilled milk together with the milk and yogurt mixture and caster sugar to taste, or whizz briefly in a blender. Serve with shortbread biscuits or Cornes de gazelle (see page 38).

Cook's Tip Lassi is an Indian yogurt drink.

SERVES 4
PREPARATION TIME: 20 MINUTES
COOKING TIME: 5 MINUTES
FREEZING TIME: 2–3 HOURS

MINT **GRANITA**

1 bunch mint
5 tablespoons sugar
Juice of 1 lime
1 dash of mint syrup (optional)

1 Wash the mint, reserve a few leaves for decoration, then tear up the rest and put them in a pan with the sugar and 500 ml (17 fl oz) of water. Bring to the boil, stirring to dissolve the sugar, then leave to simmer for 5 minutes. Add 2 tablespoons of the lime juice.

2 Strain through a sieve, crushing the mint with a wooden spoon to extract the flavour, then pour into a fairly shallow freezerproof box and cool before putting in the freezer.

3 After about 30 minutes, take it out and whisk with a fork, then return to the freezer. Repeat this procedure after 30 minutes, then repeat once or twice more. How often you do this depends on the power of your freezer or freezing compartment.

4 Once the mixture has reached the consistency of crushed ice, serve it either as it is, decorated with mint leaves, or add a dash of mint syrup.

Cook's tip Granita is a type of Italian sorbet. It is half-frozen and can be served between courses in glass bowls.

SERVES 6
PREPARATION TIME: 25 MINUTES
COOKING TIME: 40 MINUTES

LIQUORICE & OLIVE OIL
GATEAU

Butter for greasing
1 stick liquorice root (available from health food stores)
150 ml (¼ pint) milk
3 whole eggs + 2 yolks
100 g (3½ oz) caster sugar
5 tablespoons olive oil
100 g (3½ oz) plain flour
½ teaspoon salt
3 tablespoons icing sugar

FOR THE SYRUP
150 g (5 oz) sugar
1 tablespoon lemon juice
250 ml (8 fl oz) water

1 Finely grate a little of the liquorice root bark. Reserve a little to use later and add the rest to the milk with the root. Bring almost to boiling point, then remove from the heat. Cover and leave to infuse for about 15 minutes, then discard the root.

2 Preheat the oven to 180°C (350°F) Gas Mark 4. Grease a cake tin 20 cm (8 inches) in diameter.

3 Separate the whole eggs. Whisk the 5 yolks with 100 g (3½ oz) of sugar until the mixture is very pale. Stir in the olive oil and the milk. Sift the flour with the salt, fold into the liquid ingredients and gently mix together.

4 Whisk the egg whites until stiff and fold them into the mixture. Pour the mixture into the tin, put in the oven and bake for 20 minutes, then lower the oven temperature to 150°C (300°F) Gas Mark 2 and bake for a further 20 minutes.

5 Meanwhile boil the sugar, lemon juice and water in a small pan to make a syrup.

6 Remove the cake from the tin, leave to cool, then dredge with icing sugar and the reserved grated liquorice root bark. Serve the cake together with the syrup.

Cook's Tip Liquorice root, especially the bark, has a sweet, distinctive flavour similar to anise or fennel, but stronger.

SERVES 6
PREPARATION TIME: 20 MINUTES
COOKING TIME: 10 MINUTES
CHILLING TIME: MINIMUM 4 HOURS

LIQUORICE **PANNA COTTA**

6 leaves gelatine (12 g/½ oz)
450 ml (¾ pint) single cream
3 tablespoons caster sugar
1 stick liquorice root, broken in half

1 Soften the gelatine in a little cold water. Heat the cream, without letting it boil, with the sugar and half the liquorice root. Stir to dissolve the sugar.

2 Squeeze the gelatine. Remove the cream from the heat and completely dissolve the gelatine in the hot cream. Cover and leave to infuse for 20 minutes. Discard the liquorice root.

3 Grate a little of the remaining liquorice root bark into the cream, divide it between small glasses and leave to set in the refrigerator for at least 4 hours.

SERVES 6
PREPARATION TIME: 15 MINUTES
COOKING TIME: 10 MINUTES
FREEZING TIME: 4 HOURS

ALLSORTS ICE CREAM

4 egg yolks
2 tablespoons caster sugar
2 teaspoons cornflour
300 ml (½ pint) milk
300 g (10 oz) fromage frais
200 g (7 oz) liquorice allsorts

1 To prepare the egg custard: heat the milk. Whisk the egg yolks, sugar and cornflour together in a heatproof bowl. Heat the milk to boiling point and pour onto the egg mixture, stirring constantly until smooth. Return it to the pan over gentle heat, still stirring constantly, until the cream coats the back of the spoon. Pour the cream into a bowl and leave to cool.

2 Mix the fromage frais into the cooled cream. Cut the liquorice allsorts into quarters. Churn the ice cream in an ice-cream maker, or freeze in an ice-cream container, stirring at regular intervals to disperse the crystals. Mix in the allsort bits when the ice cream has begun to set but is still fairly soft.

SERVES 4
PREPARATION TIME: 45 MINUTES
COOKING TIME: 35 MINUTES

LIQUORICE **CREAM SLICES**

1 sheet pre-rolled butter puff pastry
75 g (3 oz) caster sugar
4 tablespoons icing sugar
200 ml (7 fl oz) double cream, chilled

FOR THE CONFECTIONER'S CUSTARD
3 egg yolks
50 g (2 oz) caster sugar
1 stick liquorice root
250 ml (8 fl oz) milk
1 tablespoon flour
1 tablespoon cornflour

1 To prepare the confectioner's custard: whisk the egg yolks and sugar in a heatproof bowl, then add the cornflour and whisk again. Heat the milk with half the liquorice stick to boiling point. Discard the liquorice, then pour a little of the milk onto the egg mixture, whisking constantly and gradually adding the rest. Return the mixture to the pan over medium heat, stirring constantly and scraping the bottom of the pan with the spatula. When it comes to the boil, continue cooking and stirring until it is thick enough to coat the back of the spoon. Transfer to a bowl, cover closely with clingfilm and leave to cool.

2 Preheat the oven to 230°C (450°F) Gas Mark 8. Place the pastry on a baking sheet and sift over the caster sugar. Put it into the oven and lower the temperature to 180°C (350°F) Gas Mark 4. After 10 minutes, place a light baking sheet on the pastry to prevent it from rising too much and bake for a further 8 minutes.

3 Take out the pastry and raise the oven temperature to the maximum. Turn the pastry over between the baking sheets and remove the top sheet. Sift half the icing sugar over the pastry, then replace in the oven for 5–8 minutes to caramelize, being careful not to let it burn. Leave to cool. With a sharp knife, cut the pastry into 4 equal-size pieces.

4 Whip the well-chilled cream and add a little grated liquorice root bark. Beat the confectioner's custard until smooth and mix with the whipped cream. Spread half of this cream on the caramelized side of one piece of pastry, place a second piece on it, and spread with the rest of the cream, then top with the last layer of pastry. Dredge with icing sugar to serve.

MAKES 12
PREPARATION TIME: 15 MINUTES
COOKING TIME: 30 MINUTES

LIQUORICE **MUFFINS**

150 g (5½ oz) ground almonds
150 g (5½ oz) fine semolina
1 stick liquorice root
2 teaspoons baking powder
450 g (1 lb) plain yogurt
2 tablespoons chopped or flaked almonds
150 g (5½ oz) caster sugar
15 g (½ oz) butter + extra for greasing
 3 tablespoons honey
Juice of 1 lemon
300 ml (½ pint) water

1 Preheat the oven to 180°C (350°F) Gas Mark 4. Grease a shallow square baking tin or a 12-cup muffin tin.
2 Mix the ground almonds, the semolina, the finely grated bark of the liquorice root and the baking powder in a bowl. Stir in the yogurts. Pour into the baking tin or muffin tins, filling to three-quarters only as it rises during cooking. Smooth out the top and scatter over the almonds. Put in the oven and bake for 30 minutes.
3 Heat the sugar, butter, honey, lemon juice and water in a small pan, stirring until the sugar has dissolved.
4 Remove the cake from the oven, pierce it all over with a skewer and pour over the syrup. Cut into squares to serve.

36

SERVES 4
PREPARATION TIME: 30 MINUTES
COOKING TIME: 30 MINUTES

LIQUORICE **CHOUX BUNS**

150 g (5 oz) double cream
150 g (5 oz) mascarpone
4 tablespoons icing sugar
1 stick liquorice root

FOR THE CHOUX PASTRY
125 ml (4 fl oz) milk
125 ml (4 fl oz) water
100 g (3½ oz) butter, cut into small pieces,
   + extra for greasing
1 tablespoon caster sugar
1 teaspoon salt
150 g (5 oz) flour
4 eggs

1 Preheat the oven to 200°C (400°F) Gas Mark 6. Grease a baking sheet and line with nonstick baking paper.

2 To make the choux pastry: heat the milk, water, butter, sugar and salt in a pan. Take off the heat just before it boils, put all the flour in and stir vigorously with a spatula. When the flour has all been absorbed, replace the pan on the heat to dry out the dough, stirring until it comes away from the sides of the pan, then transfer to a bowl.

3 Beat the eggs in a separate bowl and gradually add them to the mixture, beating them in with the spatula. It should not be too soft. If the dough looks right (it will gently close up if you run your finger through it), do not add all the egg.

4 Using a piping bag with a nozzle, pipe the choux buns onto the prepared baking sheet. Put in the oven and bake for 10 minutes, then increase the oven temperature to 220°C (425°F) Gas Mark 7 and cook for a further 15–20 minutes. Transfer them to a wire rack to cool.

5 Whip the cream to firm peaks. Stir the mascarpone until smooth then mix with the whipped cream, adding half the sugar and a little of the liquorice root bark, grated on a nutmeg grater.

6 Make a hole in the choux and fill them with the cream, using a piping bag or a spoon, then pile them into a pyramid and sift over the icing sugar, together with a sprinkling of grated liquorice root bark.

MAKES 12
PREPARATION TIME: 45 MINUTES + RESTING TIME
COOKING TIME: 15 MINUTES

CORNES DE GAZELLE (GAZELLE HORNS)

FOR THE PASTRY
100 g (3½ oz) butter
150 g (5 oz) plain flour
1 tablespoon caster sugar

FOR THE FILLING
50 g (2 oz) very soft butter
100 g (3½ oz) icing sugar
150 g (5 oz) ground almonds
3 tablespoons crème fraîche
1 egg, beaten
1 stick liquorice root

TO FINISH
1 egg, beaten
3 tablespoons flaked almonds
Icing sugar

1 To make the pastry: melt the butter, then mix with the flour and sugar. Add 3 tablespoons of cold water. Knead this mixture for a few minutes. It should be firm but quite pliable. Leave to rest at room temperature.

2 To make the filling: mix the very soft butter with the icing sugar, then add the ground almonds, crème fraîche and the beaten egg. Grate in the liquorice root bark with a nutmeg grater.

3 Preheat the oven to 180°C (350°F) Gas Mark 4. Grease a baking sheet. Take half the pastry and roll it out into a long rectangle 10 cm (4 inches) wide, then cut this into squares. Roll out each square a little more, place a spoonful of the filling in one corner and roll it up to the opposite corner, then curve the ends in to form a croissant shape.

4 Repeat the process with the other half of the pastry and arrange the gazelle horns on the prepared baking sheet. Brush them with beaten egg and sprinkle over the flaked almonds. Put in the oven and bake for 15 minutes. Leave to cool before dredging with icing sugar.

SERVES 2
PREPARATION TIME: 10 MINUTES
COOKING TIME: 3 MINUTES
CHILLING TIME: 1–2 HOURS

LIQUORICE **MILKSHAKE**

500 ml (1 pint) milk
1 stick liquorice root
2 scoops fromage frais or yogurt ice cream

1 Heat the milk with half the stick of liquorice root almost to boiling point, then take off the heat, cover and leave to infuse until completely cold.

2 Discard the liquorice root and refrigerate the milk.

3 When the flavoured milk is thoroughly chilled, process it with the ice cream in a blender or food processor.

4 Serve in tall glasses, sprinkled with a little grated liquorice root bark.

SERVES 4
PREPARATION TIME: 15 MINUTES
COOKING TIME: 50 MINUTES

LIQUORICE **FLAN**

1 sheet rich shortcrust pastry
Butter for greasing

FOR THE FILLING
4 eggs
50 g (2 oz) cornflour
200 ml (7 fl oz) milk
200 ml (7 fl oz) crème fraîche
1 stick liquorice root
Salt

1 Preheat the oven to 200°C (400°F) Gas Mark 6. Line a greased flan tin with the pastry, cover the base with a circle of nonstick baking paper and weight with dried beans, and bake for 10 minutes. Remove the paper and beans and set the pastry case aside.

2 Whisk together the eggs, cornflour, milk, crème fraîche, finely grated liquorice root bark and a pinch of salt.

3 Pour this mixture into the pastry case, put in the oven and bake for 40 minutes, until the filling is set and the top is risen and brown.

MAKES 18
PREPARATION TIME: 20 MINUTES
COOKING TIME: 15 MINUTES
CHILLING TIME: 30 MINUTES

LIQUORICE **FINANCIERS**

100 g (3½ oz) butter + extra for greasing
175 g (6 oz) icing sugar
1 stick liquorice root
6 egg whites
70 g (3 oz) ground almonds
70 g (3 oz) plain flour

Classic 'financier' moulds
(trays with small, rectangular indentations)

1 Melt the butter and allow it to brown slightly. Leave aside to cool.

2 Sift the icing sugar into a large bowl, then add the grated bark from the liquorice root and 3 egg whites. Whisk this mixture carefully, then mix in the ground almonds. Whisk in the remaining egg whites and sift in the flour. Gradually pour in the butter, being careful to leave behind any deposit that has formed in the pan. Place in the refrigerator for 30 minutes.

3 Preheat the oven to 220°C (425°F) Gas Mark 7.

4 Grease 18 'financier' moulds with softened butter.

5 Fill each mould to the top, put in the oven and bake for 10 minutes, then lower the temperature to 190°C (375°F) Gas Mark 5 and bake for a further 5 minutes. Take out of the oven and leave for 5 minutes before turning out the financiers onto a wire rack to cool.

Cook's tip Financiers ('gold bars') are delicious little French cakes made with almonds. If you can't get hold of the special financier moulds, use a mini-muffin tin instead.

English translation and adaptation: JMS Books LLP
Layout: cbdesign

First published in France in 2007 under the title
La Boîte à gâteau, by Hachette Livre (Marabout)
Copyright © 2007 Hachette Livre (Marabout)
Editorial: Catherine Berranger and Charlotte Müller-Buch

An Hachette Livre UK Company
www.hachettelivre.co.uk

First published in Great Britain in 2008 by
Hamlyn, a division of Octopus Publishing Group Ltd
2–4 Heron Quays, London E14 4JP
www.octopusbooks.co.uk

ISBN 978 0 600 61876 8

A CIP catalogue record for this book is available from
the British Library

Printed and bound in China

1 3 5 7 9 10 8 6 4 2

This book contains dishes that are made with raw or lightly cooked eggs.
These should be avoided by vulnerable people such as pregnant and
nursing mothers, invalids, the elderly, babies and young children.

PEACH-APRICOT

hamlyn

CONTENTS

SERVES 4
PREPARATION TIME: 30 MINUTES + OVERNIGHT SOAKING IF NECESSARY
COOKING TIME: 45 MINUTES

APRICOT **SOUFFLÉ**

Butter for greasing
2 tablespoons caster sugar for dusting
200 g (7 oz) dried apricots, (soft, ready-to-eat are easiest)
4 tablespoons soft light brown sugar
1 vanilla pod
1 tablespoon rum
1 tablespoon lemon juice
3 egg yolks
5 egg whites
1 tablespoon icing sugar
Cream or vanilla ice cream to serve

1 Put the apricots to soak the previous day. If you use soft dried apricots, you can leave out the soaking, and also Step 4.

2 Preheat the oven to 190°C (375°F) Gas Mark 5. Generously grease a 1-litre (1¾-pint) soufflé dish and dust with sugar.

3 Cut a strip of nonstick baking paper and line the sides of the dish so that it sticks up about 5 cm (2 inches) above the rim, as the soufflé will rise out of the dish.

4 Put the apricots in a pan. Cover with water, bring to the boil, then simmer for 15 minutes.

5 Blend the apricots to a smooth purée. Add the brown sugar, seeds scraped from the vanilla pod, the rum and the lemon juice. Allow to cool, then beat in the 3 egg yolks, one at a time. Beat the 5 egg whites until stiff and fold very carefully into the mixture.

6 Pour into the soufflé dish, put in the oven and bake for 35–40 minutes. Dust with icing sugar and serve immediately, with cream or ice cream.

SERVES 6
PREPARATION TIME: 35 MINUTES
COOKING TIME: 15 MINUTES
CHILLING TIME: MINIMUM 4 HOURS

APRICOT **BAVAROIS**

225 g (7½ oz) extra-soft dried apricots
1 tablespoon lemon juice
6 leaves gelatine (12 g)
450 ml (¾ pint) milk
3 tablespoons dried verbena leaves
  (or 3 sachets verbena tea)
5 eggs, separated
100 g (3½ oz) caster sugar
2 teaspoons cornflour (Maizena, if possible)
150 ml (¼ pint) double/whipping cream

1 Purée the apricots with the lemon juice and just sufficient water to give a thick, smooth purée. Soak the gelatine in a little cold water; squeeze out when ready to use.

2 Heat the milk, add the verbena leaves, remove the pan from the heat, cover and leave to infuse for 10–15 minutes.

3 Beat the egg yolks together with the sugar. Add the cornflour and beat again. Strain the verbena-flavoured milk into the egg mixture (discard the verbena leaves) and mix well, transfer to the pan and cook over very low heat until the mixture thickens.

4 Whisk the egg whites until stiff and fold into the mixture. Set aside to cool.

5 Whip the cream until it holds firm peaks and fold into the mixture. Pour into a large moistened metal mould (a fancy shape if you like) and stand in the refrigerator to set for at least 4 hours. Stand the mould briefly in a little hot water before turning out the cream as this makes the job easier.

Cook's tip Bavarois (Bavarian cream) is a delicate egg custard aerated with whipped cream and set with gelatine.

SERVES 4
PREPARATION TIME: 15 MINUTES
COOKING TIME: ABOUT 1 HOUR

PEACH & APRICOT **CRUMBLE**

1.5 kg (3 lb) apricots and/or peaches
3 tablespoons brown sugar
Peel of 2–3 lemons
150 g (5 oz) plain flour
125 g (4 oz) salted butter, cut in pieces
5 amaretti biscuits (soft Italian almond macaroons)
3 tablespoons flaked almonds

To serve: pouring cream

1 Preheat the oven to 180°C (350°F) Gas Mark 4.

2 Wash the fruits, cut in quarters and put in an ovenproof dish. Sprinkle with a spoonful of the sugar, add the lemon peel and bake for 30 minutes. Smooth the surface of the fruit by pressing with a fork. Discard the lemon peel.

3 Put the flour and butter in a mixing bowl. Rub the butter into the flour with the fingertips to the consistency of coarse breadcrumbs. Mix in the remaining sugar. Crumble the amaretti and add to the mixture.

4 Spread the crumble over the cooked fruit, sprinkle with almonds, put in the oven and bake until the top is golden.

5 Serve either warm or chilled, with cream.

SERVES 6
PREPARATION TIME: 35 MINUTES
COOKING TIME: 35 MINUTES
CHILLING TIME: 1 HOUR

BOURDALOUE

12 ripe apricots, washed, pitted, and cut into quarters
5–6 boudoir biscuits, or sponge fingers

FOR THE PASTRY
200 g (7 oz) plain flour
1 teaspoon salt
100 g (3½ oz) butter, cut into pieces
1 tablespoon caster sugar
1 egg
Vanilla essence

FOR THE ALMOND AND FENNEL CREAM
30 g (1 oz) soft butter, cut into pieces
30 g (1 oz) crème fraîche
3 tablespoons caster sugar
60 g (2¼ oz) ground almonds
1 pinch ground fennel seeds
1 egg

1 To make the pastry: sift the flour and salt into a large bowl. Add the butter and rub with the fingertips to a coarse breadcrumb consistency. Stir in the sugar, then mix in the egg and a few drops of vanilla essence with a palette knife to bring the dough together. Finish the dough by hand (adding a little water if necessary), and form into a rough ball without working too much. Put in a polythene bag or wrap in clingfilm and put in the refrigerator to rest for at least 1 hour.

2 Preheat the oven to 180°C (350°F) Gas Mark 4.

3 Roll out the pastry and line a tart tin about 23 cm (9 inches) in diameter.

4 Crumble the boudoir biscuits and spread over the base of the tart (they will absorb the juice from the fruit so the pastry does not go soggy).

5 For the filling: mash the butter with a spatula. Add the crème fraîche, sugar, ground almonds and fennel, and mix in the egg.

6 Spread over the tart base. Arrange the apricot quarters on top of the cream. Put in the oven and bake for about 35 minutes.

Cook's tip This dessert is a variation of Bourdaloue, created by a pastry chef who had an establishment on Rue Bourdaloue in Paris.

SERVES 6
PREPARATION TIME: 30 MINUTES
COOKING TIME: 1¼ HOURS

APRICOT **MERINGUE CAKE**

1 kg (2 lb) apricots, washed and pitted
150 g (5 oz) soft butter + extra for greasing
250 g (8 oz) caster sugar
4 eggs, separated
100 g (3½ oz) ground almonds
300 g (10 oz) plain flour, sifted

1 Preheat the oven to 190°C (375°F) Gas Mark 5. Grease an ovenproof dish and also a tart tin 23 cm (9 inches) in diameter.

2 Put the apricots in the ovenproof dish and bake for 30 minutes. Remove the skins.

3 In a mixing bowl, beat together the butter and half the sugar. Add the egg yolks, then the almonds and finally the flour. Press this dough into the tart tin, put in the oven and bake for about 30 minutes.

4 Turn up the oven temperature to 220°C (425°F) Gas Mark 7.

5 Purée the apricots with half the remaining sugar. Whisk the egg whites until stiff, add the remaining sugar and whisk again.

6 Cover the base of the cake with apricot purée, leaving a 2-cm (½-inch) rim. Cover the the fruit and the rim with the meringue to make a seal. Draw a pattern with a spoon. Bake for 15–20 minutes. The meringue should be golden brown in places.

SERVES 4
PREPARATION TIME: 25 MINUTES
COOKING TIME: 1¼ HOURS

PEACH **PIE**

10 peaches, washed and pitted
Rosewater or vanilla essence
2 sheets all butter puff pastry
1 egg, beaten
2 tablespoons caster sugar
Crème fraîche or whipped cream for serving

1 Preheat the oven to 200°C (400°F) Gas Mark 6. Line a baking sheet with nonstick baking paper.

2 Cut the peaches in quarters, put in an ovenproof dish with 1 tablepoon of the sugar and bake for 30 minutes. Remove the skins and crush to a compote. Flavour with a little rosewater or vanilla essence.

3 Unroll one sheet of pastry onto the lined baking sheet. With a sharp knife, score a line all the way round, 5 mm (2 inches) from the edge. Spread the compote in the middle. Brush the edge with a little water and cover with the second sheet of pastry, pressing down well to seal the edges.

4 Using your thumb, mark all the way round with regular indentations. Make a cut in the centre of the pie to allow the steam to escape. Design a 'rose' on the top with a pointed knife. Brush with beaten egg, sprinkle with the remaining sugar, put in the oven and bake for about 40 minutes.

5 Serve warm or cold with crème fraîche or whipped cream.

SERVES 6
PREPARATION TIME: 30 MINUTES
COOKING TIME: 40 MINUTES

CHOCOLATE TART
WITH A HINT OF APRICOT

A little butter for greasing
1 roll butter shortcrust pastry
200 g (7 oz) dark chocolate
150 ml (¼ pint) single cream
150 ml (¼ pint) milk
2 eggs
4–5 tablespoons apricot jam

1 Preheat the oven to 180°C (350°F) Gas Mark 4. Grease a tart tin 20–23 cm (8–9 inches) in diameter.

2 Spread the pastry over the tart tin. Cover the pastry base with a piece of nonstick baking paper and fill with beans. Put in the oven and bake for 20 minutes, remove the beans and paper, and bake for a further 5 minutes. Remove from the oven but do not turn off the heat.

3 Chop the chocolate. In a pan, bring the milk and cream to the boil, remove from the heat and add the chocolate. Melt, stir until smooth, then beat in the eggs

4 Gently heat the apricot jam and spread it over the tart base. Pour in the chocolate filling, return the tart to the oven, and bake for 15 minutes. Allow to cool before serving.

SERVES 4
PREPARATION TIME: 15 MINUTES
COOKING TIME: 15 MINUTES
FREEZING TIME: 6 HOURS

SEMIFREDDO

500 g (1 lb) well-ripened apricots and/or peaches
75 g (3 oz) hard Spanish nougat (turrón duro, or Italian torrone)
150 ml (¼ pint) milk
1 vanilla pod
2 egg yolks
2 tablespoons caster sugar
100 ml (3½ fl oz) double or whipping cream

1 Skin and pit the peaches, pit the apricots and dice the flesh. Purée half the fruit.

2 Chop or crush the nougat as fine as possible, almost to a powder.

3 Heat the milk with the split vanilla pod. In a bowl, beat together the egg yolks and sugar. When the milk is about to boil, pour it over the egg mixture, stirring constantly. Pour back into the pan and cook over low heat, stirring constantly, until the cream thickens and coats the back of the spoon. Pour into a clean container and add the powdered nougat to the cream while still hot. Allow to cool before adding the fruit purée. Whip the chilled cream until it holds firm peaks and fold in.

4 Freeze this mixture in an ice-cream maker then add the diced fruit. Alternatively, instead of freezing in an ice-cream maker, pour into a smoothly lined rectangular box and put in the freezer for at least 6 hours.

5 Take out of the freezer 15–20 minutes before serving.

6 Serve cut in slices, perhaps with a fruit coulis.

Cook's tip Semifreddo is a soft iced dessert with a texture halfway between mousse and ice cream.

SERVES 6
PREPARATION TIME: 10 MINUTES
COOKING TIME: 15 MINUTES

PEACHES IN OLIVE OIL
WITH SHORTBREAD

6 small peaches
6 rich, buttery shortbread biscuits (palets bretons, if possible)
1 tablespoon olive oil
3 tablespoons white sugar
4 tablespoons mascarpone
1 tablespoon brown sugar

1 Peel the peaches. Keep whole for preference.

2 Put 400 ml (14 fl oz) of water and the white sugar in a deep frying pan. Bring to the boil, stirring to dissolve the sugar, then simmer and add the peaches to the pan. Poach for 10–15 minutes, turning once. They should be tender, but not mushy. Take them out of the pan, turn up the heat and reduce the liquid to a fairly thick syrup but not too caramelized. Allow the peaches to cool.

3 To serve, place a shortbread biscuit on each small plate. Drizzle with syrup and spread with a little mascarpone. Put a peach on top, drizzle with olive oil and sprinkle with a little brown sugar. Keep the peaches whole if they are not too big, but they are easier to eat if cut in half and pitted. As you please!

SERVES 4
PREPARATION TIME: 15 MINUTES

STRAWBERRY & PEACH **JUICE**

500 g (1 lb) ripe (but not overripe) strawberries
4 ripe white peaches
Small piece of fresh ginger, peeled
Ice cubes
Lemon juice
Sugar

1 Wash and hull the strawberries. Peel and pit the peaches. Grate the ginger.
2 Purée the strawberries with the peach flesh and ice cubes. Add a little lemon juice, a very little ginger, and sugar only if necessary.

SERVES 4
PREPARATION TIME: 20 MINUTES
COOKING TIME: 55 MINUTES
FREEZING TIME: 30 MINUTES

ICED SPONGE WITH PEACHES

Butter for greasing
6 peaches
120 g (4 oz) caster sugar + 1 tablespoon for the fruit
4 eggs, separated
Vanilla essence
1 teaspoon baking powder
120 g (4 oz) plain flour + a little for greasing
250 ml (8 fl oz) vanilla ice cream

1 Preheat the oven to 180°C (350°F) Gas Mark 4. Grease and flour 2 cake tins 18–20 cm (7–8 inches) in diameter.

2 Wash and pit the peaches, then cut in six. Put them in an ovenproof dish and sprinkle with the tablespoon of sugar. Put in the oven and bake for about 35–40 minutes, until they have released their juices. Leave to cool and put in the refrigerator.

3 In a bowl, beat together the egg yolks and sugar. The mixture should become very light and frothy. Add a few drops of vanilla essence.

4 Sift the flour and baking powder together in a bowl and mix into the beaten eggs with a metal spoon or a whisk. Beat the egg whites until stiff and fold them in. Pour into the cake tins, put in the oven and bake for about 20 minutes. After 15 minutes, reduce the oven temperature to 160°C (325°F) Gas Mark 3 for the last 5 minutes. Turn out and cool on a wire rack.

5 To assemble the cake, the ice cream must be a bit soft: take it out of the freezer and put in the refrigerator 30 minutes beforehand.

6 Drizzle one of the sponges with the juice from the peaches and spread with a layer of ice cream, then a layer of peaches. Cover with the second sponge and drizzle with the remaining peach juice. Place in the freezer for 20–30 minutes to firm up and make the cake easy to cut. Make sure you don't forget it (set a timer)! Take out and serve immediately.

SERVES 4
PREPARATION TIME: 20 MINUTES
COOKING TIME: 30 MINUTES

PEACH & APRICOT
BREAD & BUTTER PUDDING

8 slices stale white bread
Butter for spreading + extra for greasing
5–6 apricots or 3 peaches (or a mixture of the two),
   pitted and quartered
Small strips of zest from 1 lemon,
   pared carefully to avoid any pith
150 ml (¼ pint) milk
150 ml (¼ pint) single cream
2 eggs
4 tablespoons caster sugar

1 Preheat the oven to 190°C (375°F) Gas Mark 5. Grease a medium-size ovenproof dish.

2 Spread the bread with butter. Cut the slices in half, in triangles if they are square. Arrange the slices as near vertical as possible in the ovenproof dish. Insert pieces of apricot or peach and the lemon zest between the slices.

3 Beat together the milk, cream and eggs. Pour over the bread and sprinkle with sugar.

4 Put in the oven and bake for about 30 minutes, long enough for the custard to set and the top to turn golden.

SERVES 4
PREPARATION TIME: 40 MINUTES
COOKING TIME: 45 MINUTES
CHILLING TIME: MINIMUM 4 HOURS

PEACH **CHARLOTTE**

1.5 kg (3 lb) peaches
4 tablespoons granulated sugar
5 leaves gelatine
500 ml (17 fl oz) milk
1 vanilla pod
4 egg yolks
About 30 boudoir biscuits, or sponge fingers
200 ml (7 fl oz) double/whipping cream
Peach syrup

1 Preheat the oven to 190°C (375°F) Gas Mark 5. Wash and pit the peaches and cut in six. Reserve one or two peaches for serving. Put the peaches in an ovenproof dish, sprinkle with a tablespoon of the sugar, put in the oven and bake for 35 minutes. Lift out with a slotted spoon and drain, reserving the cooking syrup.

2 Soak the gelatine in cold water: squeeze out when ready to use. In a pan, heat the milk with the split vanilla pod. Beat together the egg yolks and the remaining sugar in a heatproof bowl, then pour over the boiling milk, stirring constantly. Return the mixture to the pan, and cook over low heat, stirring constantly until the custard thickens. Completely dissolve the softened gelatine in the hot custard, then set aside to cool.

3 Whip the cream until it holds firm peaks. Mix the cold custard into the whipped cream.

4 Line a charlotte mould with a layer of boudoir biscuits briefly soaked in the diluted syrup. Pour in half the custard cream, add a layer of peach slices, a second layer of boudoir biscuits, more custard cream, more peaches and finish with a layer of boudoir biscuits to give the charlotte some firmness. Cover and put to set in the refrigerator for at least 4 hours.

5 Turn out and serve with the reserved peaches, cut in slices.

SERVES 6
PREPARATION TIME: 25 MINUTES
COOKING TIME: 40 MINUTES

BOMBE MELBA

6 peaches
100 g (3½ oz) caster sugar
1 punnet raspberries
½ litre (17 fl oz) good quality vanilla ice cream
3 egg whites
1 bought sponge base 20 cm (8 inches) in diameter
Grenadine (or pomegranate syrup)

1 Preheat the oven to 190°C (375°F) Gas Mark 5.

2 Wash and pit the peaches and cut in six. Put in an ovenproof dish, sprinkle with a tablespoon of the sugar and bake for 35 minutes. Set aside to cool.

3 The remaining preparations should be done at the last minute.

4 Preheat the oven to 230°C (450°F) Gas Mark 8. Crush the raspberries with a fork. Take the ice cream out of the freezer. Beat the egg whites until stiff, add the remaining sugar and beat again.

5 Put the sponge base on a heatproof serving dish. Drizzle, to taste, with grenadine or the lighter pomegranate syrup. Cover with peaches and raspberries, leaving a 2-cm (½-inch) rim. Spoon the slightly melted ice cream onto the fruit and shape into a dome.

6 Spread the meringue to cover the ice cream and the rim, to make a seal. Bake in the very hot oven for about 3 minutes, just long enough for the meringue to turn golden in places. Serve immediately.

SERVES 6
PREPARATION TIME: 30 MINUTES + RESTING TIME
COOKING TIME: 45 MINUTES

PEACH **TARTE TATIN**

FOR THE TOPPING
4 peaches + 5 apricots
50 g (2 oz) butter
3 tablespoons caster sugar

FOR THE PASTRY
120 g (4 oz) butter, cut into pieces
200 g (8 oz) plain flour
2 tablespoons caster sugar
1 egg

1 To make the pastry: sift the flour into a large bowl, add the butter and rub in with your fingertips to the consistency of coarse breadcrumbs. Stir in the sugar and mix in the egg using a palette knife. Add a little cold water if necessary and form the dough into a ball by hand, without working it too much. Put in the refrigerator to rest for at least 1 hour.

2 Preheat the oven to 190°C (375°F) Gas Mark 5. Wash and pit the peaches and apricots, cut in two.

3 Put the butter and sugar in a cake tin 23–25 cm (9–10 inches) in diameter, or a tatin tin if you have one. You could also use a deep frying pan, as long as it is all metal and can go in the oven. Place directly over low heat and melt the butter and sugar, until a golden caramel forms.

4 Remove from the heat and add the fruit to the caramel. Roll out the dough and cover the fruit with it, tucking the edges down between the fruit and the sides of the tin. Bake for about 45 minutes, until the pastry is golden.

5 Take the tart out of the oven, allow to rest in the tin for 10 minutes, then turn upside down onto a serving plate.

SERVES 6
PREPARATION TIME: 30 MINUTES
COOKING TIME: 1¼ HOURS

PEACH & APRICOT **CREAMS**

600 ml (1 pint) double cream
1 vanilla pod
6 egg yolks
200 g (7 oz) caster sugar
Butter for greasing
2 ripe peaches
3 ripe apricots

1 Preheat the oven to 150°C (300°F) Gas Mark 2. Stand 6 individual ramekins in a roasting tin.

2 Heat the cream together with the split vanilla pod and the seeds scraped from it. In a bowl mix the egg yolks with 50 g (2 oz) of the sugar. Add the cream when almost boiling, stirring constantly. Pour into the ramekins, and put the tin in the oven; pull out the shelf slightly and pour in hot water to halfway up the ramekins. Cover the tin with foil and cook for 1 hour. The creams should be just set. Take the ramekins out of the tin, allow to cool, then put in the refrigerator..

3 Grease a metal mould. Put 100 g (3½ oz) of the sugar and 200 ml (7 fl oz) of water in a pan. Cook until a golden caramel forms. Pour into the mould. Leave the caramel to set, then detach it and break into small pieces.

4 Wash the fruit, peel the peaches, and slice both peaches and apricots very thinly.

5 Preheat the grill. Arrange the sliced fruit on top of the cold creams. Flatten and sprinkle with the remaining sugar. Put them under the grill for just long enough for the sugar to melt and bubble. Set aside to cool.

6 Serve the creams cold, sprinkled with the pieces of caramel.

SERVES 4
PREPARATION TIME: 15 MINUTES
COOKING TIME: 15 MINUTES

APRICOT CREAM **MACAROONS**

6–8 apricots
4 tablespoons sugar
½ lemon or 1 stem citronella (optional)
200 g (7 oz) mascarpone

FOR THE MACAROONS
300 g (10 oz) icing sugar
180 g (6½ oz) ground almonds
5 egg whites
30 g (1 oz) caster sugar

1 Preheat the oven to 180°C (350°F) Gas Mark 4 (use the fan if possible). Line a baking sheet with nonstick baking paper.

2 To make the macaroons: sift together the icing sugar and ground almonds three times. Beat the egg whites until stiff, add the sugar and beat again. Fold the egg whites into the sugar and almond mixture. The mixture should collapse a little. Form round macaroons on the baking sheet using a piping bag or a spoon. It doesn't matter if they are irregular in shape. Put in the oven, reducing the temperature immediately to 140°C (275°F) Gas Mark 1, and bake for about 10 minutes until a crust forms on top, which should be quite solid. Remove from the oven, detach from the baking sheet, and put to cool on a wire rack.

3 Wash and pit the apricots and cut in half. Crush the citronella stem or peel the half lemon. In a pan or a frying pan, heat 400 ml (14 fl oz) of water, 3 tablespoons of the sugar and the lemon or citronella peel. Stir until the sugar dissolves. Add the apricot halves to the simmering syrup. Poach for 6–7 minutes, until the apricots are tender. Remove the apricots and turn up the heat to reduce the liquid to a syrup. Purée the apricots and mix with the mascarpone and the remaining sugar. Drizzle the macaroons with syrup and assemble in pairs with the apricot cream.

SERVES 4
PREPARATION TIME: 30 MINUTES
COOKING TIME: 1 HOUR
RESTING TIME: 1 HOUR

PEACH & APRICOT **CLAFOUTIS**

3 peaches + 4 apricots
25 g (1 oz) butter
90 g (3¼ oz) caster sugar
4 eggs
50 g (2 oz) cornflour, Maizena if possible
200 ml (7 fl oz) milk
200 ml (7 fl oz) heavy cream
Salt

FOR THE PASTRY
200 g (7 oz) plain flour
100 g (3½ oz) butter from the freezer + extra for greasing

1 To make the pastry: sift the flour with a pinch of salt into a mixing bowl, take the butter out of the freezer and grate into the flour using a grater with big holes. Add 4 tablespoons of cold water and mix the dough with a palette knife using 'cutting' movements. Add more water if necessary. Form a ball and put in the refrigerator to rest for 1 hour.

2 Preheat the oven to 200°C (400°F) Gas Mark 6. Line a greased baking tin with the dough, cover with a sheet of nonstick baking paper and fill with beans. Precook the tart base for 10 minutes. Take out of the oven and remove the paper and beans.

3 Peel and pit the peaches and apricots and cut in quarters. Melt the butter in a frying pan. When it has melted, skim off any foam that has formed on the surface with a spoon. Put in the peach and apricot quarters, fry on one side until golden, turn, sprinkle with 2 spoonfuls of the sugar and brown on the other side until the sugar begins to caramelize.

4 Beat together the eggs, cornflour, milk, cream, a pinch of salt and the remaining sugar.

5 Re-heat the oven to 200°C (400°F) Gas Mark 6. Spoon the fruit onto the tart base and pour over the custard-cream. Bake for 40 minutes. The custard-cream should be set and have risen and turned golden.

SERVES 6
PREPARATION TIME: 35 MINUTES
COOKING TIME: 1¼ HOURS

APRICOT & CHOCOLATE
CAKE

250 g (8 oz) soft butter + extra for greasing
250 g (8 oz) soft light brown sugar
4 eggs
1 cup very strong espresso coffee (optional)
250 g (8 oz) plain flour + extra for dusting the cake tin
2 teaspoons baking powder
200 g (7 oz) milk chocolate, chopped
200 g (7 oz) soft dried apricots, chopped

1 Preheat the oven to 180°C (350°F) Gas Mark 4. Grease and flour a 1-litre (1¾-pint) capacity loaf tin, or line with nonstick baking paper.

2 Beat together the butter and sugar until the mixture becomes very fluffy (easiest with an electric beater). Add the eggs one at a time while continuing to beat, then add the coffee, according to taste, and mix well.

3 Sift the flour and baking powder into a bowl and fold carefully into the butter-sugar-egg mixture with a large metal spoon, 'cutting' the mixture. Add the chocolate and the apricots (reserving a little chocolate to put on top of the cake). Mix just enough to blend in.

4 Pour into the loaf tin. Put the remaining chocolate on top, in the centre. Bake for about 1¼ hours. To test if it is done, Insert a metal skewer into the centre of the cake. It should come out clean.

5 Set aside to rest for 15 minutes before turning out. Eat warm or cold.

SERVES 4
PREPARATION TIME: 30 MINUTES
COOKING TIME: 15 MINUTES

APRICOT **FOOL**

About 10 apricots
4 tablespoons caster sugar
Few dried verbena leaves
200 ml (7 fl oz) double cream
400 g (13 oz) fromage frais, well drained

1 Wash and pit the apricots and cut in half. Pour 400 ml (14 fl oz) of water into a pan or a deep frying pan, then add 3 tablespoons of the sugar and the verbena leaves. Heat, stirring until the sugar dissolves. Add the apricot halves to this simmering syrup. Poach for 10 minutes, until the apricots are very tender.

2 Remove the apricots with a slotted spoon, discard the verbena leaves, and turn up the heat to reduce the liquid to a syrup. Purée the apricots with the syrup. Whip the chilled cream with the remaining sugar and fold into the fromage frais and apricot purée, without mixing too much. Pour into glasses, refrigerate and serve as soon as possible, perhaps with hazelnut shortbread.

English translation and adaptation: JMS Books LLP
Layout: cbdesign

First published in France in 2007 under the title
La Boîte à gâteau, by Hachette Livre (Marabout)
Copyright © 2007 Hachette Livre (Marabout)
Editorial: Catherine Berranger and Charlotte Müller-Buch

An Hachette Livre UK Company
www.hachettelivre.co.uk

First published in Great Britain in 2008 by
Hamlyn, a division of Octopus Publishing Group Ltd
2–4 Heron Quays, London E14 4JP
www.octopusbooks.co.uk

ISBN 978 0 600 61876 8

A CIP catalogue record for this book is available from
the British Library

Printed and bound in China

1 3 5 7 9 10 8 6 4 2

This book contains dishes that are made with raw or lightly cooked eggs.
These should be avoided by vulnerable people such as pregnant and
nursing mothers, invalids, the elderly, babies and young children.

COFFEE
VANILLA

hamlyn

CONTENTS

SERVES 4
PREPARATION TIME: 25 MINUTES
COOKING TIME: 40 MINUTES

COFFEE **CAKE**

175 g (6 oz) plain flour
1 teaspoon baking powder
150 g (5 oz) soft butter + extra for greasing
100 g (3½ oz) caster sugar
3 eggs
2 tablespoons strong coffee
100 g (3½ oz) Brazil nuts, chopped
Salt

FOR THE ICING
200 g (7 oz) icing sugar
120 g (4 oz) soft butter
1 teaspoon very strong coffee
Coffee essence

1 Preheat the oven to 180°C (350°F) Gas Mark 4. Grease 2 cake tins 18–20 cm (7–8 inches) in diameter (If you only have one tin, you can cut the cake in two horizontally).

2 Sift together the flour, baking powder and a pinch of salt. Beat together the butter and sugar until the mixture is very fluffy (easier with a food processor or electric beater). Gradually add the eggs, beating well, then carefully fold in the flour. Lastly add the coffee and three-quarters of the nuts (reserve the remainder for decoration). Spoon the mixture into the cake tins, put in the oven and bake for 35–40 minutes. Turn out and leave to cool on a wire rack.

3 Beat together 175 g (6 oz) of the icing sugar, the butter, coffee and a few drops of coffee essence to taste. Add more sugar if the mixture seems too soft. Spread over one of the cakes, reserving a little for the topping

4 Place the second cake on top of the first. Make a circle of icing in the centre of the cake and decorate with the remaining nuts. You can make a double quantity of icing and cover the top and sides of the cake as well, which makes it look richer!

SERVES 6
PREPARATION TIME: 20 MINUTES
CHILLING: MINIMUM OF 4 HOURS

COFFEE-CHOCOLATE
MOCK NOUGAT

200 g (7 oz) petit-beurre biscuits
200 g (7 oz) soft butter + extra for greasing
200 g (7 oz) cocoa powder
200 g (7 oz) ground almonds
100 g (3½ oz) granulated sugar
2 tablespoons very strong coffee
1 egg

1 Grease a 1-litre/2-lb loaf tin.

2 Break the biscuits in coarse pieces. Mix the butter with the cocoa and add the ground almonds.

3 Put the sugar in a small pan with 3 tablespoons of water and dissolve over low heat. Remove from the heat and add the butter-almond-cocoa mixture, then the egg and the coffee. Fold in the pieces of biscuit very carefully.

4 Pour the mixture into the loaf tin. Smooth over and cover with foil. Place in the refrigerator to set, all night if possible. Turn out and serve cut in very thin slices.

SERVES 4–6
PREPARATION TIME: 45 MINUTES
COOKING TIME: 30 MINUTES

COFFEE **PROFITEROLES**

FOR THE CHOUX PASTRY
150 ml (¼ pint) water
50 g (2 oz) butter, cut into small pieces,
    + extra for greasing
½ teaspoon salt
65 g (2½ oz) plain flour
2 eggs

FOR THE CHOCOLATE-COFFEE SAUCE
100 g (3½ oz) dark chocolate
3 tablespoons icing sugar
25 g (1 oz) butter
2 tablespoons very strong coffee

FOR THE FILLING
150 ml (¼ pint) double cream
2 tablespoons caster sugar
100 g (3½ oz) mascarpone
2 tablespoons very strong coffee

1 Preheat the oven to 200°C (400°F) Gas Mark 6. Grease a baking sheet or cover it with nonstick baking paper. To make the choux pastry: in a pan, heat the water, butter and salt. Remove from the heat just before it boils. Add all the flour at once and mix vigorously with a spatula. As soon as the flour has been thoroughly mixed in, put the pan back on the heat to dry out the mixture. Stir until the dough comes away from the sides of the pan. Transfer to a large bowl. Beat the eggs in another bowl, then gradually add them to the dough, 'cutting' it with a spatula. It should not be too soft. If the dough looks right (it will gently close up if you run your finger through it), do not add all the egg.

2 Using a piping bag (small nozzle), form 20–24 little balls of choux pastry spaced well apart on the baking sheet. Bake for 10 minutes, then increase the oven temperature to 220°C (425°F) Gas Mark 7 and cook for a further 15–20 minutes. Remove the choux balls from the oven and put them on a wire rack to cool completely. Make a slit in each one.

3 To make the sauce: put the ingredients in a heatproof bowl, then place it on top of a pan of hot water, off the heat. Melt and stir until smooth.

4 Whip the cream with the sugar. Beat the mascarpone with a wooden spoon until smooth, mixing in the coffee at the same time. Fold the mascarpone into the whipped cream. Fill the choux balls with this mixture, using a small piping bag. Pile the profiteroles on small plates (3–6 on each) or on one large plate, pour over the sauce and serve immediately. The sauce may be replaced with a caramel.

SERVES 4
PREPARATION TIME: 15 MINUTES
COOKING TIME: 15 MINUTES
REFRIGERATION TIME: MINIMUM 4 HOURS

MACAROONS
WITH COFFEE ICE CREAM

75 ml (3 fl oz) double cream or 4 tablespoons mascarpone
1 cup strong cold coffee + extra Amaretto (optional)

FOR THE ICE CREAM
500 ml (17 fl oz) milk
2 tablespoons coffee granules/powder
3 tablespoons barley malt syrup
4 egg yolks
75 g (3 fl oz) caster sugar

FOR THE MACAROONS
300 g (10 oz) icing sugar
180 g (6 oz) ground almonds
5 egg whites
30 g (1 oz) caster sugar
Coffee essence

1 To make the ice cream: heat the milk with the coffee granules/powder and the syrup, beat together the egg yolks and sugar, pour the milk over the mixture, stirring constantly, then pour it all back into the pan and stir constantly until the custard coats the back of the spoon. Transfer to an ice-cream maker to set.

2 Preheat the oven to 180°C (350°F) Gas Mark 4 (open the vent or use the fan, if available). Line a baking sheet with nonstick baking paper.

3 To make the macaroons: sift together the icing sugar and ground almonds three times. Beat the egg whites until stiff, add the caster sugar and a few drops of coffee essence and beat again. Fold the egg whites into the sugar and almond mixture. The mixture should collapse a little.

4 Form the macaroon mixture into rounds (about 6 cm/ 2½ inches in diameter), with a piping bag or a spoon. It doesn't matter if they are irregular in shape. Put in the oven (ideally on double baking sheets so that the bottom doesn't cook too much) and turn down the heat immediately to 150°C (300°F) Gas Mark 2. Bake for about 10 minutes. A crust should form on top, which should not be completely firm. Unstick the macaroons and put them to cool on a wire rack.

5 Whip the double cream. Soak each macaroon in cold coffee and serve with a little mascarpone or whipped cream and a scoop of ice cream.

14

SERVES 4
PREPARATION TIME: 10 MINUTES
REFRIGERATION: SEVERAL HOURS

COFFEE **GRANITA**

500 ml (17 fl oz) very strong hot coffee (about 4 good cups)
60 g (2¼ oz) caster sugar
100 ml (3½ fl oz) double cream for serving
2 tablespoons barley malt syrup

1 Dissolve the sugar in the coffee, allow to cool and put in a fairly shallow freezerproof box. Put in the freezer compartment or freezer for 1–3 hours.
2 When the mixture begins to freeze at the edges, take it out and beat briskly with a fork.
3 Return to the freezer and repeat after 1–3 hours.
4 Serve the coffee crystals in small glasses, with the barley syrup and a little chilled whipped cream on top.

Cook's tip Granita is a type of Italian sorbet. It is half-frozen and can be served between courses in glass bowls.

SERVES 4
PREPARATION TIME: 20 MINUTES
CHILLING TIME: MINIMUM 4 HOURS

LIGHT & FLUFFY
COFFEE CHEESECAKE

150 g (5 oz) sablé biscuits
50 g (2 oz) butter
3 leaves gelatine
250 g (8 oz) fromage frais
50 g (2 oz) caster sugar
200 ml (7 fl oz) single or double cream
2 tablespoons coffee granules/powder
2 egg whites

To decorate: chocolate covered coffee beans
or chocolate shavings

1 Crush the biscuits coarsely (in a food processor or put them in a polythene bag and crush with a rolling pin). Melt the butter and mix with the biscuit crumbs. Fill small individual moulds with the mixture.

2 Soak the gelatine in a little cold water and squeeze out when ready to use. Mix together the fromage frais and sugar. Heat half the cream, dissolve the coffee in it, then the drained gelatine (ensure it is completely dissolved). Mix with the fromage frais and add the remaining cream.

3 Beat the egg whites until stiff and fold into the mixture. Pour over the biscuit bases and put to set in the refrigerator for at least 4 hours (all night if possible).

4 Serve in the ramekins or turn out onto a plate (after running the blade of a knife between the cakes and the moulds), then turn them the right way up on another serving dish. Decorate with coffee beans or chocolate shavings.

SERVES 6
PREPARATION TIME: 40 MINUTES + RESTING
COOKING TIME: 10 MINUTES

CANNOLI
WITH COFFEE CREAM FILLING

FOR THE DOUGH
250 g (8 oz) plain flour + extra for dusting
50 g (2 oz) unsalted butter, cut into pieces
Salt
Oil for frying + 1 tablespoon for greasing the sticks

FOR THE FILLING
1 tablespoon coffee granules/powder
  (or more, if you like it stronger)
60 ml (2½ fl oz) milk
300 g (10 oz) ricotta
3 tablespoons caster sugar
Amaretto or coffee liqueur
50 g (2 oz) roasted almonds or hazelnuts, chopped
Cocoa powder

1 For this recipe you need cannoli moulds or improvise with small sticks about 12 cm (5 inches) long and 2.5 cm (1 inch) in diameter. (You can buy bamboo canes from a garden centre and cut them to the required size.)

2 Make the dough first. Sift the flour and a pinch of salt into a bowl and make a well. Add the butter and rub in with your fingertips, then add sufficient water (start with 4 tablespoons) to form a dough. Roll it into a ball, wrap in clingfilm and refrigerate for at least 2 hours (if possible overnight).

3 To make the cannoli: on a lightly floured work surface, roll out the dough quite thin (no more than 2 mm/⅛ inch thick). With a pastry cutter or a lightly floured glass, cut circles 6–7 cm (2½–3 inches) in diameter. Wash and oil the cannoli moulds/sticks and roll the circles of dough round them. Seal the edges tight by moistening the dough with a little water and pressing firmly.

4 Heat oil in a deep fryer to 180°C (350°F). Plunge the sticks into the oil (not too many at a time). Allow them to turn slightly golden and rise to the surface, then drain and lay them on pieces of kitchen paper. Carefully remove the mould/stick.

5 To make the cream: dissolve the coffee in hot water to your preferred strength. Mix with the ricotta, sugar, liqueur (amaretto or coffee) to taste, and the chopped almonds or hazelnuts.

6 Fill the cannoli with this cream (using a small spoon or a piping bag). Dust very lightly with cocoa and serve.

SERVES 6
PREPARATION TIME: 25 MINUTES
CHILLING TIME: 4 HOURS TOTAL

ALMOND PASTE
& COFFEE TIMBALES

Icing sugar for dusting
250 g (8 oz) almond paste
1 sponge base
2 tablespoons Amaretto or Marsala
1 cup very strong espresso
300 g (10 oz) fromage frais
100 g (3½ oz) mascarpone
1 tablespoon coffee granules/powder
1 vanilla pod
3 tablespoons caster sugar
Cocoa powder

1 Roll out the almond paste on a work surface dusted with icing sugar. Dust the inside of 6 small moulds or ramekins with icing sugar. Cut circles of almond paste the diameter of the moulds, and strips the height of the moulds. Cover the base and sides of the moulds with the almond paste. Cut circles for the tops and set aside

2 Cut circles of sponge the diameter of the moulds and lay them on the almond paste bases. Soak the sponge with the mixture of alcohol and coffee.

3 Beat together the fromage frais and the mascarpone. Add the coffee granules/powder, vanilla seeds scraped from the pod with the tip of a sharp knife and the caster sugar.

4 Fill the moulds with this mixture and cover with the almond paste lids. Stand in the refrigerator for 1 hour, then turn out onto a large serving dish or small dessert plates. Return to the refrigerator for 2–3 hours. Dust with cocoa and serve.

SERVES 6
PREPARATION TIME: 35 MINUTES
COOKING TIME: 1¼ HOURS

COFFEE, CHOCOLATE
& ALMOND **POUND CAKE**

250 g (8 oz) soft butter + extra for greasing
250 g (8 oz) brown sugar
4 eggs
1 cup very strong espresso coffee
250 g (8 oz) plain flour + extra for dusting
2 teaspoons baking powder
200 g (7 oz) dark chocolate, chopped
150 g (5 oz) whole roasted almonds, roughly chopped

1 Preheat the oven to 180°C (350°F) Gas Mark 4. Grease and flour a 1-litre/2-lb loaf tin or line with nonstick baking paper.

2 Beat together the butter and sugar until the mixture becomes very fluffy (it's easier with an electric whisk). Beat in the eggs one at a time. Mix in the coffee.

3 Sift the flour and baking powder together into a bowl. Using a large metal spoon, carefully blend into the butter-sugar-egg mixture, 'cutting' the dough.

4 Add the chocolate (reserving a little for the top of the cake) and the almonds. Do not over-mix.

5 Tip the dough into the loaf tin and put the remaining chocolate on top in the centre. Bake for about 75 minutes. Test by inserting a metal skewer into the cake. It should come out clean. Leave to rest for 15 minutes and turn out onto a wire rack to cool. Eat warm or cold.

SERVES 6
PREPARATION TIME: 45 MINUTES + RESTING TIME
COOKING TIME: 30 MINUTES

COFFEE CREAM **BABAS**

FOR THE CONFECTIONER'S CUSTARD
500 ml (17 fl oz) milk
1 cup very strong espresso coffee
5 egg yolks
100 g (3½ oz) caster sugar
2 tablespoons plain flour
2 tablespoons cornflour (Maizena if possible)
Coffee essence (optional)

FOR THE BABA DOUGH
60 ml (2½ fl oz) milk
1½ teaspoons dried yeast
1 tablespoon sugar
150 g (5 oz) plain flour
1 egg
80 g (3 oz) butter, fairly soft

FOR THE SYRUP
60 ml (3½ fl oz) water
100 g (3½ oz) caster sugar
1 cup very strong espresso
Coffee liqueur (optional)

1 To make the confectioner's custard: heat the milk and espresso coffee together. In a large bowl, beat together the egg yolks and sugar, sift in the flour and cornflour and beat again. Add a little coffee-flavoured milk that is just on the boil, beat again, then gradually add the remaining milk, beating continuously. Transfer the mixture to the pan and cook over medium to low heat, stirring constantly and scraping the bottom of the pan well. Bring to the boil. When the first bubbles appear, cook for a further 2–3 minutes, continuing to stir. Add a few drops of coffee essence (without beating), if using. Pour the cream into a bowl. Cover closely with clingfilm to prevent a skin forming and leave to cool.

2 To make the baba dough: heat the milk and pour into a mixing bowl. Mix in the yeast and sugar. Add the flour and the egg and beat (preferably with an electric whisk). Add the butter, a bit at a time, beating continuously. Continue beating for 2–3 minutes. Cover with clingfilm and set aside to rest for 1½ hours, if possible in a warm place, until the dough has doubled in volume.

3 To make the syrup: dissolve the sugar in the water in a small pan. Continue to simmer to reduce the syrup to a fairly thick consistency. Add the coffee and the liqueur, if using.

4 Grease 6 small moulds or individual ramekins. You could also make one large baba in a big mould. Take small balls of dough and fill the moulds no more than half full. Set aside to rest for a further 30 minutes.

5 Preheat the oven to 180°C (350°F) Gas Mark 4. Put the babas in the oven and bake for about 15 minutes until they have risen and turned golden. Pour the syrup over the babas and serve with the confectioner's custard.

SERVES 4
PREPARATION TIME: 25 MINUTES
COOKING TIME: 1¾ HOURS

VANILLA **TART**

FOR THE DOUGH
240 g (8 oz) plain flour
2 tablespoons sugar
1 teaspoon salt
120 g (4 oz) unsalted butter, cut into small pieces,
  + extra for greasing
1 egg white
1 vanilla pod

FOR THE CREAM
800 ml (1¼ pints) milk
2 vanilla pods, split lengthways
3 whole eggs + 3 yolks
100 g (3½ oz) caster sugar + extra for dusting

1 To make the dough: sift the flour and salt into a bowl and mix in the sugar. Add the butter and the seeds scraped from the vanilla pod and rub in with the fingertips to the consistency of coarse breadcrumbs. Add 3–4 tablespoons of very cold water and mix together with a knife. Finish off the dough with your hands, without working it too much. Form roughly into a ball, wrap in clingfilm, and set aside to rest for at least 1 hour in the refrigerator. (You can also make the dough in a food processor.)

2 Preheat the oven to 190°C (375°F) Gas Mark 5. Grease a cake tin, about 16–18 cm (6–7 inches) in diameter. (A 6-cm/2½-inch deep cake ring placed on a lined baking sheet would be ideal.)

3 Roll out the dough. Cut a circle the diameter of the cake tin or ring (using the ring as a pastry cutter). Cut a strip to make the edges and place it against the sides, sealing it well to the base. Cover the base of the tart with a piece of baking paper, cover with dried beans, put in the oven and bake for 25 minutes. Remove the beans and paper and bake for a further 10 minutes. Brush the base with lightly beaten egg white and reduce the temperature to 150°C (300°F) Gas Mark 2.

4 While the case is baking, prepare the cream. Put the milk to simmer very gently with the split vanilla pods. Remove from the heat, cover and leave to infuse for 10–20 minutes. Beat the eggs and egg yolks with the sugar, then beat in the milk. With a small knife, scrape the vanilla seeds out of the pods into the cream before pouring onto the tart base

5 Put in the oven and bake for about 1¼ hours. The filling should be set but still a little quivery in the centre. Dust with a little sugar. Serve warm or cold.

MAKES 20 BISCUITS
PREPARATION TIME: 20 MINUTES
COOKING TIME: 50 MINUTES

VANILLA **SHORTBREAD**

150 g (5 oz) caster sugar
300 g (10 oz) soft butter
1 vanilla pod
200 g (7 oz) plain flour
250 g (8 oz) cornflour (Maizena if possible)
Salt
Milk

1 Preheat the oven to 150°C (300°F) Gas Mark 2. Reserving 1 tablespoon of sugar until the end, beat together the butter and sugar with the seeds scraped from the vanilla pod, preferably using a food processor or an electric mixer, until the mixture becomes very fluffy. Sift the flour, cornflour and salt onto the butter-sugar mixture. Blend everything together carefully by 'cutting' the dough with a knife (or give it one or two turns with the blade of the food processor on minimum speed).

2 Form the dough into a ball using your hands, without working it too much. Add a little milk if necessary, but the dough should be quite crumbly. Flatten out to a thickness of 1 cm (½ inch) with the palms of your hands on a baking sheet or in a rectangular cake tin. Prick with a fork.

3 Put in the oven and bake for about 50 minutes. The dough should remain very pale. Remove from the oven. Cut into biscuits and transfer to a wire rack to cool. Sprinkle with the remaining sugar.

SERVES 4
PREPARATION TIME: 25 MINUTES
COOKING TIME: 50 MINUTES

QUEEN OF PUDDINGS
WITH VANILLA

150 g (5 oz) stale white bread or brioche
Finely grated rind of ½ lemon
500 ml (17 fl oz) milk
50 g (2 oz) butter + extra for greasing
1 vanilla pod, split lengthways
Vanilla essence (optional)
4 eggs, separated
2 tablespoons gooseberry or quince jelly
Salt
110 g (3¾ oz) caster sugar

1 Preheat the oven to 180°C (350°F) Gas Mark 4. Grease a medium-sized, shallow baking dish.

2 Process the bread into coarse breadcrumbs and tip into a mixing bowl. Add the grated lemon rind.

3 In a small pan, heat the milk with the butter and the split vanilla pod. Just before it boils, pour the hot milk over the breadcrumbs. Leave to infuse for 10 minutes, scrape out the vanilla seeds with the point of a knife into the milk and discard the pod. Add a few drops of vanilla essence to taste, if desired. Add the egg yolks and beat.

4 Pour the mixture into the baking dish. Put in the oven and bake for about 30 minutes. The cream should be just starting to firm. Set aside to cool, then chill in the refrigerator for a little while.

5 Warm the jelly and spread it over the slightly chilled cream. Beat the egg whites until stiff with a pinch of salt, add the sugar (reserving 2 teaspoons) and beat again. Spread the meringue over the cream, sprinkle with sugar and put in the oven for 15 minutes, just long enough for the meringue to brown in places. Serve hot.

SERVES 6
PREPARATION TIME: 1 HOUR + RESTING TIME
COOKING TIME: 1 HOUR

VANILLA CREAM **TARTLETS**

FOR THE SWEET PASTRY
200 g (7 oz) plain flour
75 g (3 oz) caster sugar
125 g (4 oz) butter,
   cut into pieces
1 vanilla pod, split lengthways
1 egg

FOR THE FILLING
500 ml (17 fl oz) milk
1 vanilla pod, split lengthways
5 egg yolks
100 g (3½ oz) caster sugar
30 g (1 oz) cornflour
   (Maizena if possible)
30 g (1 oz) plain flour

FOR THE CHOUX PASTRY
4 tablespoons milk
4 tablespoons water
50 g (2 oz) butter,
   cut into pieces
½ teaspoon salt
1 teaspoon caster sugar
75 g (3 oz) plain flour
2 eggs

FOR THE CARAMEL
150 g (5 oz) caster sugar
Vanilla essence

1 To make the sweet pastry: mix the sugar and flour, add the butter and add the seeds scraped from the vanilla pod. Rub the butter into the flour with the fingertips to the consistency of coarse breadcrumbs. Mix in the egg with a palette knife. Finish the dough with your hands, adding a little water if needed. Stand in the refrigerator for 1 hour.

2 To make the cream: heat the milk with the split vanilla pod. In a mixing bowl, beat together the egg yolks and sugar. Sift in the flour and cornflour and beat again. When the milk reaches boiling point, pour a little into the bowl, beat, then gradually add the remaining milk. Transfer the mixture to the pan and cook over medium to low heat, stirring constantly and scraping the bottom of the pan well. Cook for a further 2–3 minutes, continuing to stir. Pour the cream into a bowl. Remove the vanilla pod, scrape the seeds into the cream and mix. Cover closely with clingfilm and leave to cool.

3 Preheat the oven to 180°C (350°F) Gas Mark 4. Grease 6 tartlet tins.

4 To make the choux pastry, see page 10.

5 Roll out the sweet dough and line the greased tartlet tins with it. With a piping bag, draw a circle of choux pastry round the inside of the bottom of each tartlet. Bake in the oven for about 20 minutes, but check regularly. Remove from the oven and leave to cool.

6 Fill the tartlet cases with the vanilla cream and smooth the surfaces. Make a caramel with the sugar, 100 ml (3½ fl oz) of water and a few drops of vanilla essence. Pour over the cream.

MAKES 15–20
PREPARATION TIME: 15 MINUTES + RESTING TIME
COOKING TIME: 5 MINUTES PER BATCH

VANILLA **TUILES**

50 g (2 oz) butter
1½ tablespoons golden syrup
1 vanilla pod
90 g (3¼ oz) sugar
40 g (1½ oz) plain flour

1 Melt the butter and golden syrup in a bain-marie. Add the seeds scraped from the vanilla pod. Put the sugar in a bowl and sift in the flour. Pour over the butter-syrup mixture and mix well. Stand in the refrigerator for 30 minutes.

2 Preheat the oven to 180°C (350°F) Gas Mark 4. Cover several baking sheets with nonstick baking paper.

3 Make small balls of dough and place spaced well apart on the baking sheets. Cover with a second sheet of baking paper and roll the dough as thinly as possible. Using a pastry cutter, cut neat discs. Put in the oven and bake for 5–6 minutes. You will have to bake several batches.

4 Have some small glasses ready for use beside the oven. When the tuiles begin to turn golden, take them out and slip them one at a time onto the glasses (to give them their curved shape). When they have hardened, put them on a wire rack to cool.

Cook's tip Tuiles – meaning 'tiles' – are named for their curved shape, which resembles roof tiles.

MAKES 12
PREPARATION TIME: 30 MINUTES
COOKING TIME: 35 MINUTES

VANILLA **CUPCAKES**

180 g (6 oz) soft butter + extra for greasing
80 g (3 oz) caster sugar
Vanilla essence
1 vanilla pod
3 eggs
225 g (7½ oz) plain flour
2 teaspoons baking powder

For the topping
100 g (3½ oz) soft butter
300 g (10 oz) icing sugar
1 teaspoon vanilla essence
Salt
Milk

To decorate: silver balls, chocolate vermicelli,
    hundreds and thousands, etc.

1 Preheat the oven to 160°C (325°F) Gas Mark 3. Generously grease a 12-cup muffin tin or sit paper cases in the muffin cups.

2 Beat together the butter, sugar, a few drops of vanilla essence and the vanilla seeds scraped from the pod. The mixture should be very fluffy. Add the eggs one at a time, then the sifted flour and baking powder. Mix carefully.

3 Two-thirds fill the muffic cups or paper cases, put in the oven and bake for 35 minutes. (Test by inserting a metal skewer in one. It should come out clean). Take the cupcakes out of the tins and leave to cool completely on a wire rack.

4 For the topping: mix all the ingredients, together with a pinch of salt, and a little milk if necessary, so the mixture is quite easy to spread (but still firm). Spread the topping generously on the cakes when they have cooled. Decorate as desired.

SERVES 6
PREPARATION TIME: 20 MINUTES
COOKING TIME: 10 MINUTES
CHILLING TIME: MINIMUM 4 HOURS

VANILLA **PANNA COTTAS**

6 leaves gelatine
450 ml (¾ pint) double cream
450 ml (¾ pint) single cream
3 tablespoons caster sugar
1 vanilla pod, split lengthways
Vanilla essence

FOR THE SYRUP
150 g (5 oz) caster sugar
200 ml (7 fl oz) water
1 vanilla pod
1 teaspoon lemon juice

1 Soften the gelatine in a little cold water and squeeze out when ready to use. Heat the cream to below boiling point with the sugar and the split vanilla pod. Stir to dissolve the sugar. You can add more sugar, but the panna cotta is served with a syrup that sweetens it a little. Drain the gelatine and stir to dissolve completely in the hot cream. Cover and set aside to infuse for 20 minutes.

2 Remove the vanilla pod and scrape the seeds into the cream, then add a few drops of vanilla essence, to taste. Pour the mixture into small glass bowls and chill for at least 4 hours in the refrigerator.

3 Make the syrup by dissolving the sugar in the water, over low heat. Add the seeds scraped from the vanilla pod and the lemon juice. Stir to ensure the sugar is completely dissolved, then simmer for long enough to produce the consistency of a syrup (but not too thick). Serve the panna cottas with the syrup.

SERVES 6
PREPARATION TIME: 35 MINUTES
COOKING TIME: 2–3 HOURS

VACHERINS

5 egg whites
350 g (12 oz) caster sugar
Vanilla essence
150 ml (¼ pint) double or whipping cream
250 g (8 oz) fromage frais
1 vanilla pod
500 ml (17 fl oz) vanilla ice cream
Icing sugar for dusting or decorations of your choice

1 Preheat the oven to 120°C (250°F) Gas Mark ½.
2 To make the meringues: beat the egg whites until stiff. Gradually add the sugar and then a few drops of vanilla essence, to taste. Form 12 round meringues on a baking sheet covered with nonstick baking paper. As a guide, you can use a saucer to draw rings on the paper.
3 Put in the oven and 'dry out' for 2–3 hours, depending on the size of the meringues. They must dry out thoroughly.
4 Whip the cream to firm peaks. Stir the fromage frais until smooth and fold into the cream with the seeds scraped from the vanilla pod.
5 Just before serving, spread half the meringues with half the cream. Put a small scoop of ice cream on each, then add more cream and top with a second meringue, to form a sandwich. Decorate as you please.

Cook's tip To check if the meringues are ready, lift one with a palette knife. If it comes away cleanly and feels crisp on the outside, it is ready.

SERVES 6
PREPARATION TIME: 30 MINUTES
COOKING TIME: 1 HOUR

RANCHO EGG CUSTARD

200 g (7 oz) caster sugar
750 ml (1¼ pints) evaporated milk
2 whole eggs + 6 yolks
1 vanilla pod, split lengthways
2 teaspoons vanilla essence

1 Preheat the oven to 180°C (350°F) Gas Mark 4.

2 Put half the sugar in a small pan with about 100 ml (3½ fl oz) of water and cook to a light caramel. Pour into a deep metal mould (such as a charlotte mould) with a capacity of almost 2 litres (3½ pints). You could also reduce the quantities or make it in two moulds. Tip the mould in all directions to spread the caramel as much as possible.

3 Heat the evaporated milk with the split vanilla pod. Remove from the heat just before boiling point, cover and set aside to cool. Scrape the vanilla seeds into the milk and discard the pod. Beat together the eggs and the yolks, the evaporated milk and the vanilla essence. Try not to create too much froth when beating.

4 Pour into the mould and cover with foil. Place the mould in a large roasting tin, slide it into the oven and fill the tin with hot water to halfway up the mould. Bake for 55 minutes. The cream should be set but still quivery. Bake for a further 10 minutes if the custard still looks a little runny.

5 Allow to cool before refrigerating until set, or when required.

6 To serve: run the blade of a knife between the custard and the sides of the mould and turn out onto a plate.

SERVES 6
PREPARATION TIME: 15 MINUTES
COOKING TIME: 35 MINUTES

EASY VANILLA **ÉCLAIRS**

FOR THE CONFECTIONER'S CUSTARD
500 ml (17 fl oz) milk
1 vanilla pod, split lengthways
5 egg yolks
100 g (3½ oz) caster sugar
2 tablespoons plain flour
2 tablespoons cornflour (Maizena if possible)

FOR THE CHOUX PASTRY
150 ml (¼ pint) water
50 g (2 oz) butter, cut into small pieces
½ teaspoon salt
65 g (2½ oz) plain flour
2 eggs

FOR THE ICING
150 g (5 oz) icing sugar
Lemon juice
Vanilla essence
1 vanilla pod

1 To make the confectioner's custard: heat the milk with the split vanilla pod. In a large bowl, beat together the egg yolks and sugar, sift in the flour and cornflour and beat again. Add a little milk when it is just below boiling point, beat, then gradually add the remaining milk, stirring constantly. Transfer the mixture to the pan and cook over medium to low heat, stirring constantly and scraping the bottom of the pan well. Bring to the boil and cook for a further 2–3 minutes, continuing to stir, until the custard cream coats the back of the spoon. Pour into a bowl, scrape in the vanilla seeds and discard the pod. Cover closely with clingfilm to prevent a skin forming and leave to cool.

2 Preheat the oven to 200°C (400°F) Gas Mark 6. Grease a baking sheet or line with nonstick baking paper.

3 To make the choux pastry: follow the instructions on page 10.

4 Using a piping bag (small nozzle), pipe fingers of dough on the baking sheet. Put in the oven and bake for about 25 minutes, increasing the oven temperature to 220°C (425°F) Gas Mark 7 after 10 minutes. Set out on a wire rack to cool completely.

5 Slit the éclairs open and fill with the cream.

6 To make the icing: mix the icing sugar with sufficient lemon juice to give a fluid consistency. Add a few drops of vanilla essence, to taste, and the seeds scraped from the pod. Ice the éclairs and put in a cold place. Serve without waiting too long.

English translation and adaptation: JMS Books LLP
Layout: cbdesign

First published in France in 2007 under the title
La Boîte à gâteau, by Hachette Livre (Marabout)
Copyright © 2007 Hachette Livre (Marabout)
Editorial: Catherine Berranger and Charlotte Müller-Buch

An Hachette Livre UK Company
www.hachettelivre.co.uk

First published in Great Britain in 2008 by
Hamlyn, a division of Octopus Publishing Group Ltd
2–4 Heron Quays, London E14 4JP
www.octopusbooks.co.uk

Copyright © English edition
Octopus Publishing Group Ltd 2008

Original French edition copyright
© HACHETTE LIVRE (Marabout) 2007

ISBN 978 0 600 61876 8

A CIP catalogue record for this book is available from
the British Library

Printed and bound in China

1 3 5 7 9 10 8 6 4 2

This book contains dishes that are made with raw or lightly cooked eggs.
These should be avoided by vulnerable people such as pregnant and
nursing mothers, invalids, the elderly, babies and young children.

CHOCOLATE

hamlyn

CONTENTS

SERVES 6
PREPARATION TIME: 25 MINUTES
COOKING TIME: 30 MINUTES

CHOCOLATE **SOUFFLÉ**

Butter, for greasing
200 g (7 oz) dark chocolate
50 ml (2 fl oz) single cream + extra for serving
1 tsp vanilla essence, or to taste
6 egg yolks
10 egg whites (8 if large eggs)
2 tablespoons plain flour
1 tablespoon icing sugar

To serve: cream, whipped if preferred

1 Preheat the oven to 220°C (425°F) Gas Mark 7. Grease a soufflé dish well.

2 Melt the chocolate in a heatproof bowl over a pan of barely simmering water. Add the cream and vanilla essence and mix together until smooth.

3 Allow the melted chocolate to cool a little, add the 6 egg yolks and mix well. Beat the egg whites until stiff and fold them into the mixture. Then mix in the flour.

4 Pour the chocolate mixture into the soufflé dish and cook for 20–25 minutes. Dust with icing sugar and serve immediately with cream.

SERVES 6
PREPARATION TIME: 35 MINUTES
COOKING TIME: 30 MINUTES
CHILLING TIME: 5 HOURS

RICH CHOCOLATE **TART**

FOR THE PASTRY
200 g (7 oz) plain flour
100 g (3½ oz) unsalted butter, cut into pieces
1 tablespoon caster sugar
1 egg
Salt

FOR THE FILLING
500 ml (17 fl oz) milk
200 g (7 oz) dark chocolate + 50 g (2 oz) in shavings or grated
3 leaves gelatine, weighing 6 g/¼ oz
1 shot very strong espresso coffee
2 eggs, separated
150 ml (5 fl oz) whipping/double cream, chilled

To decorate: chocolate shavings

1 To make the pastry: mix together the flour, sugar and a good pinch of salt. Rub in the butter with the tips of the fingers until the mixture resembles breadcrumbs. Mix in the egg with a round-bladed knife. Add a little cold water if necessary. Form into a ball by hand, without working the dough too much. Wrap in clingfilm and put in the refrigerator for 1 hour.

2 Preheat the oven to 200°C (400°F) Gas Mark 6.

3 Roll out the pastry and line a tart tin 20 cm (8 inches) in diameter. Cover with a sheet of nonstick baking paper and a layer of dried beans, then bake for 15 minutes, remove the beans and continue baking for a further 5–10 minutes.

4 Soften the gelatine in a little cold water. Heat the coffee. Squeeze out the softened gelatine and completely dissolve it in the coffee.

5 Melt the chocolate in a heatproof bowl over a pan of barely simmering water. Stir until smooth. Add the coffee-gelatine mixture. Allow to cool, then add the egg yolks. Whip the chilled cream. Beat the egg whites until stiff. Fold the cream and egg whites into the chocolate mixture.

6 Spread the chocolate filling over the cooled tart base and chill in the refrigerator for 3–4 hours. Decorate with chocolate shavings.

SERVES 4
PREPARATION TIME: 20 MINUTES
COOKING TIME: 5 MINUTES
CHILLING TIME: MINIMUM OF 2 HOURS

CHOCOLATE **MOUSSE**

250 g (8 oz) dark chocolate
4 eggs, separated

1 Melt the chocolate in a heatproof bowl set over a pan of barely simmering water. Using a spatula, stir the chocolate until smooth and leave to cool for a few minutes.

2 Beat the egg yolks, one at a time, into the melted chocolate.

3 Whisk the egg whites until stiff and firm. Fold very gently into the chocolate.

4 Pour the mousse into ramekins or glasses, cover with clingfilm and stand in the refrigerator for at least 2 hours.

Cook's tip For a more colourful effect, use half milk chocolate and half dark chocolate. Pour the mousse into glasses in alternate layers.

SERVES 6
PREPARATION TIME: 30 MINUTES
COOKING TIME: 35 MINUTES

BROWN SUGAR **BROWNIES**

250 g (8 oz) soft unsalted butter + extra for greasing
200 g (7 oz) muscovado sugar (soft brown sugar)
250 g (8 oz) dark chocolate
4 eggs
4 tablespoons plain flour
4 tablespoons cocoa powder
½ teaspoon baking powder
Salt

1 Preheat the oven to 180°C (350°F) Gas Mark 4. Grease a 20-cm (8-inch) square cake tin.

2 Beat the butter and sugar together until the mixture becomes light and fluffy.

3 Chop up the chocolate and set 3 tablespoons aside. Melt the remainder in a heatproof bowl set over a pan of barely simmering water.

4 Beat the eggs lightly and add to the butter and sugar mixture. Add the melted chocolate, then the reserved chocolate pieces.

5 Sift together the flour, cocoa, baking powder and a generous pinch of salt. Fold gently into the chocolate mixture. Pour into the cake tin and bake for about 30 minutes. The outside edges should be shrinking away from the tin while the centre should be springy. Leave to cool and cut in squares.

SERVES 6
PREPARATION TIME: 5 MINUTES
COOKING TIME: 5 MINUTES

INSTANT SAUCE
FOR PEARS & ICE CREAM

300 ml (½ pint) milk
300 g (10 oz) dark chocolate

1 Chop the chocolate. Bring the milk to the boil, remove from the heat, add the chocolate and beat until smooth.
2 Pour the sauce over ice cream or poached pears (or both).

MAKES ABOUT 20
PREPARATION TIME: 25 MINUTES
COOKING TIME: 20 MINUTES

CHOC-NUT **COOKIES**

3 tablespoons oat flakes
125 g (4 oz) plain flour
3 tablespoons cocoa powder
¼ teaspoon baking powder
100 g (3½ oz) soft butter
125 g (4 oz) brown sugar
1 egg
Vanilla essence
100 g (3½ oz) dark chocolate, chopped
75 g (3 oz) walnuts (or macadamia nuts), chopped
Salt

1 Preheat the oven to 180°C (350°F) Gas Mark 4.

2 Toast the oat flakes briefly in a hot frying pan.

3 Sift together the flour, cocoa powder, a pinch of salt and the baking powder. Add the oat flakes.

4 Beat the butter and sugar together until light and fluffy. Beat the egg with a few drops of the vanilla essence and add to the butter and sugar mixture.

5 Gently fold in the sifted dry ingredients, then the chocolate and the chopped walnuts.

6 Line a baking sheet with nonstick baking paper. Using a tablespoon, place small mounds of mixture spaced well apart on the sheet. Put in the oven and bake for 15–20 minutes. Allow to cool on a wire rack. These cookies are delicious served warm.

SERVES 4
PREPARATION TIME: 5 MINUTES
COOKING TIME: 5 MINUTES

SWEET-AND-SAVOURY
MOMENTS

4 'lingue' (long, flat, savoury Italian biscuits with olive oil)
150 g (5 oz) dark chocolate

1 Finely chop (or grate) the chocolate. Heat the grill.
2 Sprinkle chocolate on the 'lingue', leaving one third uncovered. Grill very briefly. Enjoy!

SERVES 4
PREPARATION TIME: 5 MINUTES

ICED CHOCOLATE

4 tablespoons cocoa powder
150 ml (¼ pint) vanilla ice cream
600 ml (1 pint) milk

To serve: ice cubes

1 Mix the cocoa powder with a little hot water. Whizz in a blender with the ice cream and milk.
2 Serve poured over the ice cubes.

SERVES 6
PREPARATION TIME: 40 MINUTES
COOKING TIME: 40 MINUTES
CHILLING TIME: MINIMUM OF 1 HOUR

CHOCOLATE & PEAR
CELEBRATION CAKE

FOR THE CAKE
75 g (3 oz) butter + extra for greasing
150 g (5 oz) plain flour
2 tablespoons cornflour, Maizena preferably
2 tablespoons cocoa powder
6 eggs
150 g (5 oz) caster sugar

FOR THE TOPPING
100 g (3½ oz) dark chocolate
100 ml (3½ fl oz) single cream
150 ml (¼ pint) double cream, chilled
2 pears, freshly poached or canned in syrup

For decoration: cocoa powder or grated chocolate

1 Preheat the oven to 190 °C (375 °F) Gas Mark 5. Grease 2 round cake tins 20–25 cm (8–10 inches) in diameter or one deeper one. Line with nonstick baking paper.

2 For the cake: melt the butter and allow to cool. Sift together the flour, cornflour and cocoa.

3 Beat the butter and sugar together until the mixture turns pale and becomes very fluffy. Carefully fold in the flour and cocoa mixture and then the melted butter.

4 Pour the mixture into the cake tins, smooth off the top and bake for 30–35 minutes. Leave to cool on a wire rack.

5 For the topping, first melt the chocolate in a heatproof bowl over a pan of barely simmering water. Allow to cool. Stir in the single cream. Whip the double cream and mix into the chocolate. Place in the refrigerator to cool (at least 1 hour).

6 Slice the pears. If you baked a single large cake, cut it in half horizontally. Sandwich the two cakes/halves together with the chocolate cream and slices of pear. Dust with cocoa or sprinkle with grated chocolate.

SERVES 6 (AT LEAST)
PREPARATION TIME: 25 MINUTES
COOKING TIME: 25 MINUTES
FREEZING TIME: 4 HOURS

MOELLEUX AU CHOCOLAT

FOR THE CHOCOLATE GANACHE FILLING
200 ml (7 fl oz) single cream
200 g (7 oz) dark or milk chocolate

FOR THE CAKE MIXTURE
200 g (7oz) butter at room temperature + extra for greasing
400 g (14 oz) very dark chocolate
125 g (4 oz) caster sugar
6 eggs
60 g (2¼ oz) plain flour
Icing sugar and cocoa powder for dusting

To serve: vanilla ice cream

1 For the chocolate ganache: chop the chocolate. Heat the cream, add the chopped chocolate and beat until smooth. Allow to cool, then pour into ice-cube trays and freeze for about 4 hours.

2 Preheat the oven to 190°C (375°F) Gas Mark 5.

3 For the cakes: generously grease 6 large muffin cups or ramekins with butter. Break up the chocolate into small pieces and put in a heatproof bowl over a pan of barely simmering water. When it is almost all melted, stir until smooth.

4 Beat the butter and sugar together. The mixture should become light, very pale and fluffy. Gradually add the eggs and the flour. Finally mix in the melted chocolate.

5 Pour the mixture into the muffin cups or ramekins. Insert a cube of frozen chocolate cream into each cake. Bake for 20 minutes. Serve hot with vanilla ice cream.

Cook's tip Moelleux au chocolat are delicious little cakes with an indulgent liquid chocolate filling.

SERVES 6
PREPARATION TIME: 25 MINUTES
COOKING TIME: 2 HOURS

MELT-IN-THE-MOUTH
HEART-SHAPED CAKE

400 g (14 oz) very dark chocolate
200 g (7 oz) butter at room temperature + extra for greasing
125 g (4 oz) caster sugar
6 eggs
60 g (2¼ oz) plain flour
Icing sugar and cocoa powder for dusting

To serve: vanilla ice cream, if liked

1 Preheat the oven to 150°C (300°F) Gas Mark 2.

2 Generously grease a heart-shaped mould with butter. Break up the chocolate into small pieces and put in a heatproof bowl over a pan of barely simmering water. When almost all the chocolate has melted, stir until smooth.

3 Beat the butter and sugar together. The mixture should become light, very pale and fluffy. Gradually add the eggs and the flour. Mix in the melted chocolate.

4 Place the mould in a roasting tin, slide into the oven and pour hot water around it. Then pour the mixture into the mould. Bake for 1½–1¾ hours; the cake should just begin to firm.

5 It is advisable to wait until the cake is completely cold before attempting to turn it out of the mould. Dust with cocoa powder and icing sugar and serve on its own or with a scoop of vanilla ice cream.

SERVES 4
PREPARATION TIME: 25 MINUTES
COOKING TIME: 15 MINUTES
RESTING TIME: 1 HOUR

CHOCOLATE MACAROONS
WITH A HINT OF LIME

Finely grated rind of 2 limes
90 g (3¼ oz) ground almonds
150 g (5 oz) icing sugar
3 egg whites
2 tablespoons caster sugar
100 ml (3½ fl oz) single cream
100 g (3½ oz) good dark chocolate

1 Preheat the oven to 180°C (350°F) Gas Mark 4 (open the vent or use the fan, if available). Line a baking sheet with nonstick baking paper.

2 Mix the grated lime rind carefully with the ground almonds and icing sugar. Then sift this mixture three times. The peel will remain in the sieve. Discard it, as the lime essence will have flavoured the almonds.

3 Beat the egg whites until stiff, add the caster sugar and beat again. Fold the egg whites into the icing sugar and almond mixture. The mixture should collapse a little.

4 Form the mixture into an equal number of mounds (about 6 cm/2½ inches in diameter), with a piping bag or a spoon. It doesn't matter if they are irregular in shape. Put in the oven (ideally use double baking sheets so that the bottom doesn't brown too much) and turn down the heat immediately to 150°C (300°F) Gas Mark 2. Bake for about 10 minutes. A soft crust should form on top. Carefully lift off the macaroons and put them on a wire rack to cool.

5 Break up the chocolate into little pieces. Bring the cream to the boil, add the chocolate pieces and mix until smooth. Allow to cool, then place in the refrigerator to thicken but not set firm. Sandwich the macaroons together in pairs with the chocolate cream.

SERVES 6
PREPARATION TIME: 30 MINUTES
COOKING TIME: 40 MINUTES

EASY CHOCOLATE TART

Butter for greasing
1 sheet butter shortcrust pastry
250 g (8 oz) dark chocolate
150 ml (¼ pint) single cream
150 ml (¼ pint) milk
2 eggs

1 Preheat the oven to 180°C (350°F) Gas Mark 4. Line a greased tart tin 20–23 cm (8–9 inches) in diameter with the pastry. Cover the base of the tart with a piece of nonstick baking paper and fill with beans. Bake for 20 minutes, remove the beans and paper and bake for a further 5 minutes.

2 Chop the chocolate. In a pan, bring the milk and cream to the boil, remove from the heat and add 200 g (7 oz) of the chocolate. Beat until smooth, then beat in the eggs with a whisk. Spread the remaining chocolate over the tart base. Pour over the chocolate cream and return the tart to the oven for 15 minutes. Allow to cool before serving.

SERVES 4
PREPARATION TIME: 30 MINUTES
COOKING TIME: 1 HOUR

BEETROOT & CHOCOLATE **CAKE**

Butter for greasing
250 g (8 oz) cooked beetroot
120 g (4 oz) dark chocolate
5 tablespoons cocoa powder + extra for dusting
180 g (6 oz) plain flour
2 teaspoons baking powder
175 g (6 oz) caster sugar
200 ml (7 fl oz) olive oil
1 teaspoon vanilla essence, or to taste
3 eggs
Salt

1 Preheat the oven to 180°C (350°F) Gas Mark 4. Grease a heart-shaped cake tin or a round cake tin 20 cm (8 inches) in diameter.

2 Put the beetroot through a blender to give a smooth purée. Chop the chocolate.

3 Sift together the cocoa powder, flour, baking powder and a pinch of salt. Mix in the sugar and add the olive oil, vanilla essence and the lightly beaten eggs. Mix well before stirring in the beetroot purée and chocolate pieces.

4 Pour the mixture into the cake tin and bake for 50 minutes to 1 hour. Test by sticking a metal skewer into the cake; it should come out clean.

5 Leave to cool for 15 minutes in the tin before turning out onto a wire rack to cool completely. Dust with cocoa powder and serve.

Cook's tip The beetroot does not flavour the cake, it simply makes it velvety soft!

SERVES 6
PREPARATION TIME: 20 MINUTES
CHILLING TIME: MINIMUM OF 4 HOURS; PREFERABLY OVERNIGHT

TRIPLE CHOCOLATE **SLICE**

100 g (3½ oz) chocolate sablé biscuits
   or double choc chip cookies
50 g (2 oz) milk chocolate
   (with almonds or hazelnuts if desired)
200 g (7 oz) soft butter + extra for greasing
200 g (7 oz) cocoa powder
200 g (7 oz) ground almonds
100 g (3½ oz) caster sugar
1 egg

1 Crush the biscuits into coarse pieces. Chop up the milk chocolate. Mix the butter with the cocoa powder and add the ground almonds.

2 Put the sugar in a small pan with 3 tablespoons of water and dissolve over low heat. Remove from the heat and add the butter-almond-cocoa mixture, then the egg. Very gently mix in the crushed biscuits and the chocolate.

3 Grease a loaf tin (large enough to contain the mixture to just below the rim) and pour in the mixture. Smooth over and cover with foil. Place in the refrigerator, if possible overnight. To serve, turn out and cut in very thin slices.

SERVES 6
PREPARATION TIME: 25 MINUTES
COOKING TIME: 15 MINUTES

CHOCOLATE **POTS**

120 g (4 oz) dark chocolate
150 ml (¼ pint) milk
150 ml (¼ pint) single cream
2 vanilla pods, split open
1 egg yolk
1 tablespoon cornflour
2 tablespoons caster sugar
2 tablespoons butter
150 ml (¼ pint) double or whipping cream

1 Chop the chocolate.

2 Heat the milk and single cream together with the vanilla pods. Remove from the heat just before boiling, cover and leave to infuse for 15 minutes. Scrape the seeds into the liquid and remove the pods.

3 Beat together the egg yolk, cornflour and sugar, then pour in the milk and cream mixture. Beat well and pour back into the pan over fairly low heat. Heat, stirring constantly, until the cream thickens. Then beat in the chocolate and butter.

4 Pour into small pots (small glass yogurt pots are ideal), allow to cool and store in the refrigerator. Whip the double or whipping cream and divide it between the pots. Refrigerate again, then serve.

SERVES 6
PREPARATION TIME: 30 MINUTES
COOKING TIME: 1 HOUR
CHILLING TIME: 24 HOURS

DOUBLE CHOCOLATE
CHEESECAKE

175 g (6 oz) chocolate-coated sablé biscuits,
   or plain chocolate digestives
75 g (3 oz) butter
175 g (6 oz) dark chocolate
375 g (12 oz) fromage frais
200 g (7 oz) mascarpone
75 g (3 oz) caster sugar
3 eggs
2 tablespoons plain flour

1 Crush the biscuits into crumbs.

2 Melt the butter, mix with the biscuits and press into the base of a cake tin 20 cm (8 inches) in diameter (springform if possible). Place in the refrigerator to set.

3 Preheat the oven to 150°C (300°F) Gas Mark 2. Melt the chocolate in a heatproof bowl set over a pan of barely simmering water, or in the microwave. Stir until smooth.

4 Beat together the fromage frais and mascarpone until smooth, then add the sugar. Beat again before stirring in the eggs one at a time. Finally mix in the flour and the melted chocolate.

5 Pour over the biscuit base and bake for 45 minutes to 1 hour. The filling should be set but still slightly quivery. Leave to cool in the oven, then take it out, remove carefully from the cake tin and place in the refrigerator overnight.

SERVES 3
PREPARATION TIME: 30 MINUTES
COOKING TIME: 30 MINUTES
RESTING TIME: 30 MINUTES

SABLÉ BISCUITS
WITH PASSION FRUIT
& CHOCOLATE FILLING

75 g (3 oz) caster sugar
120 g (4 oz) butter + extra for greasing
4 tablespoons cocoa powder + extra dusting
150 g (5 oz) plain flour
200 ml (7 fl oz) single cream
100 g (3½ oz) dark chocolate
100 g (3½ oz) mascarpone
2 passion fruit

1 Preheat the oven to 190°C (375°F) Gas Mark 5. Grease a baking tray, or line with nonstick baking paper.

2 Beat together the sugar and butter. Sift the cocoa and flour into the mixture. Work into a dough (but don't over-work). Line the baking tray with a 5-mm (¼-inch) thick layer of this soft dough. The dough is difficult to roll out but you can always place it with your fingers, a little at a time. Smooth the surface. Bake for about 20 minutes.

3 Heat the cream and pour over the chopped chocolate. Stir until smooth, allow to cool, then place in the refrigerator until set.

4 When set, mix the chocolate with the mascarpone and the juice and flesh of the passion fruit (don't worry if the cream is not smooth, it should be lumpy).

5 With a pastry cutter, cut out small circles (about 3 cm/ 1¼ inches in diameter) of the chocolate pastry. Sandwich them together in pairs with the chocolate and passion fruit cream.

Cook's tip A sablé is a crumbly biscuit, usually round. There are many French regional varieties.

SERVES 6
PREPARATION TIME: 30 MINUTES
COOKING TIME: 15 MINUTES
CHILLING TIME: ABOUT 2 HOURS

SEMIFREDDO

120 g (4 oz) dark chocolate
50 g (2 oz) butter
150 ml (¼ pint) milk
150 ml (¼ pint) single cream
2 vanilla pods, split open
3 egg yolks
2 tablespoons caster sugar
1 packet tuiles aux amandes (almond biscuits)
A 50 g (2 oz) Toblerone

1 Chop the chocolate and cut the butter in pieces. Heat the milk and cream with the vanilla pods to boiling point. Remove from the heat, cover and leave to infuse for 15 minutes. Scrape the seeds into the liquid and remove the pods.

2 Beat together the egg yolks and sugar in a bowl, then pour in the milk and cream mixture, beat again and pour back into the pan. Cook over fairly low heat, stirring constantly, until the cream thickens. Finally beat in the chocolate and butter. Allow to cool.

3 Break the tuiles aux amandes into small, but not too small, pieces. Chop up the Toblerone. Fold both into the cream. Pour the mixture into a loaf tin lined with clingfilm or several small moulds. Stand in the refrigerator for 2 hours. The dessert must be cold enough to slice but still a little soft. Check occasionally, as refrigerators do not all chill equally efficiently.

4 Turn out and serve cut in slices.

Cook's tip Semifreddo is a soft iced dessert with a texture halfway between mousse and ice cream.

SERVES 4
PREPARATION TIME: 10 MINUTES
COOKING TIME: 15 MINUTES

PIQUANT
HOT CHOCOLATE

150 g (5 oz) very dark chocolate
  (at least 70% cocoa solids)
500 ml (17 fl oz) goat's milk
  (it's delicious! Otherwise use ordinary milk)
2 tablespoons cocoa powder

1 Chop the chocolate.
2 Heat the milk with 250 ml (8 fl oz) of water and the cocoa powder. Bring to boiling point, beat in the chocolate, reduce the heat and simmer over a low heat for 10 minutes. Strain and serve immediately, or put in the refrigerator and reheat when required.

English translation and adaptation: JMS Books LLP
Layout: cbdesign

First published in France in 2007 under the title
La Boîte à gâteau, by Hachette Livre (Marabout)
Copyright © 2007 Hachette Livre (Marabout)
Editorial: Catherine Berranger and Charlotte Müller-Buch

An Hachette Livre UK Company
www.hachettelivre.co.uk

First published in Great Britain in 2008 by
Hamlyn, a division of Octopus Publishing Group Ltd
2–4 Heron Quays, London E14 4JP
www.octopusbooks.co.uk

Copyright © English edition
Octopus Publishing Group Ltd 2008

Original French edition copyright
© HACHETTE LIVRE (Marabout) 2007

ISBN 978 0 600 61876 8

A CIP catalogue record for this book is available from
the British Library

Printed and bound in China

1 3 5 7 9 10 8 6 4 2

This book contains dishes that are made with raw or lightly cooked eggs.
These should be avoided by vulnerable people such as pregnant and
nursing mothers, invalids, the elderly, babies and young children.